THE COMMITTED PROFESSOR

THE
COMMITTED
PROFESSOR

A MEMOIR

My Fall from the Lectern to the Psych Ward

KATHI N. MINER, PhD

ISBN: 979-8-9906535-0-4

Disclaimer: The events, places, and conversations in this book are a good faith and truthful recollection of the author that have been recreated from memory and/or supplemented. It is acknowledged that some people may have memories of certain events that differ. When necessary, the names and identifying characteristics of individuals and places have been changed to protect their privacy. All indented text in italics is from actual text messages, emails, or other documents. The author of this book disclaims liability for any loss or damage suffered by any person or company as a result of the content in this book.

For more information, the author can be contacted at:
kathiminerphd@gmail.com

AUTHOR'S NOTE

As a feminist psychology and women's and gender studies professor, I dedicated my life to researching, understanding, and teaching others how gendered power dynamics, sexist oppression, and patriarchal social structures affect women's lives. Little did I know that this intellectual sanctuary would be juxtaposed against the stark reality of my own life, one marred by the insidious grasp of a narcissistically abusive relationship that pushed me to the brink and nearly claimed my very existence.

The process of penning this experience was neither easy nor immediate. It took me over a decade to complete this book, with many stops and starts, and breakdowns and tears, in between. My strong belief that our personal stories have the power to resonate with and help others while at the same time bring people together to challenge oppressive social systems that influence those experiences motivated me to finally finish it.

In the pages that follow, I invite you into the most intimate and darkest corners of my life where I share my experiences of betrayal, abuse, and suffering. As I recount the most tumultuous period of my life, I aim to shed light on the complexities of narcissistically abusive relationships—especially when men are the perpetrators and women are the targets—in a society that privileges men and subjugates women. I also describe how my fall from the esteemed academic lectern to the bleak corridors of a psychiatric ward has been nothing short of personally transformative, challenging the very foundations of my identity as a woman, a scholar, and an advocate for gender equality. Ultimately, mine is a story of self-love, resilience, and personal growth.

The first chapter of the book briefly explains my upbringing, educational trajectory, and relationship with my husband. The remaining chapters illustrate the devastating demise of my marriage and horrific divorce, covering a period of roughly two years: January 2011 to December 2013. Everything I portray in the book is true and accurate to the very best of my recollection. My narrative of events is accompanied by actual text messages, emails, reports, and records to substantiate and exemplify my story; these instances are indented and in italics. To protect the identities of those mentioned in the book, I have changed their names and, as much as possible, any identifying details. I have also included material on many of the topics I have discussed in the book—for example, narcissistic abuse, parental alienation, betrayal trauma, and complex post-traumatic stress disorder—that did not exist or that I was unaware of when I was going through those terrible two years but will help the reader understand those concepts more fully. Thankfully, there are many more resources available to women in narcissistically abusive relationships today than there were when I was in the brunt of it.

There are a few caveats. First, while I focus on women's experiences of narcissistic abuse from men, and how living in a patriarchal culture exacerbates the negative effects of those experiences, I also fully acknowledge that men can be victims of narcissistic abuse from women and that men are also harmed by patriarchy. These topics are for another writer and another book. I also recognize that many of the interpersonal dynamics and situations I have discussed in the book may occur in same-sex couples. I purposely focus on heterosexual couples in the present work because it is closest to my own lived experience. Finally, many subjects in the book may trigger some readers. Those who may be uncomfortable reading about psychological abuse, harassment, stalking, suicide, and trauma, among other related themes, should proceed with caution.

To my family, friends, colleagues, and students who provided unwavering support and compassion during my dimmest hours, I extend my heartfelt gratitude. Your presence helped illuminate my path to liberation, and this memoir is as much a tribute to the strength found in collective as it is an account of personal triumph.

As you, the reader, embark on this journey with me, I ask for your kindness, empathy, and an open heart. May the words within these pages foster conversations about gender inequality in intimate relationships and society and, above all, inspire courage in those who need it the most. I hope that, by sharing my story, I can provide solace to those who have felt the suffocating clutch of a narcissistically abusive male partner and empower those who may still be navigating the labyrinth of his abuse.

With humility and strength,
Kathi

I dedicate this book to women.

TABLE OF CONTENTS

Silence about trauma also leads to death—the death of the soul.
—Bessel V. van der Kolk

CHAPTER 1: THE MOVES

Yee-haw! It was the summer of 1995, I had just turned twenty-five, and I was moving across the country from Southern California to Texas. I never dreamed I would leave the Golden State. I loved living there and fit right in. Aside from school and my job waiting tables, I spent most of my time by the pool or at the beach in flip-flops and shorts with my blond hair in a ponytail hanging out with friends or a steady boyfriend. All of my family lived close by, too, and they were my rock. But I had big plans for my life—getting a PhD and becoming a college professor—and I was dead set on achieving them. My goals hadn't always been so lofty, though. In fact, it took me a while to figure out what I wanted to do with my life.

After graduating high school and spending years waffling at the local community college, I finally got it together and started taking school seriously. The turning point came when I took an Introduction to Psychology course. The instructor was a laid-back cool dude with a pot belly and an unmaintained large dark beard. He taught the class in such a way that kept me glued to his every word; he augmented the sometimes-bland material with captivating stories and a phenomenal sense of humor. I was especially intrigued by the class material on social-psychological development, specifically the area of gender socialization and gender roles. That is, I was fascinated by the myriad of ways in which society and culture influence how we develop the sense of ourselves as women and men, including our traits, behaviors, goals, desires, and relationships. I was particularly interested in how society influences women's important life decisions like career and marriage. I enjoyed learning, reading, writing, and thinking about the subject so much I decided to become a psychology major with the ultimate career ambition of becoming a college professor in psychology with expertise in women and gender.

My interest in societal influences on women's life decisions stemmed from the experiences I had as a child and young adult. I had a wonderful childhood in an upper-middle-class nuclear family with my mom, dad, and sister, Kenzie, who was three years older than me. I also had three older half-siblings—Lance, Jill, and Milly—whom I was very close to even though they were roughly a decade older than me and had moved out of the family home. My parents were traditional in the sense that my mom did all of the shopping, cooking, and cleaning and my dad took care of the yard and pool. My mom also did all of the relational work: planning family parties and events, buying Christmas and birthday presents, checking on relatives, and listening to and supporting family members when they had problems. She did all of the scheduling of my sister's and my appointments, enrolled us in all of our extracurricular activities, chauffeured us around town, and took care of all of our school-related needs including homework, project supplies, and parent-teacher conferences.

On top of that, my mom worked full time as a successful newspaper journalist; she was the food editor of the *Orange County Register* newspaper. My dad was the breadwinner and spent most of his time working at his certified public accountant (CPA) practice to provide for the family. They seemed authentically happy and in love. One of my favorite memories of them is when they would affectionately snuggle up together on the living room couch chatting, listening to classic tunes, and sipping Kahlua. I would sometimes sit on one of the four stairs leading down to the living room and watch them, overcome with feelings of warmth and refuge. I can still recall nearly every word of the 5th Dimension's Greatest Hits on Earth album, especially "One Less Bell to Answer."

I felt very loved and cared for by my parents and have warm-hearted memories of family dinners while watching *The Love Boat*, water skiing and camping, trips to Hawaii, Mexico, and up the Pacific Coast, backyard barbequing, and swimming in our pool and jacuzzi. I think pool time was my favorite. I was a good swimmer, having learned how to swim at age two, and swam constantly. My blond hair was green in the summer from the pool chlorine, and my family was always commenting on how cute my little tan body was in my swimsuit. In the summer evenings, we would often sit together as a family in the jacuzzi with the warm bubbles swirling around us overlooking the city lights below. My mom would bring out roasted potato "bites" with butter, garlic, and parmesan cheese for us and red wine for her and my dad. She would call for me "Kath-i-a, sweet-e-a, love-e-a! Your bites are ready!" I loved her nickname for me.

Holidays, especially Christmas, were a big deal in our home. Each December, my mom would decorate the house with Santa Clauses, snow families, and big red-and-gold bows, and my dad would line the outside roof of the house with festive glimmering lights. In our home entryway, we had a mechanical plastic Santa Claus that lit up and bent forward and back to welcome you. He seemed so big to me as a little girl but was only about three feet tall. On Christmas Eve, the whole family—my siblings, aunts, uncles, cousins, and grandparents—would come over for a delicious turkey dinner with all the fixings, followed by a gift exchange in the living room by a roaring fire with Stevie Wonder, The Supremes, or Johnny Mathis playing in the background. My parents would always let my sister Kenzie and me open just one present from them on Christmas Eve; we would open the rest of our presents Christmas morning. The Christmas Eve present always contained new pajamas, which we would immediately and delightfully don. The excitement about Santa's arrival would overwhelm me and lead me to bed earlier than any other day of the year. The morning would be full of ripping paper, laughing, and running around while eating candy from our stockings. It was the very best day of the year!

All of this changed after the unexpected death of my mom when I was fifteen. She was doing a newspaper story on the California Strawberry Festival in March of 1986. She and my dad did the two-hour drive to Oxnard, California, to partake in the festivities. At a restaurant one evening, she had an allergic reaction to sulfites that made her vomit uncontrollably. She died from asphyxiation and was pronounced dead at the restaurant. She was forty-seven.

My dad arrived back home in the middle of the night that night and woke us by screaming throughout the house: "Mom's dead! Mom's dead!" He was completely distraught and in shock. There, in that exact moment, my world and life trajectory changed forever. I no longer had a mom. The loss of her was my first true heartbreak. I would sit in my bedroom for hours listening to Bread's "Everything I Own" over and over and cry. I cried so much I was sure I would have permanent tear tracks down my cheeks. It was a grim and depressing time for me. I was in a constant and overwhelming state of longing and heartache. It followed me wherever I went, like a ton of gray cinderblocks on my shoulders. For her wake and funeral, my dad told my sister Kenzie and me that we could pick out her outfit. We chose a beautiful deep purple jumpsuit that she would wear out on special occasions with my dad. I can still smell her Estee Lauder Youth Dew perfume she would douse on herself on those evenings. Even now when the smell passes by me, memories of her come flooding back and the tears start flowing. It was tough to be a grieving motherless daughter as a young teenager; it still is.

My dad was in a deep depression for years after that night and would just sit in the dark in our family room watching murder mystery TV shows and drinking red wine. There was no laughter or happiness in our home, just sadness and loss. We didn't celebrate Christmas, our family's most special holiday, for three years after my mom died; we didn't even get a Christmas tree. We finally got a tree the fourth year after my mom's death but only because Kenzie and I went out ourselves to buy the tree. We decorated it alone, too. Everything that usually brought Christmas tree joy—the lights, the ornaments, the angel at the top of the tree—only brought grief and sorrow. Shortly after that Christmas, my dad remarried a wonderful woman who not only brought a smile to his face again but ours too.

Kenzie and I also started taking care of the household and my dad when mom died. We began doing grocery shopping, cleaning, and cooking for ourselves and for him. I distinctly remember the clerk at the Alberton's grocery store giving me a confused look as I paid for a family's worth of groceries at age fifteen with my dad's credit card. I washed, dried, and folded my dad's clothes, made his bed, and put his dishes in the dishwasher. I made him spaghetti and potato salad. I hated it. I loved him, but I detested having to take care of him and what felt to me like being a wife. One day when I was in the garage putting his bedsheets from the washer into the dryer, I thought to myself: *Why would any woman do this? This sucks! I hate doing all this cooking, cleaning, and shopping. Why did mom do all this? She was working full time, too. That doesn't seem fair. I guess it's just what society expects women to do in a marriage.* It was in that exact moment that I became a feminist and realized that we live in a patriarchal society, though I had not yet been introduced to those words or their meaning.

Well, not me, I decided. *If I ever get married, my husband will do his share; we will be equal. He will respect me and all women. I am going to get a good education and have a career where I can take care of myself. I don't ever want to have to rely on a man or be his caretaker.* I began to contemplate the kind of marriage I wanted and confirmed it was one where both partners contributed, not where housework and childcare were considered "women's work" or where the wife's sole purpose was to cater to her husband. That day catapulted my interest in why women make the life choices they do and how society influences those decisions.

I began to study and learn about the role of society in women's major life decisions in a more erudite way when I transferred from the community college to a four-year university. I attended the University of California, Irvine (UCI), and graduated with a bachelor's degree (BA) in psychology and social behavior. Through my studies, I recognized the incredible pressure that society puts on women to get married and to stay married. Marriage is still considered to be women's ultimate life goal (she can get an education and have a career, but it's *really* about being married). Moreover, women are duty bound to do everything in their power to keep the relationship going and their husband smiling, even at the expense of their own happiness. The whole societal narrative of men as uninterested in a committed relationship (the whole ball-and-chain thing) and being forced to marry doesn't help. I again committed myself to eventually having a relationship that was based on fairness, integrity, loyalty, and respect. If I decided to marry, it would be with someone I truly loved, not just to have someone to call husband. And I certainly wouldn't stick around if the relationship lost the qualities that were so important to me. If I wasn't treated well, I would bolt. A good education and job would guarantee I could.

My last year at UCI, I applied for admission to numerous universities to begin graduate studies toward a PhD in psychology with a focus on women and gender. I was rejected from every single school. It was much more difficult to gain entry into a PhD than I had anticipated. Although I had a 3.8 grade point average (GPA) and some good research experience, it simply wasn't enough. Fortunately, my undergraduate mentor and advisor, Dr. Gray, encouraged me to also apply to one MA-level program in addition to the PhD programs. She obviously knew what I didn't: that getting into a PhD program was a long shot and I needed a back-up plan. She had a close colleague at Southern Methodist University (SMU) in Dallas, Texas, so was able to put in a good word for me. And I got in! It wasn't my first choice, but I was steadfast on getting my doctorate and researching women's lives as a university professor. If that meant I had to move halfway across the country by myself to get more experience and show I could do graduate-level work to get into a PhD program, then that's what it meant. I decided to attend SMU and was off to the land of big hair and cowboy hats!

I packed up my shitty college apartment and stuffed everything into my black Toyota Celica, including my little black-and-white Papillon dog, Precious. So that I wouldn't have to do the trip alone, my close friend Maggie agreed to drive with me and then fly back to California. We filled up the car with gas, put on Garth Brooks' "Against the Grain," lit a cigarette, and headed west on I-10. I was extraordinarily terrified but also excited.

Before leaving California, I had secured a tiny one-room efficiency apartment off Southwestern Boulevard, an area of Dallas filled with apartment complexes. The one I had selected was made of pink stucco buildings similar to those I'd find back home. I wished I had chosen a complex with brick buildings; they were so beautiful and rare to me. We didn't often see brick buildings where I grew up, apparently because of the possibility of earthquakes. Nonetheless, I was happy about my apartment given I signed the lease sight unseen. It was on the second floor with a nice view of some trees. The all-white kitchen was small but had good cupboard space for its size. The apartment also had a big closet that you had to walk through to get to the bathroom. The apartment was nothing special, but it was totally doable and, more importantly, all mine. And I loved the area. It was close to shops and restaurants and a trendy neighborhood called Lower Greenville. I can still taste the lime margaritas and smell the chicken fajitas from the Blue Goose Cantina.

I spent my first few days in Dallas shopping for things for the apartment. I bought a full-size mattress that I put on the floor, a build-it-yourself white laminate bookcase, a TV, pots and pans, some dishes, and a dog bed for Precious. Then I hit Tom Thumb, a nearby grocery store, and stocked up on food for the kitchen. The first meal I made in that kitchen was one of Oprah's favorite recipes: angel hair pasta with lemon and garlic. I poured myself a glass of red wine, turned on *Melrose Place*, and sprinkled some fresh parmesan cheese on my meal. I loved my little apartment and was proud of myself for making such a big move on my own.

I then visited the SMU bookstore to purchase the books for my classes. What a stunning campus! The buildings were made of that gorgeous red brick I loved and abundantly surrounded by southern large oak, crape myrtle, and Shumard red oak trees. I spent the necessary hundreds of dollars on books and supplies and bought myself a large oversized bright-red SMU hoodie and a SMU Mustangs car decal. I also went by the office of my research advisor, Dr. Karl, to say hello. She was tremendously hospitable. I was so excited to start my MA program! I was committed to acing every class and gaining critical research experience. I only had one year before I would (again) be submitting applications to PhD programs and I had to have stellar performance.

Next, I needed to find a part-time job. I had waited tables at Mimi's Café for years in California, so it made sense to start with the restaurant scene. But I didn't really know where to start. I didn't recognize any of the restaurant names and didn't want to work in fast food or somewhere too fancy. Luckily, my neighbor had a great suggestion. Chrissa knocked on my front door the week after I moved into my apartment. She and her dad lived in the apartment directly across from mine. She was young, maybe nineteen or twenty, with long brown hair, a darling fit body, and a spectacular tan.

"Yes?" I said as I opened the door.

"Hi! My name is Chrissa and live right here with my dad. I just wanted to say hello and welcome you. If you ever need anything or just want to hang out, let me know!" She oozed friendliness and warmth.

I spent time with Chrissa nearly every day after that, and we became best friends. Chrissa mentioned that she worked at a nearby restaurant and brewery.

"Do you know if they are hiring?" I asked.

"Absolutely, and it's a really fun place to work. I'll bring you an application tomorrow. It would be so fun to work together!"

I completed the application, walked it over the next day, and was hired on the spot. And she was right—it was a blast working there, especially because we often worked the same shift and made a ton of money on tips during dollar beer night.

It was easy to acclimate to Dallas life because the vibe was a lot like Southern California. There were a lot of young and beautiful people, and everyone was really laid-back and, just like back home, oftentimes pretentious. It mattered what you drove and what area of town you lived in. And you best keep your body in shape; fortunately, I was a frequent gym goer, so I checked off that box at least. Funny though, not one person said heehaw, women didn't use as much hair spray as I had imagined, and I saw only a handful of cowboy hats my entire two years living there. This girl felt right at home. And I made a ton of friends at the restaurant.

On Halloween evening, just three months after I'd moved to town, Precious and I were settling in to study when Chrissa knocked on the door. She explained that our friend Jenna from the restaurant was having a last-minute costume party and that we just *had* to go. I really had no desire; my number one commitment was always studying (I had a PhD program to get into after all!), and I hated costume parties because they always felt like too much pressure. She pleaded, and I finally conceded. She went back to her apartment to throw together a cat costume, and I borrowed a karate gi from a friend at school.

We arrived at Jenna's apartment shortly after 9:00 p.m. The party was packed, mostly with our friends from the restaurant. Chrissa suggested we grab a beer and do a roundabout to see who else was there. We walked into a room with only a handful of people and started chatting with them. It was an approachable and outgoing group, and the conversation was easy and enjoyable. I found one of the guys really funny, smart, and absolutely gorgeous. He was around 6'2" with broad shoulders and beautiful longish straight brown hair that stopped at his shoulders (I wasn't into guys with longer hair, but he wore it well). He had deep hazel eyes with long black eyelashes, a perfectly proportioned nose, and big sensual lips. I wondered what it would be like to kiss him. He had a beautiful smile as well, straight whites with a small adorable gap between his top two teeth. It looked like he too had thrown together his costume. He was dressed as a prisoner: he had on blue jeans, a blue button-down long-sleeve shirt with a piece of masking tape over the shirt pocket with a prisoner number on it, and a black-and-white striped hat. He completed his look with black Dr. Martens boots. He was exactly my type. And from what I could tell, he was the type for most of the women at the party. I think every woman that walked by him did a double take. I quickly decided he was too good looking for me and out of my league. I let the attraction go and took a sip of my beer.

Soon after, Jenna popped her head in the room and said, "Hey y'all, we're fixin to get outta here. We're gonna all head on over to the Lizard. Y'all come!"

Chrissa looked over at me with a slanted smile. "Wanna go?"

"Nah, I think I'll just head home. I have so much schoolwork to do," I replied reluctantly.

At that moment, I felt a tap on my shoulder. I turned around. It was the gorgeous prisoner.

"Hey Kathi, I really enjoyed talking with you tonight. I wanted to introduce myself. I'm Seth. I was wondering if you'd like to go out some time?"

I just about died! The out-of-my-league guy had just asked me out!

"Um, sure, I'd love to. Let me see if I have a pen." I fumbled through my purse.

When I found one, I wrote down my phone number and handed it to him while trying to contain my excitement.

"Thanks. I'll call you," he said and left.

I was on such a high after that!

"C'mon, are you sure you don't want to go to the Lizard?" Chrissa asked, clearly wanting to go.

"Well, maybe," my voice now extra cheerful, "but what is the Lizard?"

"The Lizard Lounge. It's a nightclub down the street. It'll be fun. And the prisoner might be there," she said teasingly.

"One drink!" I countered.

A lot of people from the party were at the Lizard when we arrived, including the hunky prisoner. He and I immediately grabbed two round black leather barstools and started talking and asking the typical get-to-know-you questions like "Where do you work?" and "Did you grow up in Dallas?" He moved to Texas with his mom and sister when he was in middle school. He attended a Texas university on a football scholarship and got his BA in psychology and criminal justice. He now lived in Dallas and worked at the juvenile detention center with at-risk kids. I loved that he had been a psychology major and was making a contribution to society by helping teenagers who had lost their way. It seemed he was equally impressed with me just starting an MA program in psychology with the goal of getting a PhD and becoming a college professor.

It was evident that he and I really liked each other. I was a little worried, though, because every time I left to use the restroom or chat with a friend, one of my coworkers from the restaurant, Sidney, would immediately start schmoozing him. I could tell she was into him. Was he also interested in her? No way was he flirting with both of us. That would be really douchey, and he was such a nice guy. And, of course, women would talk to him given how good looking he was! I decided it would be something I would have to get used to if we were to date. The last thing I wanted to do was fight with other women, my sisters, over a man. As it approached midnight, I realized I better get home; I had class in the morning and Precious was at home waiting for me. Seth gave me a big heartfelt hug, and I drove myself home. Then I hoped and prayed I would receive a phone call. Two days later the phone rang.

"Hello?" I answered.

"Hi, Kathi? This is Seth. I met you the other night at Jenna's Halloween party."

"Oh yeah, hi. How are you?" I replied, my face beaming.

"I'm great. How are you?" I could tell he was smiling.

We continued talking for several hours, and by the end of our conversation, I was undeniably smitten. He was caring, polite, ambitious, intelligent, loved his family, and had a great sense of humor. He was complimentary and took a real interest in me and my life. He was even genuinely interested in my perspective about sexism in society and relationships; he didn't yawn or run for the hills like most men I encountered. This guy was the whole package. And it seemed like he really dug me, too. The only issue was the warnings I received the next day.

Several of my friends at the restaurant cautioned me about dating Seth. Apparently, he was known for being a "player" and never settled down with one person. I wasn't totally surprised; he was gorgeous and charming and would have his choice of whom to date. Sidney, my coworker who kept approaching him at the Lizard Lounge the night I met him, confirmed that fact. But I wasn't into a fling or hookup, and I certainly didn't want to go out with someone who didn't respect women. He didn't come across as wanting a one-night-stand, though, and was very respectful in interacting with me. Even so, I was extremely hesitant. After speaking with Seth a few more times on the phone, and confirming with a close male coworker that a promiscuous guy can commit to one woman if he really, really likes her, I decided to go out with Seth.

Our first few dates were magical. They were nothing special—just dinner and drinks—but our connection was palpable. By our fourth date, we could hardly contain ourselves when we saw each other; we had big grins spread across our faces, and we would go straight for a big hug and kiss. We were constantly holding hands and always had to be right next to each other. The conversation was easy and lighthearted, and he made my sides hurt from laughing so hard. We were both crushing, hard. It was clear to me that I had likely met my soulmate and that he felt the same way.

On our fifth date, we decided to go to Snuffer's in Lower Greenville for a bite to eat. On our way there, Seth pulled his truck over to stop at the bank.

"I'll be just a minute," he said.

"Ok, no problem."

When he returned, he gave me a smooch and we were on our way. When we got to the restaurant, we both ordered a burger and a beer and enjoyed each other's company. After an additional round of beers, we decided we were ready to go. Seth asked for the check, and I went to use the restroom. When I sat back down, Seth had a strange look on his face.

"Hey, we just got the check," he said pointing to a slip of paper on the table. "Thing is, I forgot my wallet. I'm so sorry. Do you mind paying?"

"Oh, ok. Sure. That's fine." I was caught off guard.

I scrabbled for my purse and began to take out my wallet. In that moment, I felt an overwhelming wave of suspicion. I felt like he was lying. I looked at him curiously, my eyes squinted and head titled to the side.

"You forgot your wallet?" I asked. I wanted him to say it again for confirmation.

"Yes, I did. You don't mind paying for me, do you?" he purred with a sweet docile smile.

"Um, no I don't mind paying. But I'm a little baffled. You're just now realizing that you forgot your wallet? You didn't realize that when you stopped at the bank?" I questioned disbelievingly.

"Yeah, I just now realized."

He was starting to get a little nervous and his eyes started darting around the room. I spoke to him straight.

"That doesn't make any sense. I think you're trying to con me into paying because you don't want to. I'm not stupid, Seth. Men don't just forget their wallet on a date. They *plan* to forget their wallet. I feel like you're trying to dupe me."

He just looked at me like a deer in headlights. He shrugged his shoulders. He had no idea how to respond.

"You know this is a real bummer," I continued. "I really, really like you, but I know you're lying. So, yes, I'll pay, but this will be our last date."

"I'm sorry you feel that way," he retorted. "I'm not lying."

"Take me home please." I got up from our table.

We didn't talk on the short ride back to my apartment. He pulled up to the curb near my door, and I got out.

"See you around, Seth," I exclaimed as I shut his truck door.

I don't know what it was, but I just knew something was off. I truly felt in my gut that he was being dishonest. I was so disappointed because I liked him so much. He had been so wonderful before that. Maybe he really was the player I had been warned about. *Thank God I didn't sleep with him*, I thought. When I arrived at school the next day, my fellow classmates were eager to hear about how our most recent date went. I told them about what had happened. They wondered if perhaps I had overreacted. Maybe he wasn't lying and really did innocently forget his wallet. But that didn't explain him going by the bank. I was so puzzled.

"How about this?" I told my classmates. "If he is really telling the truth and likes me as much as I think he does, he'll reach out to me. Who knows? Maybe he'll send me flowers as a gesture of his enduring love," I laughed sarcastically.

I was certain my short-lived relationship with Seth was over. But then, that night when I got home and was making dinner, there was a knock on the door. I opened the door, and standing there was a delivery boy with a huge bouquet of red roses. I couldn't believe it! I signed for the flowers and put the vase down on the table. I opened the small envelope and read the card.

"Dear Kathi, I'm sorry for lying. Will you please give me another chance? Love, Seth."

Wow! Was Seth a mind reader? He actually did send flowers! And more importantly, he admitted he was lying. Although I was upset that he lied to me, I was thrilled by his big gesture. After all, what did I expect? I'm sure he was used to getting away with murder with women because of his charisma and good looks and probably had little remorse when he did because of societal gender norms surrounding men's conquest of women. I decided he would definitely require some rehabilitation but that his honesty demonstrated he had potential. I immediately called him to tell him I had received the roses and would give him another chance. He was ecstatic to hear it and divulged that it was now crystal clear to him that I was not a woman he could mess around with and that he respected me for standing up for myself and sticking to my guns. We went out the next evening and picked up right where we left off. The topic of the wallet never came up again.

By Christmas, Seth and I were dating exclusively and head-over-heels in love. We officially announced our status when I brought him as my date to the restaurant Christmas party. Some of my coworkers seemed a little surprised given his history as a player, and Sidney was definitely not happy. I shrugged it off and decided not to worry about it. I was in love, and he was too. It was obvious to me that I was absolutely the only woman he wanted to be with. Seth and I spent the next two years really getting to know each other and falling more and more in love. He started spending the night at my place, and we slowly began talking about the future.

One thing that really solidified the deal for me was how caring he was when I had to put my little dog, Precious, down. She was an old girl of fourteen years and began to go downhill quickly that spring. I took her to the veterinarian, and they recommended euthanasia. She was ready, they said. I was utterly devastated. I left the doctor's office that day without her. I was so upset I cried all the way home, nearly hyperventilating. I was depressed for weeks. I often woke up crying, and Seth said I even cried in my sleep.

One morning, he subtly demanded, "It's time for you to get a new dog. You are so depressed over Precious passing, and I think you need another dog to love. I hate seeing you like this."

"I think you may be right," I agreed.

About a month later, he and I drove out to the country to take a look at some Beagle puppies. We left with one in my arms. We named her Daisy, and we instantly became a family.

I started looking into psychology PhD programs late that summer and narrowed it down to those I thought were a good fit. I was especially interested in working with professors who focused their research on women and gender, especially how society influences women's life choices around work and family. These programs fell into two broad domains: social psychology, which focuses on the influence of interpersonal relationships and social groups on human behavior, and organizational psychology, which focuses on human behavior in the workplace. (By the way, clinical psychology, which most people think of when they hear psychology, usually involves having a therapy practice. This area of psychology never appealed to me. In fact, in all of my schooling, I only took one clinical psychology course.) I felt optimistic about my chances of getting into a PhD program this time; I had a 4.0 GPA in graduate-level work and gained plentiful research experience having worked on several projects with my advisor, Dr. Karl. I submitted my applications that fall, prayed to the universe, and then patiently waited.

A few months later in early March, I received a phone call from Dr. Gray, my undergraduate advisor and mentor from UCI.

"Kathi! I think they are going to admit you!" she bellowed to me on the phone.

"What? Where?" I was so excited I could barely contain myself.

"The University of Michigan in Ann Arbor! I just spoke with Dr. Olivia Steward, one of the most well-known and prolific research professors in the area of psychology and women and gender, and they are really interested in you. She wanted to know if I thought you could do PhD level work. I told them you were one of the best students I ever had. She's going to call you in a few minutes!" she said enthusiastically.

"Yes, yes, I know who she is! Thanks, Dr. Gray. I'll be ready!" I hung up the phone and breathlessly started pacing my living room.

Soon after, the phone rang.

"Hi, Kathi. This is Dr. Olivia Steward from the University of Michigan in Ann Arbor."

"Hi, Dr. Steward! It's so nice to hear from you." I tried to act calm.

"I have some good news. We've read over your application and think you are a really good fit for a new PhD program we have here at the university. We would like to offer you admittance to our joint program in psychology and women's studies."

"That is such great news! Thank you so much!"

As a psychology major, I had heard about the discipline of women's studies but didn't know much about it. I was definitely interested, though, and wanted to know more. I continued.

"Can you tell me a bit more about the program?"

"Of course. It's a combination program in both psychology and women's studies. It's the first of its kind and focuses on combining the two disciplines to provide students an interdisciplinary lens to study women's lives. In essence, you would be earning two doctoral degrees: one in psychology and one in women's studies. It's a lot of work, but we feel your interests align perfectly for what we're looking for in students for this novel program. We are holding a recruitment weekend in a few weeks and would like to invite you to come, meet all of us, and hear more about the program. We hope you accept our offer of admittance after learning more about us."

"I would love to come for recruitment weekend. I will absolutely be there!"

A few weeks later, I flew to Michigan to visit the U of M campus, meet faculty and graduate students, discover what life would be like in Ann Arbor, and gather more information about the program. The university is one of the oldest and most prestigious public universities in the U.S., consistently ranking among the top educational institutions. The sprawling campus was breathtakingly beautiful, adorned by a combination of historic and modern architecture, luxurious green lawns, and maple and pine tree-lined footpaths. The current and other potential graduate students hailed from schools like Harvard, Berkeley, Purdue, and Rice, and the faculty were top scholars in their fields. Ann Arbor was a quaint, hip, and bustling midwestern college town with a vibrant arts and music scene. It was so amazingly different from Southern California and North Texas. What an adventure it would be to live and go to school there!

The University of Michigan's joint program in psychology and women's studies, I learned, was a pioneering academic initiative integrating the two disciplines to foster in students a deep understanding of how social and cultural factors like patriarchy and gender oppression shape human behavior and experiences. Students in the program are encouraged to explore topics such as sexuality, women and work, violence against women, marriage and family, and women in science using a feminist lens while developing the skills to address these topics through research, advocacy, and social change. The goal of the program is to empower students to become critical thinkers about gender and society, contributing to the advancement of academic knowledge and to gender equality in real-world settings. *Wow, I thought, it's perfect for me!*

Seth picked me up at the airport with a huge smile and hug. I missed him while I was away, and I could tell he missed me as well. I couldn't wait to tell him all about the university, Ann Arbor, and the joint program.

"I really want to accept U of M's offer," I told him. "I have been working so hard for this, and it's such a great opportunity for me."

"I completely agree. Go for it, babe! Call them right now and tell them you accept!"

I could tell he was trying to be supportive and was happy for me, but he also seemed a bit disappointed. I think maybe he thought I would stay and continue on at SMU. My advisor, Dr. Karl, had been impressed with my performance and encouraged me to stay and complete my PhD at SMU, so it was an option. SMU wasn't the caliber of program that University of Michigan was, though, and none of the psychology professors focused their research on women and gender. I wanted to go to Michigan!

"Thank you so much for your encouragement, Seth. It means so much to me. Not only do I want to go to Michigan more than anything I've ever wanted in my life, I am also completely and totally in love with you. I know it's a lot to ask and you can certainly think about it, but I would love for you to come with me. Will you move with me to Michigan?"

His despondent voice instantly turned overjoyed.

"I am in love with you, too, and I will absolutely move with you!"

It was confirmed—we were moving together to Michigan! Almost immediately, we started planning for the big August move. We also decided that, to do it right, we should get engaged before we took off to the Great Lakes state. He proposed that June with a ring we had chosen together.

Asking Seth to come with me to Michigan and saying yes to his proposal were easy decisions for me. Just as I had never lost sight of my career goals, I also never discounted the kind of relationship I wanted to have with a lifelong partner. Seth had all of the qualities I wanted in a husband and proved time and time again that he was the man for me. Perhaps most importantly, he embraced the ideals of egalitarianism and mutual respect that were so important to me in a marriage. He wasn't hung up on "wearing the pants" in the relationship or being the patriarch of the family. He didn't care if I was more educated than him, if I made more money than him, or if we moved to help build my career as long as we did what was best for us as a couple and our family. And he didn't expect or even want me to be a "little wifey" and do all the cooking, cleaning, and childcare; he wanted to be an involved husband and father. He wanted to make me happy, smile, and laugh even if it meant less for him and more for me. He wanted me to feel extraordinarily special, and I did. I was thankful that I had met such an incredible person and that he wanted the same type of relationship and things from life that I did.

We decided to take his truck up to Michigan, so I sold my Toyota Celica, which by this time had a broken air conditioner (yes, in Texas!) and multiple cigarette holes in the upholstery. I was happy to get rid of it. Seth put a hitch on his truck, and we rented a small U-Haul trailer to carry our few belongings. Then, one evening in mid-August, just as the sun was setting and with our pup Daisy nestled in between our laps, we jumped on I-30 East. My eyes filled with tears as I looked out the window as we drove off. I could feel my life in transition once again. I affectionately looked over at Seth who had his eyes on the road. I was overwhelmed with gratitude and appreciation.

GO BLUE!

The drive to Michigan was pretty uneventful; we stopped only for food, gas, and if we had to go, pee. Seth and I played games along the way to pass the time. Our favorite was "Where are we now?" At some undefined moment, he would blurt out the question and my job was to announce where we were, how much longer until we arrived in Michigan, and several facts about the location like what it was known for or the state flower. When we finally crossed the state line into Michigan, we couldn't believe our eyes. So many trees—it was so beautiful.

We were equally enchanted when we entered Ann Arbor. Everywhere we looked we saw University of Michigan's maize and blue: on clothing, posters, banners, car decals, and flags in windows and off balconies and porches. We looked at each other smiling and yelled, "Go Blue!"

We drove through the city directly to the apartment I had leased for us in Ypsilanti, the much less expensive town next to Ann Arbor. We slept that night on the blow-up mattress we brought with us from Dallas. The change from fiery Texas to chilly Michigan was a bit tough for us, but we embraced it. In fact, aside from waiting for the shuttle bus in five layers of clothing in blizzard-like conditions, being a PhD student at Michigan was absolutely remarkable.

Seth started searching for a job in juvenile detention soon after we arrived in Michigan but wasn't having much luck, so he got a job at a nearby pet store and began substitute teaching. He continued to submit job applications in the area of juvenile detention and, after about six months, received an offer as a social worker in an emergency youth center in Detroit. He took the position even though he had a grueling seventy-mile commute with low pay. I was so impressed by him and his selflessness. He had already made so many sacrifices and here was another one, taking a less-than-ideal job that was beneath his education and salary level to support me in my dream to get my PhD and become a professor.

Things started changing for the better after the first year. We moved from the Ypsilanti apartment to a house with an Ann Arbor zip code. It was a small blue rental on a cul-de-sac in the "iffy" part of town. We loved that little house. It had four tiny bedrooms, one full bathroom, and a huge chain-link-fenced backyard for Daisy. Seth was also finally offered and accepted a job just a few miles from our house at the local juvenile detention center and stayed at that job until we left Michigan. He also decided to go back to school and get an MA degree. He didn't know exactly what he wanted to do for the rest of his life, but he knew he didn't want to stay in juvenile detention forever and an MA credential would provide a lot of opportunities for him. I fully supported him in his decision to return to school. To help with all of our school and family expenses, I took out numerous student loans to supplement my meager stipend as a graduate student and his low salary as a juvenile detention social worker. His work and school schedule kept him really busy, which made me feel better given I was always overwhelmed by my constant reading, writing, and teaching as a PhD student.

We got married in May 1999, roughly two years after moving to Michigan. We decided it would be easiest to plan and have the wedding where we lived, so that's what we did. In essence, we had a destination wedding but for all of our friends and family. We had people fly in from California, Texas, New York, and Washington. It was an incredible weekend full of festivities. We were so in love. It felt amazing knowing I was marrying such a wonderful man. We then spent two romantic weeks in Italy for our honeymoon and started trying for a baby a few months afterward given my excellent health insurance from the university.

Seth and I had a fun and solid social life including with his coworkers at the detention center. They would frequently go out for a few drinks after their 3:00-11:00 p.m. work shift, and I would sometimes meet them if I needed a break from the endless books and articles I had to read for class. We would also occasionally have them over to the house for grilling and hanging out. I was especially thrilled that Seth had made a best guy friend at work, Gus, which helped ease Seth's transition to Michigan. I really liked Gus and his wife, Nikki. Nikki worked at finding kids foster homes, so our connection on social justice issues was instant.

Seth also became good friends with one of his female coworkers, Angela. Angela was tall with short spiky brown hair. She wasn't beautiful but wasn't unattractive either. She was one of those women with a cool rough edge, like Gwen Stefani, Miley Cyrus, or P!nk. I could tell Seth liked Angela by the way he talked about her. He would say things like "Angela is really cool" or "Angela is so funny." I never thought more than *hmm* about it. I trusted Seth, and it was important to me to be the kind of wife who had no qualms about her husband having female friends. Several occurrences did unsettle me, however. For example, Angela began regularly calling the house looking for Seth. "Hi, Kathi. I'm just wondering if Seth has left yet," or "Hi, Kathi. Is Seth home? . . . Well, then can you have him call me?" Was this simply a friend calling another friend, or was there something more to their relationship?

Then, one weekend when I was at a psychology conference out of state, I called Seth and could hear that he had people over at the house. It was his friends from work (Gus, Angela, and some others) just having some drinks. *No big deal*, I thought. *Certainly, he can have friends over when I'm not home.* When I returned from my trip, I noticed that the sheets on the guest room bed were off. I looked around and found them clean and in the dryer. *Let me get this straight. Seth had (1) taken the sheets off the bed, (2) washed them, and (3) put them in the dryer.* That was some very strange behavior for him as I was the one who usually cleaned the linens. When I asked him about it, he told me that Angela had gotten so drunk that she couldn't drive so he let her spend the night in the guest room and that he washed the sheets because "that's what you always do when we have company." I was really conflicted by this: I wasn't happy that he let her spend the night at our house when I was out of town, but at the same time, he cared for a friend who couldn't drive. If it had been Gus, I wouldn't have thought twice about it. *Thank goodness we have a guest room*, I remember thinking.

A few months later, Nikki, Gus's wife, and I went out to a local brewery for dinner. She revealed to me that she thought Seth and Angela might be having an affair and disclosed that Gus had told her that Seth had asked him to lie to me when I called asking about his whereabouts one night after work. Gus had told me he didn't know. But he did know; Seth was with Angela. I couldn't believe what Nikki was telling me and was devastated about the possibility that Seth was having an affair. Would he really do such a thing? I knew he was sort of a player when we met but since then (several years ago now) gave me no reason to question him. Moreover, we had only been married a short time and, in my view, were very much in love. But evidence was evidence. Not only were there Angela's frequent phone calls to the house and the weird sheet washing incident after Angela spent the night while I was away, but now my husband was asking a friend to cover for him so he could spend time with Angela. I quickly left the brewery and raced home to begin packing. My intuition told me to leave him. I didn't have time for a cheating husband, especially one I had just married and was trying to have a baby with!

I decided I needed the support of my family, so I flew back to California to stay with my sister Jill for two weeks to plan my next steps. It was probably the most distressing *and* enjoyable two weeks of my life. Jill would go to work, and I would stay at her place and sleep and cry during the day and we would have great meals to great music at night. Our favorite was to sit on her quaint patio overlooking Anaheim Hills and grill steaks and veggies, accompanied by red wine for her and Hefeweizen wheat beer with lemon for me. Lots of cigarettes were smoked those two weeks. I think ultimately the music of Lucinda Williams saved me. She was all we listened to; "Side of the Road," over and over and over.

Seth fought for me. He called multiple times daily to talk, explain his behavior, and profess his love and commitment to me and our marriage. He had made some stupid mistakes but had not been unfaithful, he promised. He cried and begged and begged and cried. I so badly wanted to believe him. I loved him. I decided I needed to make a few phone calls. I smoked a cigarette on the patio, headed straight to my sister's bedroom, and plopped down on the partially made queen-sized bed. I took a deep breath.

The first call was to Angela. We talked for a long time, and she assured me Seth was just a good friend and that they had never been together intimately. I felt that she was being genuine and could tell she was concerned that her behavior might be misinterpreted. By the end of the conversation, we were laughing. I remember I told her, "If you're lying to me, you deserve an Academy award!" We hung up the phone, and I took a big sigh of relief.

I then called Gus. He corroborated what both Seth and Angela were saying. While my husband and Angela may have engaged in some seemingly questionable behavior, Gus had no knowledge of there being anything more between them than friendship. When I asked Gus about the lie, he admitted he did, that it was stupid, and that he regretted it. "Seth loves you," he said. "He wants more than anything to be with you." Another sigh of relief.

It was confirmed. My husband had had some really poor judgment, but he had remained faithful and did love me. He didn't cheat on me and would never cheat on me. I had no doubt that he was being authentic and truthful. I decided I would return to Michigan. Good thing, too. My period was late (from all the stress, I assumed), and the pregnancy test came back positive. We were having a baby!

Seth started working on gaining my trust back. Even though his fidelity was intact, some of the behaviors he engaged in (letting Angela spend the night when I was out of town, going to bars with her after work and not telling me, etc.) damaged my trust in him, so we decided to attend counseling to help regain confidence in our relationship. We attended marital counseling for several months, and it was helpful, mostly because it gave me a place to vent, cry, and share my feelings.

Seth also changed shifts at work. He began working the 7:00 a.m. to 3:00 p.m. shift to have no contact with Angela. He said that, even though they had become friends, it wasn't worth our marriage and that he just wanted to focus on us. He even stopped going out altogether. Although I didn't ask him to make these changes, they were bold proof that he was committed to me and our marriage. I loved my husband and soon-to-be father of my first child, more than ever. The focus was us, our growing family, and our careers.

Nine months later, our beautiful, sassy, energetic, strong-willed daughter Gracie was born. We took her home to that small blue rental home in the iffy part of town and officially began our little family. Henry, our handsome, athletic, affectionate, laid-back son, was born two years later. From the start, I wanted Gracie and Henry to have the kind of life I had growing up: a childhood full of laughter, love, and affection. I wanted them to know they were special, important, and wanted. I sought to build wonderful memories of us as family. After all, I knew all too well how losing a mom and one's family life could affect them and how important my presence was in their lives. So, from the moment they were born at the University of Michigan Women's Hospital, they became the center of our world.

Seth was extremely involved with the kids' day-to-day care and everyday house chores. I just loved that about him. We had a perfect arrangement, and everyone knew who was doing what. It went like this: Seth and I would trade off cooking each night, which usually consisted of salad, tacos, pasta, or something grilled. And we always sat and ate together as a family. While the chef for the evening was in the kitchen, the other parent would entertain the kids and clean up after dinner. The chef was then in charge of baths and would read a bedtime story and sing to Gracie; the other parent would read a bedtime story and sing to Henry. The kids knew the arrangement, too. If they wanted to know who would be reading to them that night, they would ask "Who is making dinner?" We also traded off grocery shopping, each did our own laundry, and hired a monthly housecleaner for deep cleans. We each had our own domestic responsibilities as well. He managed the money and paid the bills and took care of the yard and landscaping. I scheduled and took the kids to their appointments and planned their birthday parties and play dates, just as my mom had done. Our system worked so well for us that we rarely argued about childcare or home tasks. Seth and I made a great team, and my hope to have an egalitarian marriage built on dignity and respect materialized.

Although Seth and I were busy with the kids and work, we still made time for each other whether it be watching TV together after the kids went to bed or working out together at the gym. We also did our best to regularly go on date nights. I became really good friends with another mom and would trade off childcare with her and her husband. Sometimes, Seth and I wouldn't even go out; we would just use our date night for sex. As anyone with young children knows, it can be difficult to find time for intimacy. And sometimes you just don't feel like it; breastfeeding and wiping poopy butts all day hardly puts you in the mood. Even so, we made an effort. The last thing I wanted was for him to feel unwanted or rejected, so I began living by the motto "Always say yes" and I stood by it.

I began applying for academic jobs the year before graduation (the norm in the academic job market) and went on several on-campus interviews. Seth and I ultimately decided that I should accept a tenure-track position as an Assistant Professor of Psychology at Western Kentucky University (WKU) in Bowling Green, Kentucky. Kentucky was definitely not our first choice, but neither of us realized how competitive the academic job market is and that you often have to take a job, at least when you're starting off, in locations you're less than thrilled about. Naively, we both thought I'd be swimming in job offers with a PhD from the University of Michigan and a strong curriculum vitae. Not so. And in fact, I was incredibly lucky to get any tenure-track job; they were extremely coveted as there are always more PhD graduates with hopes of landing an academic position than there are available jobs.

Seth, again, agreed to go where my career took us, and I was so appreciative of him for it. Eventually, though, it started to be difficult for him to be a "trailing spouse." He would sometimes disclose that he felt his career was on the back burner, or he would talk about how he gave up his juvenile detention job in Dallas to move with me and "could have had a leadership position by now." I always felt so guilty that we made so many decisions to foster my career, especially when he got increasingly angry during our discussions about it. I even suggested I not take the position in Kentucky and we move back to Texas, our ultimate goal, and figure out our job situation when we got there, which likely meant me taking a non-academic job. We agreed that it was too risky to not take the WKU position—if I left the academic track now, it would be unlikely I would ever be offered another tenure-track position again. I had invested so much time and energy in getting a PhD and to abandon my dream of being a college professor seemed foolish. And I had done really well at Michigan, leaving with numerous publications in peer-reviewed academic journals, receiving several grants for my research, and winning awards for my writing. When I arrived at Michigan, some seven years earlier, I was an unexperienced student, and now I was a budding scholar. I had become an expert in the psychology of women and gender and, in particular, women's experiences in the workplace. I grew both professionally and personally during my years in Ann Arbor, and I didn't want to throw it all away. It was tough for Seth and me to make that final decision to move to Kentucky because we would be again focusing on my career. But it was our decision, and we made it together.

So, in April of 2004, we packed up the little blue house and said our goodbyes to all the wonderful friends we had made in Michigan. Seth's dad came to help us with the move. He drove with me and the kids (now one and three years old) as we followed Seth, our pup Daisy, and a new member of our family, our gray American Shorthair cat Lily, in a large U-Haul truck on I-75 South toward the Bluegrass State.

BIG RED AND BLUEGRASS

We arrived at our home in Bowling Green, Kentucky, late at night. It was our first home purchase, and we were so excited to move in. The house sat atop a small hill on a quarter acre of beautiful lush grass and dogwood trees. A huge step-up from the little blue house in Ann Arbor, the charming one-story white colonial was more than we could have imagined for ourselves. It had four bedrooms, including a huge primary bedroom with a large walk-in closet and bathroom with two sinks. There was an additional full bathroom off the hall. We were so excited that we now had two full bathrooms including one with two sinks. What a joy! The house also had a two-car garage, an enormous backyard, and a beautiful white mantle fireplace in the living room. The house even had a red front door with a gold door knocker and a little white wooden bridge covering a ditch in front of the house. It was perfect!

Seth decided not to rush his job search and instead suggested he take his time and find something he really liked while staying home with Gracie and Henry. In essence, he became a stay-at-home dad. I was thrilled about the idea. I so badly wanted him to be happy and it gave him the opportunity to take his time to find the ideal job. Moreover, the kids had not yet been in full-time day care and if he and I both worked full time that would be a necessity. I also now made enough money to hold the family over for a while until he found something. He stayed home with the kids for an entire six months and repeatedly commented how grateful he was for that time with them. Even so, the trailing spouse issue kept coming up and his resentment that my career took precedence grew, sometimes causing severe conflicts between us. I felt so badly for him and hoped that once his job situation changed, his level of anger toward me would as well. Seth ultimately got a job at the university, which we were ecstatic about. Although his anger toward me remained, his new job definitely helped. And because our buildings on campus were so close, we were able to regularly see each other during the workday. We would frequently have lunch together or surprise each other by popping into each other's office, and that was wonderful.

We spent a lot of time outside while living in Kentucky because the weather was always so nice. At the end of the backyard against the tree line, Seth built not one but two cedar-wood swing sets that were connected at one end. Together, they had four swings, two slides, two play decks with canopies, a rock-climbing wall with rope, a sandbox, and, my favorite, a double adult swing. Seth and I spent many hours on that swing talking about our future as a couple and a family while the kids played around us. It was perhaps the place that he and I felt most connected; we would discuss our hopes, dreams, and aspirations while slowly swinging back and forth with the tree leaves rustling above us. When our dog Daisy passed away suddenly our first year there, we wrapped her up in her favorite blanket, along with love notes written by the kids, and buried her in that backyard. After Daisy's death, we decided to adopt another dog, so we headed to the nearby animal shelter. We ultimately came home with two dogs, a one-year-old Treeing Walker Coonhound we named Penny and a Yellow Labrador Retriever puppy we named Frosty. It was at that time we decided we needed a fence around the backyard. Seth built the cedar-wood fence himself, and it looked incredible. I'll never forget him working out on the fence in the winter while the kids and I were snuggled up warm by the fireplace.

All of the family habits we had developed in Michigan came with us to Kentucky. We ate dinner together every night, and the chef always bathed the kids and read to Gracie before bed. But as the kids grew, so did our routines. Often after dinner when the weather was nice, Seth and I would put leashes on Penny and Frosty, and we would go for a family walk. The kids' bedtime routine expanded too, especially with me. When I was the reader, I would always read two books, one that they selected and one that I selected. True to form, my choice usually consisted of something about diversity, combatting societal oppressions, or personal empowerment. After reading, I would sing exactly four songs to them. They, and I, would be exhausted by the end of the process; more than once I fell asleep before they did.

Seth and I continued to have a strong relationship, too. We continued our date nights, this time switching childcare with a couple from church. They too had kids around our age, so it worked out perfectly. This time, though, we actually would go out on our date nights. With our bigger home in Kentucky, the kids were less likely to hear us being intimate and we were able to lock our bedroom door. Funny, though, many of our intimate moments were spent in the large walk-in closet in the primary bedroom in the mornings. Seth was usually feeling frisky in the mornings, so it was common for us to have a quickie hidden behind hanging shirts and blazers while the kids ate their breakfast and watched TV. Although we were swamped with work and small kids, we always found time to talk, hug, and connect.

Things were about to change once again, though, when I received an email about a new job position. The job was as an Assistant Professor of Psychology and Women's and Gender Studies at Texas A&M University, one of the biggest and most esteemed universities in the country. I handed Seth a printout of the email as we walked toward the outside swing that evening.

"Look at this!" I said enticingly. "I'm not sure I have a shot, but it's worth trying. We could move back to Texas and be back near family and friends! And with the focus on women and gender, it's a perfect position for me. What do you think?"

He took only a minute to read over the email. "Let's go for it!" he agreed enthusiastically.

I applied the next day and soon after was asked to come to campus for an interview. A few weeks later, I was offered the job and would begin that August. After four years living in Kentucky, our family was moving back to Texas, y'all!

Once the academic year was complete, we sold the house with the red door and again packed up a U-Haul, this time an extra-large truck, and headed toward Texas on I-40 West. I again drove with the kids (now five and seven years old) and Seth's dad who again came to help. Our pets Penny, Frosty, and Lily drove shotgun with Seth in the U-Haul. *Aggieland, here we come!*

HOWDY, GIG'EM, AND WHOOP!

Seth and I purchased a big beautiful home in one of the nicest neighborhoods in College Station, Texas, where Texas A&M University is located. Our home proved that we had finally "made it." It was a large four-way split: a primary bedroom, full bathroom, guest bedroom, and full bathroom in one section; a family room and dining room in the next section; a kitchen with eating area and den in the next; and two bedrooms with a Jack-and-Jill bathroom in the final section. So, four bedrooms, three full bathrooms, and a den. Three full bathrooms! All of the rooms had beautiful crown molding and high ceilings. The family room had a stunning white mantel fireplace and high built-in bookcases. The kitchen had all stainless-steel appliances and a huge semicircle counter and bar. I especially loved the flooring in the kitchen and den area; it was made of gold, brown, and white brick. It was gorgeous! We also had a large backyard with a patio, a large front yard, and a driveway with extra parking and a basketball hoop.

We only had Seth for a few weeks, though. When I accepted the job at Texas A&M, Seth and I found ourselves in the exact same situation as we did when we moved from Michigan to Kentucky: I had the great job, and he had not yet secured one. This time, he did not want to move until he had a job he was enthusiastic about. We both agreed that his bitterness of being a trailing spouse had become an issue and we would limit it getting worse if he stayed behind in Kentucky until he was employed in Texas. I understood his perspective, and he had already done so much for me and my career so I was open to whatever he wanted to do if it would make him happy. So, I started my incredible new job, set up our lovely new home, and got the kids enrolled and settled in school (Gracie in second grade and Henry in Kindergarten) on my own. Seth stayed with a friend of ours, Tim, in his spare room back in Kentucky. I missed my husband terribly during that time. We spoke on the phone every night, and he missed me and the kids, too.

The kids and I did well, though. I kept up with our family routines as much as I could and, because they were starting a new school (and for Henry starting *any* school) in a new city with their dad living in another state, I made sure I was completely present for them. Because of the flexibility in my work schedule as an academic, I was able to be there for them when they weren't in school. When they were in school, I became hyper focused on preparing my class lectures and working on journal publications and grant applications. Their elementary school was just a few blocks away, so the kids and I would ride our bikes to the school in the morning and I would come back when they were released from school to ride home with them in the afternoon. We would then have snacks, do homework and relax, and start our dinner and bedtime routine. Once they were in bed, I would turn on my laptop and work for a few more hours. How I got my daily workout or the dogs' walk in, I have no idea.

After six months being apart, Seth secured a position at Texas A&M and left Kentucky to join us. Our family was now complete! We were so happy to have him back with us and to be together again. We continued right where we left off with our family schedules and habits. We equitably shared the cooking, cleaning, and childcare and continued to eat dinner together. Like we did in Kentucky, we would often go for a walk as a family after dinner, including Penny and Frosty, now with the kids on their bikes.

One of the biggest changes with this move was how incredibly busy we all were. I was now at a leading research university where the expectation of research publications in top-tier academic journals and large federal research grants was through the roof. Seth too was moving quickly up the ranks to more responsibility. Although we were swamped, we each now had a full-time career we enjoyed, and I was thrilled about that. Whoop! Whoop!

The kids were also super active, especially with sports (softball, baseball, swimming, football, basketball, etc.) and other activities (music, dance, art, martial arts, etc.). As a huge sports guy, Seth encouraged them both to be involved in multiple sports at once (often to my chagrin) and often served as a coach on their teams. Being a coach was convenient for the family in that he would take the kids to their practices and games. I attended most of their games, especially during the summer. During the school year, I would usually prepare dinner and do homework with one child while Seth was coaching the other during a practice or game. It worked out well and retained the structure of the family routine. When the kids got older, they were both on elite tournament teams, Gracie for softball and Henry for baseball. I can't tell you how many weekends we spent sweating bullets at the ballpark or on the road to away games. Even when we were home, our lives revolved around sports. Many an evening I would watch Seth throw the softball or baseball to the kids in the front yard while relaxing on a camping chair with a glass of cabernet and waving hello to the neighbors. We were a full-fledged ball family!

We started taking family trips too. Our family trip to Mexico was especially memorable. I was turning the big forty and wanted to do something special for my birthday. We decided to take an all-inclusive week-long family trip to a beautiful resort on the beach over

Thanksgiving in 2010 when the kids were on school break. We ate good food, played with the kids in the pool, went souvenir shopping at a local flea market, and danced to live music. Seth and I even got a little frisky on the hotel balcony one night! He really let loose during our trip. He enjoyed cocktails at the bar, took much-needed private time relaxing in our hotel room during the day, and even participated in a poolside belly flop contest.

I'll never forget that belly flop contest! The task of the men who entered was to take a bucket of water and pour it erotically over their head, do a sensual dance, and then do the biggest, splashiest belly flop they could do. With dance club music blaring from the resort's speakers, Seth went to the microphone to say his name and where he was from. He did the bucket pour and then began moving his hands up and down his face and moving his hips back and forth in a thrusting motion. Everyone was laughing and clapping. He then began to dance salsa style directly toward me on the other side of the pool. Was he planning to involve me somehow? I was freaking out but kind of excited! He didn't, though, and instead approached a beautiful young woman who was an employee at the resort. He went up to her, grabbed her, and dipped her back with a seductive dance move. Her long brown hair flew back and her muscularly toned tan leg went straight up into the air. I was a little bummed he didn't do that with me but let it go. We were having such a good time after all. He danced back around the pool and jumped belly first into the pool, water spurting up all around him. Everyone uproariously applauded and cheered! Although he didn't win the contest, it was a fun day. Seth became known as "Texas" around the resort after that.

Thank goodness we took a ton of pictures that trip to remember what a great time we had. One evening we were listening to some live music in the bar and I began taking pictures. Seth said, "Take a few of me." And then he started to . . . pose sexily. One move he seemed to especially like was his hand on his forehead brushing his hair back like he was looking down and then someone called his name. He cracked me up! We had such an amazing time during that trip but were also happy to get back to our family routines and the dogs.

Although we didn't have a swing in the backyard at the house, we did purchase a set of beautiful brown leather couches we loved to snuggle up in to have our chats about the kids, our careers, and our future as a couple and family. We also enjoyed watching our TV shows together after the kids went to bed—well, at this point more his TV shows because I was always so busy working on a class lecture, research paper, or grant application. I always made it a point to be right next to him while he watched so we could at least chat and be affectionate. And truth be told, I did get sucked into some of his favorites, especially *True Blood* and *The Amazing Race*. I checked out when he watched *Sunday Night Football* or *The Bad Girls Club*, a reality show about young attractive unruly women living together, though.

And as I had done since we lived in Michigan, I kept my promise to "always say yes" to sex, which kept him cheerful and, by extension, me happy. I also threw some role play into the mix. He especially loved it when I would play the sexy secretary; he'd go crazy when I put on glasses, a tight skirt, button-down blouse, and high black or red stilettos with my hair up in a bun. All I had to do was walk into the room and his jaw would drop to the floor like we were Jessica and Roger Rabbit. He loved it, so I loved to do it for him.

Life was so goddamn good . . . until it wasn't.

CHAPTER 2: THE REVEAL

It was two months after our trip to Mexico to celebrate my fortieth birthday. I was in the family room folding laundry, and Seth was working in the garage when he received a *ding* on his phone, which was lying on one of the shelves of the bookcases only a few feet from me. A minute later, there was another *ding*. And then another *ding*. Somewhat annoyed by now, I went over to his phone to see who was persistently texting him. The messages were from a woman named Jackie.

"Hi!" "What're you up to today?" "Everything going okay?" her messages read.

Well, that's interesting, I thought. I had never heard of a Jackie. Maybe she was someone from work? A doctor? An old friend? I was sure it was nothing, but still I felt a gulp in my throat and an ache in the pit of my stomach; my gut told me something was wrong. I decided to ask him about it. I walked out to the garage.

"Honey, can I talk to you for a minute inside?" I motioned toward the door behind me.

"Sure." He put down the tools in his hands and headed in my direction.

I walked straight to our bedroom, him following behind me, and sat on the bed.

"Your phone kept dinging, so I picked it up. Who is Jackie?" I queried holding his phone in my hand.

He sat down on the bed next to me, his head down. He was quiet as a mouse. I could hear only the hum of the ceiling fan.

"Honey? Who is Jackie?" I repeated, a little louder this time.

"Um, well, she's a woman I've been talking to," he answered nearly whispering.

My heart sank. I knew by the way he said "a woman I've been talking to" that something was way off. Jackie was not a friend, or a doctor, or any other innocuous person I could think up.

"What? What do you mean? A woman you have been talking to? What does that mean?"

A ton of questions flooded my mind. Who was she? Where did he meet her? Were they sleeping together? There was no way; Seth would never cheat on me. I would have bet my life on it.

"I just wanted someone to talk to for fun. It made me feel good. I've never even met her in person. I met her on a website," he admitted, like it was no big deal.

"Website? What website?" I said confusingly.

"On a website called Married and Flirting," he answered hesitantly. "I've only been on the website for a few weeks, I promise. It was just something entertaining to do."

It was interesting that he came right out and told me. He didn't even try to lie. Did he think I wouldn't be upset about it? Did he know I'd sense he was lying? I felt like I was going to vomit.

"I don't understand. You've been chatting with a woman you met on a website called Married and Flirting? Like a website to have affairs?" I asked with my eyes bulging and brows so high they nearly touched my scalp.

"No, no, nothing like that. I would never do that. It's just friendly talking," he responded somewhat defensively.

"What the hell, Seth? I don't even know what to say. That's cheating! I can't be around you right now!"

I stormed out of the room and out the front door, which slammed behind me. I then furiously walked across the street and took out his phone that was now in my pocket. I stood there looking at the phone screen and contemplating my next move. Should I, or shouldn't I? *Fuck it*, I thought to myself, then I called Jackie's number. My heart was hammering as the phone rang.

"Hello?" a woman's voice answered after two rings.

"Jackie?" I demanded more than asked.

"Yes?"

I got straight to the point. "This is Seth's wife. Why are you talking to Seth?" I asked, my voice trembling.

"It's no big deal," she said nonchalantly. "We met on a website and became friends. It's just a place to talk to people and get advice. And flirt a little bit. You really shouldn't overreact," she advised condescendingly.

I was like, *Oh, hell no.* "Don't contact Seth again," I ordered as I hung up the phone.

I marched back into the house and saw Seth sitting in one of the chairs in the backyard patio with his head dropped. I was so angry I wanted to claw his face off. I tossed his phone onto the table next to him.

"Here's your phone so you can call your girlfriend back. Oh, and you're sleeping on the couch tonight," I said indignantly.

The rest of the day I only spoke to him when I had to. I couldn't even look at him because I was so boiling with anger and disbelief. When the kids were finally tucked in bed, I sped to our bedroom and slammed the door. I took a long hot shower, put on my pajamas, and got into bed. I stared at the ceiling incredulous about what had happened and what Seth had revealed to me. I started searching Google for articles on whether or not flirting counted as cheating. For the most part the answer was no. "Everybody flirts," "It's normal," It's healthy for a relationship," blah, blah, blah. Well, it sure felt like cheating to me. Seth literally went out of his way to connect with women by signing up on a website and was actually communicating with another woman behind my back in a flirtatious way. I couldn't even think straight, my mind was so overwhelmed with chatter. What did they even talk about? Did they talk about having sex or just run-of-the-mill daily life? Did my name come up? Why did he feel the need to talk to a woman in the first place? What did he type in the Google search box to even find that website? By the way he described it, it was something he was looking for, not something he simply came across out of the blue. I was so confused about the man who was sleeping on the couch. My Seth would never do something like this. Although he had made mistakes in the past—like his stupid decision to philander with Angela over a decade prior when he was working at the detention center in Michigan—he gave no indication of being on the brink of cheating. His fidelity never gave me pause or concern. We loved each other. Oddly, I kept thinking I wanted to go talk to that guy, the one who would never engage in such behavior, about it. Obviously, I couldn't. So, I cried myself to sleep instead.

The next morning, he quietly came into our bedroom to get ready for work. I closed my eyes tight, held the blanket taut in my hands against my chin, and buried my head in the pillow pretending to sleep. I had nothing to say to him. Before he left, he sat down on the bed next to me, stroked my head softly, and lovingly kissed me on the forehead.

"I love you and I'm so sorry. It was only the past few weeks. It was only talking. I'll take care of the kids this morning and drive them to school. They are already up and getting ready. You rest and I'll call you later," he said.

I could smell his cologne on his fingertips. I wanted to puke. To me, he had been unfaithful, even if it wasn't physical. He got up from the bed, gathered the kids, and they were off. He closed the front door, and the house fell silent. I was so thankful I didn't have any classes to teach that day; I was a complete wreck, fluctuating between being furious and crying, and never would have been able to make it to campus. I sat up in bed and grabbed my laptop that was sitting on the bedside table. I sent him a simple email:

> in·fi·del·i·ty
>> /ˌɪnfɪˈdɛlɪti/ [in-fi-del-i-tee]
>>> —noun, plural -ties.
>> 1. marital disloyalty; adultery.
>> 2. unfaithfulness; disloyalty.
>> 3. a breach of trust or a disloyal act; transgression.

He instantly replied:

> There was nothing physical or emotional. Just to feed my ego. I was disloyal. Dishonest. Just to feed my ego. It was not worth it. I wish I was thinking of the consequences. At the time I didn't. Or, I justified it to myself that it wasn't cheating b/c nothing was physical. But, I was wrong. I hate myself for what I have done. I love you. I love our kids.

I didn't know what to think. I knew he loved me and our kids, but I couldn't understand how he would do something so immature. Why would he jeopardize our relationship for a quick self-esteem boost? Was I not making him feel special or wanted? Did I do somehow to bring this on? To me, we had a good marriage, one built on a sturdy foundation of loyalty and respect—the pillars of the feminist principles I worked so hard to incorporate into my personal and professional life. He had lied to me, though, and that was a behavior contrary to the egalitarian marriage I sought, and I thought I had. I wondered if I should forgive him. People make mistakes, right? And they hadn't been physical. But he could be lying about that, too. Maybe they had met in person. Oh my god, maybe they kissed. Ugh. I couldn't think straight. I felt sick.

I decided to call my friend Chrissa for support. I told her about what had happened. She was also shocked. No one would have guessed that he would ever be on such a website as he was always the exemplar of a committed and faithful husband and family man.

"You know, there is probably more to the story. And Jackie might not be the only woman he's talking to. Have you checked his Married and Flirting account? How about his Facebook account? Email accounts?" she queried.

Good idea, I thought, though I was sure I wouldn't find anything. I so badly needed confirmation that this was an isolated incident.

I first typed in "Married and Flirting." Indeed, it was a real website. The first thing that caught my eye was the logo. It said "Married and Flirting: Looking for Something Extra?" The word "Married" was in big red curvy letters, you know, for that fun and whimsical feeling. Gross. Right below that it stated, "Looking for Something Extra?" I also noticed a big colorful advertisement in the top middle of the page for AshleyMadison.com. The ad cycled between several taglines including "Life is Short. Have an Affair," "The Facebook of Sex," and "When Divorce isn't an Option." It was obviously a website for married people to have secret affairs. I wrote it down as an additional place to check out, just to be sure I'd covered my bases.

From what I could tell, Married and Flirting was a bunch of chat rooms. I needed to get in and check it out. I wanted to see what people were talking about on the site and if it was as harmful and innocent as Seth and Jackie had made it out to be. Even more so, I wanted to see Seth's conversation with Jackie. I thought about creating an account, but that wouldn't get me the depth of information I needed. I decided to try to log in as Seth. I first typed in his email address as the login ID. It didn't work. Dammit. I then tried his nickname and, oh my god, it worked! Now, the password. I tried his usual letter-number combination password. My computer sat idle while the page was loading. Then, *bam*, I was in! How stupid of him to use his typical login credentials! There I was, in my husband's Married and Flirting account. I was terrified about what I might find. *Please be nothing. Please be nothing*, I prayed over and over in my head.

His name on the website was identical to his email username, so it confirmed to me that it was him. The profile picture, however, was not Seth. It showed a man with no face, only a body. The image had two full sleeves of tattoos (which Seth also had, several of which represent me and the kids—go figure), but the body was that of a gorgeous muscular model. It was definitely not Seth's body; he obviously got the image online somewhere. Next, I read his "About me." Below is what he wrote on the website:

> *Hello! I am a 39 yr old straight educated professional good looking (w/ a bad boy look) in shape male from the great state of Texas! I have an erotic list of things I want to do b/f it gets too late, but the Mrs. has no interest in helping me out. I have finally gotten to the point in my life that I am confident enough to explore new exciting things. In the last few years I have become very inhibited and become more romatic and looking for new thRills! Exciting thrills that is. I am close to the Houston area, but I can easily get to Austin and DFW. I am looking for that confident person b/n 27-45 that is adventurous and wants to explore new things that the Mrs. does not want to do or can't b/c of jealiousy issues. Discretion is a must. So what is the best way to find a "friend" like that? Suggestions would be helpful. Or if your in the area . . .*

To say I was shocked and outraged by what I read is an understatement. I sat there completely disorientated, my eyes darting around the room trying to make sense of what was happening. Did Seth actually write that? Not only could he not spell for shit (which was a total ick), but he was unequivocally, without a doubt, 100 percent soliciting sex—on a website! All of the air spewed out of my body, and I started violently gasping for breath. I grabbed my neck as if someone was strangling me, my eyes now motionless and protruding from my head. Seth told me he was just flirting for fun with Jackie, but this discovery irrefutably begged to differ. He wanted to have an affair, and he was actively trying to make that happen. It was a well-thought-out and intentional decision for him. He knew exactly what he was doing. Acid started creeping up my esophagus, and I began gagging as the vinegary liquid reached the back of my tongue. I grabbed the snot- and tear-stained ball of tissues that had sustained me throughout the night from my bedside table and started heaving into it. I coughed up so much yellow bile that the now repulsive ball of tissues began breaking into pieces in my hands. I got up and went to the bathroom, tossed it in the toilet, and flushed it down.

"What is going on?" I bellowed into the house beams. I swear the house shook in fright.

I raced back to my bed, picked up my laptop, and started examining the pictures he had posted on his profile. *Are you kidding me?* I immediately realized that I had taken every single picture. One was from Christmas day, only a month before, a photo of him proudly holding up the football encyclopedia book I gave him as a gift. The others were from our family trip to Mexico, only two months earlier. Wait . . . that night in Mexico when we were in the bar listening to live music and I teased him that it looked like he was sexily posing for something, he actually was! His favorite pose, the one with his hand on his forehead brushing his hair back, landed right in the middle of his Married and Flirting profile page. I rested my forehead in my hand incredulously, still looking up at the computer screen. What in the world was happening?

Just then, I noticed the "Your posts" tab. I moved the computer mouse over to it and hovered there for a few moments. I was conflicted; I didn't think I could handle finding out more, but I had to know if he had posted anything and how often. I clicked on the tab. Oh my god! He was one of the most active members on the website! He had dozens of conversations with different women and had posted over five hundred times just in the previous month! I started to read some of his posts. Some were friendly, some were flirty, and some were down-right raunchy. Some even put me down. He even gave me a name: "Mrs. Tattoo." Here are some of his actual posts:

— *Well move over and share the bed w/ me. i am up. in more ways than one.*
— *OK. just give me that ass. looks so much better w/ my hands on it.*
— *If I were you I'd be very careful if you turn your back. You never know what might poke you from behind. ;)*
— *ok im horny. who's first.*
— *i was thinking bed post. I bet you'll cum b/f me!*
— *Um, I just got hard. Really hard. Gulp.*
— *Apparently, all the single moms in the neighborhood want to fuck me because they smile and say hi.*
— *Mrs. Tattoo is the most selfish egocentric person in the world.*
— *i'll have sex with her instead of Mrs. Tattoo lol*
— *Name me a public place. I probably fucked there.*
— *Yes dreams do come true!! Spanking that ass!!!!*
— *Now get that sexxxy ass over here and workout that frustratoin on me.*
— *well. show me that ass. and lets do it again.*

I took my trembling hands off the computer keyboard and slowly lifted them to my face, tenderly cupping my nose and mouth. I
sat there in complete disbelief. I then grabbed the pillow next to me
and put it over my face. I screamed out my rage and hurt into that
pillow so earsplittingly loud that this time not only did the house
shake, but Frosty, who was lying on the bed with me, started barking
and Penny ran in from the other room to check on what was causing
me such distress.

"It's alright boys. I'm okay," I told them.

They both immediately came up to me and started licking my
face like I was a bowl of beef-flavored ice cream. Thank goodness
they were there. They calmed me down, and I began to gain my composure. I started to question what the fuck was going on. Was this
a joke? Was someone messing with me? Was it really Seth posting?
He wouldn't do this. This can't be real. No way was this real. *I don't
believe it.*

While I sat there on his Married and Flirting profile in utter
astonishment, an ad kept running for Find New Passion, another
website that seemed to be geared toward spouses looking to cheat. I
impulsively clicked on the link, convincing myself that there was no
way he would have a profile on another duplicitous website.

Find New Passion seemed to be a higher caliber of the cheat-
on-your-spouse genre and offered "a time out from your difficult,
sexless, or loveless marriage" and claimed to be "the place to start a
marital affair." I decided to try and log in with the credentials Seth
used for Married and Flirting, praying the entire time that he did not
have an account. I exhaustingly typed in his login name and password, hit Enter, then put my hand over my eyes. I took a deep breath
and opened my eyes through my fingers like I was watching a horror
movie and someone was about to be bludgeoned to death. "Welcome
back!" appeared across my screen. My chin immediately hit my chest
and tears flooded my eyes. I looked back up at the screen.

"You asshole!" I screamed as I slammed my laptop shut.

I shot out of bed and started pacing the room like a frantic lunatic. Who was this person I was married to? How could my amazing and committed husband do something like this? How could this possibly be true?

In the end, Seth had accounts on at least five websites catering to martial cheating. One account I tried to crack but just couldn't was AshleyMadison.com. AshleyMadison.com is apparently the crème de la crème of infidelity websites, so I just knew he was on it. But I couldn't prove it. All of my attempts using his typical login information proved useless. Then, in 2015 (some four years later), Ashley Madison was hacked and their users revealed to the world via an online searchable database. All you had to do was type in the potential cheater's email address to get the result. Do you think Seth had a profile on AshleyMadison.com? Yes, he did. Of course, he did.

Like an indomitable force of nature, I went back over to the bed, sat down, and opened my laptop. I typed Facebook into the search box, then logged into Seth's Facebook account using the same username and password as Married and Flirting and Find New Passion. I started scouring his account. I first inspected the people who had liked or commented on his posts. Everything seemed legitimate. I next went to his messages. There were a few to and from his buddies, one from his mom, and—*oh, what is this? . . . A message to someone named Veronica.* Who the hell was Veronica? I read the message. Seth had sent this woman a message asking her to meet him in Las Vegas only a few weeks before:

> *I will be going with some friends but they will be leaving a few days before me. so I'll be all alone* ☹ *so yes, you are invited.*

There were no previous messages between them, just the one. A

Las Vegas trip was certainly news to me! And inviting this Veronica to join him? I clicked on her name.

Veronica was a young woman with a *Jersey Shore* vibe. She looked about twenty-something and had long dark straight hair, dark eyes, and huge boobs. She wore lots of makeup and seemed to love to wear short tight dresses and stilettos. In all of her pictures she was standing with her hand on her hip and leaning forward to display her cleavage, which she was clearly very proud of. I didn't recognize her at all, but as I was sifting through her pictures, I stumbled across one that looked really familiar. I stared at it for a while trying to figure out why it seemed so memorable to me. Then, it clicked. The location of the picture was the resort we had stayed at in Mexico. Oh my god, that was how he met her. He met her on our Mexico vacation—on our *family* vacation! But how was that possible? I was with him nearly the entire time, except for when he went to relax in the hotel room. Or, oh my god, maybe he met her when he stayed out at the bar one night while the kids and I went back to the room for bedtime. Maybe he had sex with her! Would he really do such a thing, while the kids and I are in the hotel room sleeping? Only a horrible satanic person would do that. Am I married to Satan? Am I dreaming? What is going on? First the marital cheating websites and now this? Who is my husband? Who is he?

Fury and suspicion propelled me to keep searching. I next went to his Yahoo! email account. It was harder to crack the code. I couldn't get the username and password correct, so I had to answer some security questions. Shit.

First one: "In what city did you meet your spouse?"

Easy: "Dallas."

Second one: "What is the name of your first dog?"

Crap. This one was more difficult. He talked a lot about a dog, Shadow, he had in college. But that was in college. Surely he had a dog before that, but I couldn't recollect. Dammit.

I typed, "Shadow."

The page started loading. Did I get it right? Indeed, I did! Just as I began inspecting my deceitful husband's account, an instant message popped up!

Hey! Just checking in to say hi.

Then another instant message from a different person:

Hi Seth. I'm totally not stalking you. Just wanted to tell you I'm still thinking about you and hoping for the best.

I quickly looked at their names: *Stacy and, let's see . . . Tessa. Who in the world are Stacy and Tessa?* I immediately responded to both of them:

This is Seth's wife. Who are you?

Tessa responded that they had been talking and apologized, but Stacy was dead silent. What the fuck! So now we had Jackie, the Married and Flirting woman, Veronica from our Mexico vacation, and Stacy and Tessa from Yahoo! How many women was my lying husband talking to? How many was he having sex with? How did I not know? How stupid could I be? I must be blind! I'm here thinking we have an amazing marriage, and he's the lying cheater of the decade! Rage was pouring out of every crevice of my body, seeping from my veins and arteries. My jaw clenched and my breathing became fast and deep. How dare he do this to me and the kids, to the woman he vowed to be faithful and loyal to, the woman he promised to honor and love until death? And to think he was trying to convince me he was only talking to Married and Flirting Jackie and it was only the last few weeks. What a deceiver! Who is this man I call my husband? The husband I know would never do this. Does he have different personalities? Is he a compulsive liar? How could someone disregard and lie to their spouse like this? One thing I knew for sure, I wasn't going to stand for it. This was way over the line. Regardless of how much I loved him, I could not stay in a marriage with someone who would do these things. It had to be over. There was no other option. I refused to be the stupid wife who would stay with such a lying, cheating womanizer. I sent him this message:

> *Seth - My newest finds! You were talking with the one woman when we were in Mexico - last few weeks my ass! By the way, I just had some fun conversations with some of your "friends" on yahoo chat. WE ARE OVER FOREVER! Seth - I loved you with all my heart. I completely loved you. I am just totally shocked. I didn't know you at all.*

After I hit Send, I quickly went back to his Yahoo! email account. Could there possibly be more? Could it get any worse? *Please don't let me find more. Please don't let this get sorrier.* At this point, though, I couldn't stop myself. I checked his email inbox but didn't see anything suspicious. I next went to his sent messages. That's when I discovered Carly. Carly's email address had her last name and her place of employment, which made it easy for me to look her up. She worked at a large public university in their Office of Research Ethics and Compliance (Ha! Ethics!). I didn't recognize her and had never heard her name before. She was younger than me, maybe in her early thirties. She had long wavy blond hair, blue eyes, and a quirky smile. She was attractive but nothing special, sort of the girl-next-door type. She could pull off being stunning when dressed up for a special occasion but also someone you would pass by without taking a second look on an average day.

I instantly assumed they met at a conference or some other

work-related event given that they both had jobs in university research compliance. In fact, he had attended a conference the month before our Mexico trip. Come to think of it, I recall when he went to that conference that he left without his wedding ring. I was doing some straightening up in our bedroom and came across his ring in a small dish on top of our dresser. I remember thinking, *Huh, he forgot to put on his ring.* And then I didn't think about it again. After all, it was a common occurrence. He said it hurt because of the worsening arthritis in his fingers. His grandmother had terrible arthritis in her hands, so it seemed like a valid reason. Just like when, around the same time, he decided to try full manscaping just because he was "curious how it would look and feel." I can still remember his chubby pale, hairless body in our bathroom. *Okay, whatever,* I thought. Thinking back, how dumb could I be? Manscaping and not wearing his wedding ring—those are classic signs of cheating. How could I be so clueless and so trusting? Certainly, going out of town without his wedding ring and doing a full manscape suggested that he was preparing to be unfaithful! I'm so stupid!

As I began to read the email thread between Seth and Carly, it became clear that, not only was my husband interested in meaningless flirting and hookups, but a more substantial adulterous relationship as well. Carly and my husband's conversations read like two people, just beginning their love story, who couldn't get enough of each other, and thought constantly about being together. They liked each other, a lot.

The anger I felt from discovering his deceitful online behavior turned to anguish as I realized he had been, without a doubt, physically unfaithful and with a woman he seemed to have feelings for. Although the possibility that he had begun a real relationship with someone wasn't a stretch based on everything else I found, it still felt different. I now had confirmation that Seth was having a full-fledged physical and emotional connection with another woman, along with all the sickening online treachery. I could feel my head slowly drop and my body contract as if my back was enveloping my heart. It was the final stab to what felt like my already cut-up and bleeding body.

The dates on their emails documented that the email thread had taken place during our family trip to Mexico. Seth had communicated with Carly all throughout the trip. They sent sweet compliments, described everyday tasks and events like laundry and watching football, talked about being together sexually, and discussed spending more time together. It was clear that Carly knew he was in Mexico at a beach resort with his kids; it wasn't clear if she knew about me. It was also obvious that spelling and grammar weren't their strong suit. Here's the actual thread I found in his email, with my thoughts interspersed.

> Carly: *The beach looks freaking amazing! I love the water, be it pool or beach. I had a lot of fun living so close to the beach this summer.*
>
> Seth: *they do a good job here at the resorts keeping them clean. next time i am in CA can we go for a walk on the beach?*

Clearly, Seth was sending Carly pictures of our hotel, as you would to someone you're thinking about and wishing they were there. And he asked her if they can go for a walk on the beach the next time he's in California. The only time he ever went to California was when we were visiting my family. Did he plan on seeing Carly on our next family trip? Was he going to make up some excuse to get away for a few days?

> Carly: *We can definitely go for a walk on the beach when you are in CA. That would be nice. Do you think we'll actually get together again? It's fun to talk about, but I wonder. I hope so. So what are the plans*

for tomorrow? You guys just going out to dinner or something?

It now sounded to me like they had met at the Washington, DC, conference and had only been together during that one trip. One thing was clear: they really hit it off and were undeniably interested in spending more time together. That realization felt like a kick in the face. All this time, I believed Seth and I had something genuine and unique and that there was no one in the world he would rather spend time with than me. I thought—no I *knew*—he loved me and that he didn't want any other woman in his life. But this new knowledge was showing me I wasn't special at all. For the first time in my life, I felt entirely unexceptional. I felt replaceable, common, basic, dull, and, above all, dumb. I wondered who "you guys" was; who was she referring to when she wrote that? Who did Seth tell her he was with traveling with?

> Seth: *Will we get together again? My gut says yes. sooner than later. but yes, it is very fun to talk about. no plans for tomorrow*

Sooner rather than later? Was he going to make up a trip, like he did with Veronica and Las Vegas? And I was just thrilled to hear that he was having so much fun talking about cheating on me! My thoughts became jumbled and chaotic. I was once again utterly bewildered by the man whose conversation I was reading. This was not the man I was married to. This was not the loyal husband and father I loved so dearly. This was not the man I laughed with and made future plans with on the swing in Kentucky or loveseat in Texas. Every word I read fractured my reality of my happy life. None of it made any sense. I couldn't wrap my mind around it. Did he even love me? Did he love our family?

Carly: *I prob shldnt be sending this but I'm on the road for the nxt 3 hrs. You prob can't but here's my # if u somehow get the chance to call.*

Seth: *I just tried calling and i cant get service on my phone :(i don't know if it is just where i am at in the hotel or b/c i am in mexico. let me try to figure this out.*

When did he try to call her? I was with him the entire time we were in Mexico. Oh wait—he spent all that time alone "relaxing" in the hotel room. Was he going to the room to talk with her? Oh my god, he was talking with and emailing her all that time he was in the room! And the night he stayed at the bar when the kids and I went to bed, maybe he called her then too!

Carly: *I just pulled up to my parents house. I didn't even think abt u were calling out of the country. That cld be expensive & some phones won't call if u haven't set up an international plan. if u can I will def do everything I can to get to my phone to talk to u!*

Seth: *oh, i just made it work!! i just left a silly message, not really silly, just me rambling. i was lost for word. sorry i didn't catch you. maybe later. bye bye*

Carly: *I love your v oice! I can't believe I missed ur call. I was having coffee downstairs w/ my parents. I was actually talking abt u to my parents a few min ago. So big step I guess- my parents know abt you. Haha. Ok, I gotta get moving! So so happy to hear ur voice. I def saved that message & will listen again later.*

Ok, last email for the night! Just listened to your message just to hear your voice. I hope that doesn't sound too creepy or crazy. :) I hope u get another chance to call! I want to give u a giant bear hug w/ my arms and legs wrapped around you and listen to you say hi and how happy u are to see me and whatever else just so I can hear your sexy voice. Nighty night. Kisses!

Another hard kick in the gut—I actually put my hand to my stomach to lessen the blow as my brow furrowed and my face scrunched in pain. Carly was talking to her family about my husband as if he was her new boyfriend. She was envisioning them together in a serious relationship, and he certainly wasn't stopping her. I so badly wanted to know if she knew he was married. Was he going to eventually leave me for her? Was he falling in love with her? I started thinking about them having sex, and then about he and I having sex. He was talking to her while having sex with me! We even had sex several times on our trip! Would he go back and forth chatting with her about having sex and then come have sex with me? Nauseating! I kept reading. Apparently, they had been successful talking over the phone but the called dropped:

Seth: *Sorry! We got cut off. I wanted to at least say bye! mmmmm. i like the sound of your morning voice. very nice. well, i guess i am off to the beach. have a great lazy friday!! did i tell you that your pretty today. and oh, well, you are. :) i will chat w/ you later*

Mmmm . . . very nice? Sounds like a creepy guy at a peepshow. Gross.

Carly: *We wld probably never get out of bed or leave the house so you would get my morning voice all the time! Do you talk during sex? And/or laugh? I do some-times. Not the best conversations since ideally both participants are distracted, but it can be fun. Hope ur relaxing & thinking of me!*

Sounds to me like their rendezvous may have been quick and boring—no talking or laughing? That made me feel a little bit better at least. Obviously, I was better in bed than her (like that mattered). And yes, he does talk and laugh during sex, Carly. I know that because I have sex with him all the time and have been for the last fifteen years.

> Seth: *yes, i bet we wouldn't get out of the house until late late afternoon, and that would be to eat. then while eathing you would look at me a certain way, which would turn me on and i'd have to have you again so we would quickly get back home and make each other feel good again. lol. yes i can talk during sex. about what? depends on what's going on. and laugh too? Of course!*

See, Carly, I told you. And what is "eathing"? Would the kids and I also be there for that late afternoon meal, dear husband?

> Carly: *our fantasy world where we could see each other all the time and would have our all over each other. We wld be that sickening couple that you just want to tell to get a room or grow up! Ha. Well I think it's abt shower time for me. Need to clean myself up before we have some fam over for dinner. I will def think of u! There's a removable shower head so I can really clean some of those dirty dirty spots on my body. And lucky for me that usually feels pretty effing good! Wld be more fun if u were here to help me wash up and then make me a dirty girl all over again! Mmmm I'm*

so ready to hop in the shower. Haha, so think of me! ;)
you a little excited? Evil grin!

Are the kids and I dead in your fantasy world, Carly, so that you can be with my husband all the time? Or would you simply like the family to break up? It was interesting how much my emotions fluctuated while reading their short conversation: furious at him one moment and livid with her the next, hurt by his comments and disgusted by others, embarrassed by my stupidity while at the same time wounded by his betrayal. Incredulous and devastated, all around.

> Seth: *ok. i am being scarry stalker guy and rereading your emails. lol. hey, what can i say, some of them are really hot and fun to reread. sometime i get turned by the thought of having sex half clother. skirt pulled up. panties to the side. shrit on, but unbuttoned w/ breast hanging out of bra. that is usually being done at a place other than home. i kind of get turned on by sexy bras. somethings i'd prefer to leave them on and just pull out the breast. i just think that look is hot and sexy. i bet you can pull that off. :)*

His elaborate description of having sex with her with her skirt pulled up, shirt unbuttoned, breast out . . . It sounded exactly like the sexy secretary role I often played for him. It made me sick.

> Seth: *wake up sunshine. you have a cute boy in mexico to email. lol. didn't you know the world is much more of a beautiful place when you up and about flashing that pretty smile. i hope you have a wonderful day!*

Nice how Seth was giving her compliment after compliment when I was the one actually there all decked out in outfits I bought for the trip to look good for him. All for a lying cheating husband!

Carly: *Again, another amazing email to make me smile. Now watching some college football & helping my sis clean up. Left the coffee shop and put the top down on my car. It's a beautiful day! Just put my USC shirt on, ready for football & beer. When I was changing into my USC shirt, I noticed my boobs in the mirror and thought, wow they look good right now. Seth would love them right now and we wld both love it if u came up from behind and cupped them and caressed them. Out shopping w/ mom & sis & saw some shirts that remind me of u & what u were wearing that night.*

Seth: *Oh, my Orange Crush shirt. lol. I plan on wearing my "Lucky Charms" one tomorrow. lol. i like those types of shirts. one of those, some faded jeans, my docs, and a cool hat and i am all set to start firting with you. lol. keep thinking of me. i like it.*

He didn't even respond to her boob comments. He is only concerned about his dumb vintage tee shirts. What a selfish, egoistic, misspelling jerk!

Carly: *Yep. Love the look. Heard iowa lost. Hope ur boy wasn't too upset. Keep your fingers crossed that SC kills ND!*

Okay, so she knows Henry is with him. How about his wife and daughter?

Seth: *okie dokie. fingers crossed.*

Carly: *U need to cross ur fingers harder!*

Seth: *OK. i am doing it harder. mmm. why does that sound dirty?*

There's that "mmm" again. Ewwww. I read on.

> *i got to know a guy today and we hit it off at the pool. i later saw him at the hotel lobby bar and we started talking. after the fam and i ate dinner and watched a show we were at the bar and we talked to this guy and his fam. the families went down for the night and me and this guy stayed and bullshitted for the night. it was crazy as soon as the families left we had all of these people come up to us and started asking me and him if we were cage fighters. lol. do i look like a cage fighter to you? but i shit you not, i have been asked at least once a day here if i am a professional cage fighter. how funny is that? i have participated in a couple of "games" around the pool area and people have seen me i guess. they call me "Texas". we were sitting at the bar and like, all these people started coming up to us talking to us out of nowhere. we had a group of younger girls come talk to us all flirty and ask about our tats and if we were professional fighters. it was so funny. they were cracking us up. i just shook my head and we got out of there after a while to avoid trouble. but the experience was good for my ego. of course, not as good as you are:) so i get back to my room move my boy over to his side of the bed pick up my laptop and check to see if you emailed me. is that normal? you're just a really cool person. i know that is corny to say, but alot of things you say you do or talk about just click in my head a certain way*

This text got me thinking back to some of the details of our Mexico vacation that gave me pause. Seth did engage in some strange behavior during that trip. I think I tried to suppress those instances because I only wanted to have wonderful memories of our family time together. First, I was surprised that he wanted to stay at the bar and have a few drinks with the guy he met at the pool earlier that day. Seth was not much of a drinker. I was always the one with the party streak. I was always like, "Let's get a six-pack and listen to the concert in the park," or "Let's get a bottle of wine with our fancy dinner"; the answer was always "no." Seth's jam was eating nachos with a glass of milk in front of the TV watching whatever football game was on or the latest episode of that stupid *Bad Girls Club* reality show he watched (I always thought that was an odd choice for a dedicated family man). As such, it was very peculiar that one evening in Mexico he wanted to stay up at the bar and have some drinks while the kids and I went back to the hotel room. It felt like something was off that night, and now I knew there was.

I also started thinking about that stupid belly flop contest. The men who entered the contest were to pour a bucket of water over their head, do a dance, and then do a belly flop into the pool. Seth did the bucket bit and then started dancing directly toward me on the other side of the pool. I excitedly thought he was going to involve me somehow, but he didn't. Instead, he went to up to a gorgeous young employee of the resort, grabbed her arms as if to start dancing with her, and dipped her down. Then, he danced back around the pool and did his flop into the water. Everyone cheered and laughed. I did too. I was right there clapping and hollering along with everyone else. But in reality, I felt humiliated. No one knew it, but I felt about one inch tall when Seth didn't choose me. I thought maybe I was being jealous or overreacting, so I let it go. Everyone, especially Seth, was having such a great time after all.

I remember waking up and seeing Seth get into bed with Henry. He was clearly hyped up by all the people that flocked to him because they thought he was a professional cage fighter (sense my sarcasm) and couldn't wait to share it with Carly. The thought blew me away. He sat next to his young son who was fast asleep, his wife and daughter sleeping in the bed next to them, to begin emailing a woman he was having an affair with during their family vacation to celebrate his wife's milestone birthday. Who does that? Apparently, my cheating husband—that's who.

Seth, I was learning through my discoveries, needed constant and overwhelming attention and adoration from other and many women to feel good about himself. As he even alluded to several times in the text to Carly above, it was good for his ego. You can almost feel the rush of adrenalin he felt when the young flirty girls asked him, like people did incessantly throughout the vacation (again with sarcasm), if he was a cage fighter (clearly Seth didn't realize the bullshit some women will say to get men to buy them drinks, dumb ass). It was interesting how he told Carly he got out of there to avoid trouble; if she (or I, for that matter) had known that he shared contact information and perhaps more with at least one of the women (Veronica) he talked to at the bar that night, she would have been really upset. It was weird how I almost felt bad for Carly in that moment; she was really digging him, and he was flat out lying to her.

Carly must have been sleeping because she didn't respond to his message that night. He sent her a follow-up message the next day after we, as a family, had returned from a day of flea market souvenir shopping. We were headed toward the pool when Seth announced he had to send a quick email to a work colleague. The kids and I had already donned our sunscreen, hats, and towels, so we decided he would meet us at the pool when he was done. That must have been when he sent Carly the message below. It was the last one in the thread and the last I found of their communications:

Seth: *Well, good afternoon beautiful! i just back from a flea market and had to put my bartering skills and spanish to the test. i have had a crazy and funny 24 hours. i will tell you about it later. another gorgeous day. i gonna go eat lunch now. hopefully we'll chat online soon. i finally figured out the skype, so i have it now. oh, has anyone told you that your are pretty today? well, they should have. kisses*

I forwarded the email thread between them to Seth's work email. I wanted him to know I found it and that I knew he had, without a doubt, cheated on me. I didn't send a message along with the email, just the thread. I had no words to say.

It was the last piece of evidence of my husband's other life that I found. Sadly, as is usually the case when deceit is involved, I knew it was likely only the tip of the iceberg. But it was more than enough. I didn't need to find or see anymore. Aspects of Seth and my marriage had been revealed to me that I couldn't even imagine existed. It was clear that I had been with a man for fifteen years that I did not know, could not relate to, and had characteristics that were alarming and creepy. All the features that I thought Seth had—integrity, honesty, selflessness, trustworthiness, solid moral character, and a strong sense of duty and obligation to his wife and family—were a farce. My husband was a full-fledged liar and cheater. He was a womanizer and a sexist. He was everything I detested. My marriage did not have a foundation built on love, respect, and equality but on lies, infidelity, and disrespect. I had no choice but to leave him and file for divorce. I took a deep breath. And then I collapsed.

CHAPTER 3: THE COLLAPSE

I dropped to the floor clutching my knees into my chest, my head slowly falling toward my heart. I lay there in a fetal position, just sobbing. Actually, it was more than sobbing. Merriam-Webster Dictionary defines sobbing as "noisy crying." Yes, I had tears flowing from my eyes, but it wasn't just noisy. It was an emanation of sorrow and pain from deep within my body. I experienced intense and overwhelming groans of agony that came from my toes, stomach, and eyelashes. Hurt and anguish came from every cavity of my body. Heartbreak enveloped me. My husband Seth was dead. I had felt that horrific soul-crushing grief before when my mom unexpectedly died when I was a teenager, and I was back in that hell once again. A blanket of disbelief, shock, anxiety, and despair tightly wrapped around me making it difficult to even breathe. I couldn't bear to suffer through the torture of another traumatic loss, but like when she died, I had no choice.

Of course, Seth hadn't really died, but it felt like it to me. It felt like the man I was in love with, wedded, had children with, and had spent the last fifteen years of my life with had been overtaken by some extraterrestrial entity, morphing my incredible husband into a completely different person. This other man, a living stranger, was a man who cheated on and deceived me. Who was my husband, really? How could he be such a good husband and father yet be so selfish and mendacious? Or maybe I was just super-fucking dumb and completely bought into some fictitious relationship. My entire life—my sturdy marriage and ideal family—was a sham. It was a stupid bullshit theatre performance, and I was the leading lady.

After hours of lying there on the floor, I finally started to get up when I realized it was time to pick the kids up from school. But my body was heavy against the floor, as if it had become a pallet of bricks. I was completely emotionally and physically depleted.

"You can do this, Kathi," a tender whisper encouraged me.

I now believe it was my mom who motivated me to move and that she sat there with me for those hours holding and kissing me. Still in a fetal position, I put my palm against the floor and started to slowly push myself up. I sat there for a moment, tasting the salt from my tears on my lips. Then I started to bumpily rise, putting my arms out to maintain my balance. I sluggishly walked over to my purse, clutched my keys, walked out the front door, and got into the family van. I was thankful Seth had driven the kids to school that morning; there was no way I would have been able to ride my bike to pick them up from school like I usually did. I took a deep breath, turned the ignition, and headed toward the elementary school. As always, the kids were excited to see me when I arrived. But they could tell I had been crying.

"Are you okay, Mommy?" asked Gracie.

"Yeah, I'm ok. I just had a really hard day. I'm not feeling 100 percent. How was school?" I held back the flood of tears nearly bursting from my eyes.

"School was fine. Who is making dinner tonight?" she asked.

"I'll call and order a pizza. So, I'll be reading to you."

"Yay! Pizza!" Henry added.

The kids were a welcome reprieve from the hours I had spent crying on the floor. It pained me, though, to know their lives were about to drastically change. I wished that I had been more present the evening before so that I could have savored our regular family time together. A typical evening with dinner at the farmhouse table, sudsy baths, and story time and songs with the kids, followed by a TV show while sitting on the couch chatting with Seth seemed like paradise. It was never, ever, going to happen that way again.

Not long after, Seth arrived home from work. We went through the tasks of the family evening routine, but it was filled with silent joyless agitation. When the kids were tucked in bed, he and I sat down in the family room, each on our own couch. He looked at me lovingly and apologetically.

"I am so sorry. I know I am a horrible person and what I have done is unforgiveable. But I love you and I want to make it up to you. I want to fix this." He sounded genuinely regretful.

My elbow was on the arm of the couch, and my chin rested in the palm of my hand. I was looking away toward the fireplace, my eyes staring deep into the glowing embers bouncing and crackling around the hearth. I turned my head toward him and looked directly and seriously into his eyes.

"I want a divorce. And I want you to leave immediately. And when I say immediately, I mean right now. Get the fuck out!" I demanded as my arm stretched out and my finger pointed toward the front door.

He closed his eyes and slowly lowered his head toward his chest. He stood up and walked to our bedroom and gathered some of his things. He left without saying a word. I had no idea where he went, and I didn't care. I just wanted him out of my sight. I went to the kitchen and poured myself a glass of cabernet. Then I resumed sobbing...and didn't stop. I cried everywhere. I bawled in my bed, in the shower, in the car, cooking dinner, checking email, and walking the dogs. I wailed anywhere and everywhere. I even cried while sleeping, which was usually accompanied by nightmares of Seth cheating on or abandoning me. I always had tissue with me to wipe my runny nose and had a constant ponytail so as to not have my wet hair sticking to my face because my cheeks were constantly saturated with tears. Just when I would start to feel a little better or would be distracted for a moment, it would all rush back. It felt like I was continually getting punched in the face, over and over and over, with a constant stream of blood running from my nose.

Seth ultimately rented a room somewhere (I still have no idea where; he could have easily stayed with someone he was seeing), while the kids and I remained in the family home. I also enrolled the kids and myself in therapy. It was without a doubt the most painful and devastating time in my life. I was mourning the loss of the husband who now felt dead to me but who was still very much alive. It was confusing and surreal to miss someone who never really existed. I adored the man I thought my husband was, and I longed for him. I wanted to go to him and nuzzle my head into his strong chest, his arms around my body comforting me. I just wanted to be with him and share what was happening with this imaginary man. But, of course, I couldn't. That man, the one I was so in love with, wasn't real. I often felt like I was in a movie, watching someone else's life disintegrate.

Making it especially difficult to keep it together, Seth was constantly calling, texting, and emailing me to apologize and try to get me back. He admitted his culpability, said he would do anything to gain my trust and forgiveness, and wanted desperately to be a family again. He was extraordinarily repentant, as can be seen in some of his actual messages to me:

> *Every thought I have is ravaged with regret and despair. I miss you so much. I am working everyday to be a better man, partner, and father. There are so many things I wish I would of done differently. Just know that I am working tirelessly to be a better person and*

restitute for the things I have done wrong. I love you. I love our kids. I want them to be happy. I want to earn your respect. My heart tells me you are my love. I love you.

Please know that I will continue to work on and improve myself as a father and partner. I was in a dark place and I don't ever want to return there. I love you very much and I know this has been extremely difficult for you and the kids. I hope that you will soon get to a place where you will consider to come to counseling sessions with me to figure out how and why this all happened. I care and love for you deeply and I suffer constantly in grief and anguish over how this has played out.

I miss you so much Kathi. I am not trying to compare the agony you are going through w/ mine, but I had an extremely rough night and currently having a hard time functioning here at work. I am haunted by how I let you and the kids down. I am so remorseful and sorry. I would do anything to get you back. Get our family back. I want you. I want our family together again. Our poor kids never deserved this. I need to do all I can to make it up to them to you. I am so sorry Kathi. I am so sorry.

Seth's messages only amplified my pain. The man who was sending such sweet and compassionate notes was the man I fell in love with. I continued to be profoundly in love with him, and I missed being together as a family. But that man also had a side of him that was chauvinist, sneaky, and selfish. He was opposite to my feminist values of integrity, respect, and care. The amount of manipulation and dishonesty needed to keep me in the dark about all he was doing, when he knew I would end the relationship if I was aware, was astonishing. He gave me no option to consent to actions that would affect my health, safety, and livelihood, ultimately making his behavior, in my mind, a form of physical and sexual exploitation. He put me in danger, just to stroke his ego and get himself off. There was absolutely nothing feminist about that.

It was hard for me to understand how the man I had given my heart to, and who was supposedly so in love with me, could behave that way. I just couldn't wrap my mind around it. Was it possible he could love me so deeply yet still seek the attention of so many other women? Was it possible he could have sex with me regularly yet yearn for so many extramarital affairs? Could he respect me as a woman yet still treat women as prey to be chased? And if yes, was he the norm or the anomaly? Is this just how men are? Was I simply naïve to the typical behavior of men? Perhaps I shouldn't have been surprised given how society socialized men to be overly consumed with sex. Was Seth simply succumbing to the aspect of toxic masculinity that sexually objectified and used women? My head was swirling and spinning with questions that I could never figure out how to answer. What I did know, and ultimately would conclude again and again, was that whether or not it was "just how men are" or the fault of the societal construction of masculinity, it was not the kind of relationship I wanted. I had always sought, and retained my desire for, an egalitarian relationship. Maybe it was unattainable, but that didn't matter. I would rather be alone than be in a relationship built on anything less.

THE DIVORCE ATTORNEYS

Soon after the reveal, I began asking friends and colleagues if they knew any good divorce attorneys. One name repeatedly came up: Harry Kaitling. He was considered "the shark" of family law attorneys in our area. I did a quick search online, found his number, and made an appointment for a consultation. I arrived at Harry's office a few minutes before our 9:00 a.m. appointment. The young receptionist offered me a cup of coffee and motioned for me to take a seat. I declined her offer for coffee and sat down on a long brown tweed sofa near the window. The sofa was scratchy against my skin, but the warmth from the sun coming through the window made up for it. I wanted to wrap that warmth around me like a weighted blanket and hide under it to keep myself safe. At the same time, I wanted to scream at the top of my lungs so the world would feel my pain, hurt, and betrayal. Those conflicting feelings felt like I was in a constant state of agitation, never able to relax and always on the verge of a breakdown. I looked around the office, disbelieving where I was. Was this real? Was I in a nightmare? A divorce attorney's office was the last place I ever thought I'd be, and yet, there I was. *Fuck you, Seth.*

I could hear Harry on a phone call in his office, laughing heartily and loudly. I wondered how long I would be sitting there and hoped he wouldn't linger. Thankfully, only a few minutes later his office door swung open and he began to approach me, his arm held out to shake my hand. He was a tall, lengthy, older man, in his early sixties I'd say, with thick gray hair and matching eyebrows.

"Hi there, Kathi. How are ya? I'm Harry." He was upbeat and friendly, almost too happy for this time of the morning, especially given his profession as a divorce lawyer.

"I'm okay, thanks. Nice to meet you." I shook his hand.

"Please, c'mon in. Let's chat."

His office was large and disorganized and felt dusty and damp. The furniture was old and worn. I wondered for a moment if I had slipped back in time to the 1970s. There were stacks of papers every-where, including the floor. His desk, though, was free from clutter and on it had only a pad of paper and a pen. We both sat down. At least the chair was comfortable.

"How can I help you today, dear?" he asked paternalistically.

I wondered if I would even be able to speak, my chin was quiv-ering so badly trying to ward off the imminent deluge of tears. I quickly lifted my hand to my chin and forcefully cupped it to stop it manually. It helped a little.

"Well, I recently left my husband. I discovered that he was be-ing unfaithful. There is no possibility of reconciliation and I want a divorce. I'm completely devasted and heartbroken. I have been committed to him, our marriage, and our family for fifteen years and I feel like I don't even know him. I don't want this to be a long, drawn-out process. I just want this to be over so I can begin to heal. It's already been tough enough on me and our two kids." I was proud of myself that I was able to get the words out.

Harry slowly stood up and went to the large black-paned win-dow directly behind him. He looked out the window for a few mo-ments before he spoke, still peering out.

"I'm so sorry, Kathi. Adultery can be very tough to deal with. Are you sure you don't want to try and make your marriage work? Cheating is very common, and many couples are able to get through it. It doesn't always have to end in divorce."

Uh, yeah, I'm fucking sure, Harry. He clearly wasn't understand-ing the gravity of Seth's cheating.

"Yes, I am absolutely 100 percent sure I want a divorce. There is nothing that can be done to make my marriage work. It is in no way salvageable. There were a slew of women." My chin was now steady as a racehorse. "And I want to come out on top in this divorce. I want someone who will fight for me."

He sighed long and slow while nodding in agreement. He then turned, looked at me donning a genteel smile, and sat back down in his chair.

"Ok, well, if that is the way you feel, I am happy to represent you and will do what I can to help. I have been in this game a long time, for over twenty-five years, and have a solid history of getting people what they want from their divorce. I do have a $4,000 retainer fee, and once that's paid, we can begin the paperwork. You can pay the retainer fee on your way out with the receptionist. She will give you the forms to fill out and schedule a time for us to meet next week," Harry explained.

"That sounds good. I would definitely like you to represent me, and I'm ready to get started."

I didn't let it show, but I was completely taken aback by how exorbitant the retainer fee was and couldn't help wondering how women with fewer resources would ever be able to hire an attorney of his caliber. I hardly could, but I wanted the best so I chalked it up to the price I had to pay for good representation, even if it meant putting it on a credit card.

"Oh, and I have some advice for you."

"Sure, I'll take anything." I listened attentively.

"Because you are the woman in the divorce, you should not have a social life, date, or be seen drinking alcohol. You don't want your husband to be able to paint you as a bad person or a bad mother. Do you work?"

I was completely taken aback. What fucked-up double-standard bullshit was this? Not have a social life? Not date? *Let me get this straight. Seth can fuck everyone in town while he's married and I can't go on a goddamned date?*

"Yes, I'm a professor at the university. At Texas A&M. In psychology and women's and gender studies." I wondered what working had to do with anything.

"Hmm . . . so you work full time. It's good that you can support yourself and the kids, but it's not good in that you might be perceived as a career woman who puts work before her kids. This is especially the case because you're a professor; we all know how grueling that can be. I tell you what: go to work, but spend the rest of your time taking excellent care of your kids. Be the absolute best mother you can be. You can have a life of your own later. Right now, your focus has to be on pleasing the court. And that means being an impeccable mother who has no other needs than her children."

I became clearly irritated. *Dammit, here come the waterworks again.* Why did I have to cry all the time, even when I was pissed off?

"But that's not fair. I haven't done anything wrong. I have been a faithful and devoted wife and mother. And I've worked hard getting where I am in my career. Why should I have to limit my life? He's the one who cheated and lied. He's the one who destroyed our family. And he works full time, too!" I explained defensively. I wiped under my eyes with the knuckles of my index fingers.

"That's just the way divorce works, honey," he said unempathetically.

I sighed deeply. "Well, that's total bullshit, but I'll do my best." I don't think he caught on to my sarcasm.

I left his office and handed the receptionist my credit card. In return she handed me a large manila envelope filled to the brim. I left that office completely discouraged. I went home and wept.

Harry and I met a few times after that initial meeting to discuss the heap of forms I had completed. We talked about child custody, assets and debts, and the kind of life I wanted after the divorce. As Harry had initially warned, the divorce process was going to be very different for me as a woman than it was for Seth as a man. Not only did the family law system seem to care very little about Seth's adultery, but there was a microscope on my behavior and a lackadaisical attitude toward his. How I represented myself as a woman and mother appeared to be the only thing that really mattered. There was the constant threat of me losing the kids as a result of having a career, social life, or lapse in mental health. Although Seth was the adulterer, my behavior seemed to be the real focus. It seemed Seth's behavior was irrelevant, no matter how egregious. He simply could do things as a man that I could not as a woman. Seth seemed to know this and would later use that knowledge to either threaten me or to relaxedly engage in behaviors that would have been catastrophic for me.

Harry continually reminded me of this double standard during our meetings, and I always left feeling pissed off and defeated. I began to wonder the extent to which his cautionary advice stemmed from his own prejudiced attitudes toward women. That is, was his chauvinistic counsel coming from his own gender bias or from his experiences with the family court system? Indeed, his paternalistic treatment of me during our meetings—calling me "dear" and "honey," for example—were a dead giveaway that he just might be a bigot. I decided I needed to be careful and interpret his guidance using a critical feminist lens. The more and more I met with him, the more his sexism was revealed. I began to feel that Harry was more on Seth's side than on mine. One day Harry and I met to discuss the financial deal I sought. When I explained my requests and my rationale to Harry, he laughed and said, "Kathi, do you really think this is fair to Seth? How is he going to afford all this?" My mouth dropped to the floor. Was Harry looking out for my best interests or for my cheater husband's? After that moment, I felt like I could no longer trust Harry. So, I fired him, right there, on the spot. Back to the attorney drawing board, so to speak.

This time, I interviewed several attorneys in town and decided to go with my gut rather than the big name. I settled on Lyle Lexington. Lyle was short in stature but represented all things Texas. He wore a big black cowboy hat, had office furniture covered in leather and studs, a rifle and bullets donning his office wall, and a brown-

and-white cowhide rug in the middle of his office floor. Although testosterone oozed from his strong southern accent, he was gentle and empathetic. I just had a good feeling about him. His office got straight to work and had all my paperwork moved from Harry's office the same day I signed on. It was Lyle who guided me through the remainder of the divorce. I felt like Lyle had my back and he didn't take any shit. And he didn't give a damn about what was good for Seth. Lyle too warned me to watch my behavior as to not give Seth ammunition signifying I was a bad mother and person, but not with the same misogynistic overtones of Harry. Nor did he seem to have the contempt for women that Harry had. Our relationship was extremely professional and respectful.

BARELY SURVIVING

Although I now had the backing and support of my new badass attorney Lyle, I could hardly take care of myself. All of the limited energy I had went toward the kids. It took everything in me to take care of them. We stopped riding our bikes to school, we had take-out or macaroni and cheese nearly every night for dinner, and we watched every kid movie in our DVD collection at least three times. I tried to have some stability for them, but it was tough. I continued to keep up on their school assignments, take them to their appointments, and run the family home. I still did baths and bedtime stories after dinner but couldn't wait until they were asleep so I could emotionally vomit in my journal or smother myself in music. I would listen to how-could-you, I-miss-you, or fuck-off songs on YouTube over and over on my laptop, especially Ben Harper's "Widow of a Living Man" and Adele's "Rolling in the Deep." My most common activity, though, was to sit on the phone in the living room while lamenting to anyone who would listen and provide comfort and encouragement, usually one of my sisters, friends, or my stepmom. They were all so supportive and really helped me survive those initial months.

My work at the university also suffered. I cancelled half of my classes that first month. After getting the kids to school, I would just go back to bed and cry. My colleagues knew I was not doing well. One day, while at home in the middle of one of my sobbing sprees, I heard a knock at my front door. It was my colleague, Wendy, and her husband, Raymond. They had come over to check on me and bring me food. They actually brought me prepared meals, you know, as people do in times of stress and transition. The last time I had people bring me prepared meals was when I gave birth. The time before that was when my mom died. I appreciated it so much during those times, and I did so when Wendy and Raymond did it for me.

Even when I could seem to get myself to campus, I would just sit in my campus office and weep. When it came time to teach a class, I would clean myself up and become an actress for a few hours. I would drudge across the campus quad to the classroom where I was teaching, attempt to give an informative and engaging lecture, and slog back to my office. Most people had no idea how badly I was suffering internally, doing everything in my power not to lie down on the quad asphalt and bawl. Wendy and Raymond could tell, though. In fact, Raymond taught at the same time as me in the classroom across from mine. Every day before our class, he would appear at my office door to walk me to class, giving me reassuring looks along the way. When we each finished our class, he would walk me back to my office. I'm convinced these comforting walks with Raymond to and from class kept me from falling over the edge at work that semester. Not that I didn't come close many other times.

It wasn't uncommon for me to break down in a colleague's office, in a faculty meeting, or at a university event. It got to the point that I could tell when a sob was coming on and I would quickly and quietly remove myself and head to the women's restroom. One day, I was walking from the parking structure to my office and could feel an impending eruption. It was only about a five-minute walk, but I just could not complete it. About two minutes in, I could feel my mouth begin to turn downward and my eyeballs begin to drown. As I approached my office, I began to walk faster and faster, just as you do when you really need to pee and the toilet is just within reach. You fear the pee might start running down your leg, so you quicken your pace as to thwart the possibility. I didn't make it to my office. But I did reach my neighboring colleague's office. Jane was standing in the doorway of her office holding what seemed to be student papers.

"You ok?" she asked.

I said nothing but walked directly toward her and wrinkled in her arms. It resembled the scene where a runner just crosses a marathon finish line and collapses from exhaustion and dehydration. I was like that runner, and Jane was the medical personnel there to aid me.

I worried about how I was going to keep up my productivity at work. As an academic at a research-focused university working her way toward tenure, my job relied entirely on my cogent intellect. But my brain was mush. I couldn't think clearly and was constantly distracted. Still, I was expected to publish in prestigious academic journals and secure million-dollar research grants. I had no idea how I was going to reconcile my new reality with the demands of academia. Was I going to lose my job too? Although I tried with all my might, I just could not seem to check my grief at the workplace door.

Moreover, even with all that Seth had done, his remorse would sometimes sway me and I would have to remind myself of everything he had done—the websites, the women, the infidelity, the deceit, and the sexism. I would have to repeatedly reread the messages between him and Carly, the woman I had proof he had an affair with, or all his posts on Married and Flirting, to jolt my memory of why I was divorcing him. I had to walk myself through every piece of evidence, draw pictures, and write pros-and-cons lists. I even made a PowerPoint presentation (an informational mechanism I was very comfortable with as a professor) that included everything I had found about his other life, complete with custom animation and images. This would sometimes make me tough and resilient. He would text or call and lovingly ask to talk or come by, and I would refuse and demand he leave me alone. Or I would cry and scream and tell him to go fuck himself.

Other times, though, when I felt hopeless and helpless, I longed to be with him. He was the man I had children with, snuggled and watched movies with, and planned a future with. I missed our dumb inside jokes and his silly nature. And I was still attracted to him; I had always found him incredibly handsome and that never waned. I would reminisce about us sitting and chatting together on the outside swing in the backyard in Kentucky while the dogs and kids ran around the just-mowed green grass. I missed that man, and I missed him with all of my broken heart. But like Liz Phair sings in "Friend of Mine," it had been a long time since he'd been a true friend to me. And Seth's messages continued:

> *I really wish we could be salvaged. I want to save it. Us. I have done horrible deplorable things. I have taken responsibility for them and I continue to punish myself every minute. I am driven to be a better man and overcome my mistakes. I owe to you and the kids. I want to raise our kids together. just please give it some thought. I know you are trying to show the kids how to be strong in the face of adversity. I hope to show and teach them about redemption and overcoming mistakes. just please put some thought into it. I love you. I love our kids.*

> *I am so sorry how this is all playing out. I understand that you now see me differently. I am determined to*

show you, the kids, our families, and my friends, that the events that have occurred during this past year are not who I am, nor who I ever wanted to be. I am ashamed, regretful, and penitent for what I have done. I am standing up and taking responsibility for the situation I got myself into. I am more determined now than ever to show that to everyone, and especially you, that I am a man of strong character and loyalty. You probably laugh after reading that and I don't blame you. In time you will see. Or at least you'll be open to seeing. But, that will take time. I love you with all my heart. I love our kids with all my heart. I miss our little family.

I was doing fine for the last week or so, but I'll be honest, the last 4 days have been pure hell. I miss you so much. I miss our family. Sometimes, I just want to hear your voice and I will listen to old voice mails. I know that sounds crazy, but I still yearn for you and my heart still needs you. I am so sorry. I hope you believe me when I say that. I am truly sorry for this.

Sometimes my heart, brain, and body craved his attention to the point that I had to surrender. I would find myself reaching out to him. Even though I wanted to disconnect from him and move on, I also wanted his love and affection. I wanted him on his knees in tears pleading for forgiveness and reconciliation. If he didn't contact me for a few days, I felt completely lost and out of control. I was an emotional yo-yo, devastated and furious by his behavior one moment and longing for him and his affection the next.

The pull to him was so strong that occasionally I agreed to see him, especially if the kids had gone to bed and I was making my way through a bottle of wine. He was so kind and tender when he would come over. We would sit together on the leather loveseat accompanied by firelight and soft music. He would sit so close to me our thighs would touch and put one arm around me and the other on my leg while tightly holding my hand. He would be tearful and repentant. I usually sat there, head down, and cried. He would dotingly wipe the streams coming from my eyes and the tear-wet hair out of my face and put it behind my ear. It was such a strange feeling to have the person that hurt you also be the one to console you. These dysfunctional encounters lasted hours.

Ultimately, we would begin to embrace and then kiss—long, deep, intense, romantic kisses with our mouths pressed hard against each other and our tongues slowly churning together. We would end up having sex, and not just regular sex—hands-all-over-each-other sex, you-are-the-love-of-my-life sex, we-are-soulmates sex. It felt amazing to have his adoring devotion and strong arms around me. I tried to stop myself from spending these nights together, but his attention was like a drug; my physical body just couldn't get enough. I never felt good about it afterward. I would promise myself I wouldn't be with him again, but like a recovering addict confronted by their drug of choice, it was hard to resist and I always regretted it when I used. The lure was just too appealing. Even one time, when I was filled with rage about his deceitful behavior—enough to cause him a bloody nose from the thumps of my fists—did we begin to ultimately kiss, bright-red blood streaming from his nose to our pressed lips, our bodies eventually entangled in rapturous coition. We had these late-night rendezvous repeatedly. Before long, I stopped having sexual relations with Seth, and never did resume, mostly because of his falling mask.

CHAPTER 3: THE COLLAPSE

THE FALLING MASK

Things began to happen that made me question the sincerity of Seth's remorse. While he did the "I love you," "I miss you," "I can't live without you" bit, I continued to find or hear more information about his previous and ongoing betrayals. For example, several of my female colleagues who I had become close friends with revealed to me that Seth had made them feel very uncomfortable when we spent time with them socially. My friend Emily, at dinner one night shortly after my divorce process began, divulged that my husband made her feel squeamish when we got together with her and her husband. She said Seth would stare at her as if imagining having sex with her. She said she always felt like something was off with him. Another friend, Nia, disclosed something similar. Nia, more direct than Emily, told me that "Seth always acted like he wanted to fuck me. It was creepy." Interestingly, these two colleagues did not know of each other and had never met. Other colleagues told me, "None of us could ever understand why you were with him" and "Why do you think we never invited you over?" It all completely baffled me.

Other questionable incidents happened as well. I was shocked, for instance, by who Seth hired to represent him in the divorce. Chelsea Lord was a no-name divorce attorney hired by few people in town. She was an eye-catching blonde in her mid-thirties who was more known for her skin-tight zipper dresses and stilettos than for her legal skills. Of all the attorneys in town, Seth hired *her*? Now, I wholeheartedly believe women should be able to wear whatever they want and be taken seriously. It just seemed like an odd choice for a man trying to win back his wife and family after engaging in rampant adultery. I was sure he was going to try to date her or at the very least have sex with her. There was really no other reason for his selection; she definitely wasn't known for her stellar counsel. I'm not saying she slept with her clients, but my husband probably thought he'd take his chances. Their flirtatious interactions suggested she just might be open to it.

For example, one day Seth came over to spend some time with Gracie and Henry. He greeted them, and then they went outside to play in the backyard. As he was walking outside, he placed his phone on the kitchen counter. Right as he shut the back door his phone buzzed; he had received a text. I peeked my head out the window to see if he'd heard it. He hadn't. I walked over to his phone and looked down at it. It was Chelsea Lord. I was so curious I couldn't help myself. I touched the screen and it opened; he must have been texting with her when he arrived. I was shocked by their conversation. I quickly took screenshots and sent them to myself in case I needed proof of their inappropriate relationship. Here are some excerpts of their actual text thread:

> Seth: *I have had a crazy week . . .*
>
> Chelsea: *here's my advice for when the loneliness you feel is physically painful [she goes on to provide some tips] . . . My cell # is 220-XXXX. I rarely become pals with clients, but you're cool and I feel your pain . . . if u ever need to talk just let me know.*
>
> Seth: *Thanks for the advice . . . Mmmm, now I'm tempted to call. Are we becoming pals? I may just call.*

These messages confirmed to me that Seth was interested in more than counsel from Chelsea. And there was that "Mmmm" wording again that he used trying to be flirty with the woman he'd definitely had an affair with, Carly. Ew!

Then, one morning I logged into his email account to see if he had been communicating with Carly (or any other woman) and found that he had created a profile on the online dating site Match.

com only the day before. He used his real name but lied about his marital status (divorced rather than separated) and about where he lived (he said he lived in a neighboring city to ours). He had posted numerous pictures on his profile, all of which I took. My mind was deluged with perplexity and disbelief once again. Not only had we been having our teary late-night lovemaking episodes pretty regularly, but he continued to send me heartfelt messages urging reconciliation.

I was fuming when I found the Match.com account. Why would you be on an online dating site when you're trying to get your wife and family back and so deeply regret cheating and lying? Later that day, when he arrived to visit the kids, I wrathfully marched straight up to him as he approached the house and put my phone right up to his nose.

"You're on Match.com now? Really? What happened to you'll do anything to get your family back and you're so in love with me you can't survive without me? What happened to all your fucking regret?" I raged.

I then grabbed the object nearest to me—a lawn chair—and threw it in his direction, just barely missing him.

"I hate you! You liar!" I yelled through tears, apparently loud enough for the neighbor, Doug, across the street to hear.

"Everything okay over there?" Doug bellowed.

"Yes, everything is fine," Seth loudly replied with a wave.

Seth looked me straight in the eyes and said, "No, Kathi, I am not on Match. I created an account, but it's not active. You keep telling me you won't take me back and are going through with the divorce, so what choice do I have? I love and want to be with you, but you keep telling me it's over. And stop looking through my email! My email is none of your business. We wouldn't be in this horrible mess if you would have respected my privacy!"

His response sent me over the edge. How dare he turn this on me and make it seem like my fault! He then walked through the garage and into the house. My heart began to hammer, pulsating nearly out of my chest, and my blood turned hot. Adrenaline burst throughout my body. Amygdala hijack. I was instantly in full-fledged fight mode. I furiously followed him into the house, grabbing an empty beer bottle from the recycle bin along the way. We were standing across from each other at the semicircle kitchen counter. In a fury of tears, I lifted my arm high, my hand tightly gripping the beer bottle, aiming straight for his head. I could feel the vehemence moving through my core as my arm moved through the air toward his scalp. I couldn't wait to hear the beer bottle crack against his head and watch the blood stream down his face. Maybe then he would hurt as bad as I did. I wanted him to feel intense, gripping pain. I wanted him to bleed a river of red, at the very least, to show me he was a real person who could feel. As Ben Harper croons, "Please Bleed."

Then I saw Gracie and Henry out of the corner of my eye. They were watching the entire interaction. Gracie quickly grabbed Henry and moved him out of the kitchen and into her bedroom to protect him from what would come next. That move jolted me out of fight mode and back into reality. With the bottle only a millimeter from Seth's skull, I stopped myself and slowly lowered my arm. I gently placed the bottle on the counter. I then grabbed his phone on the counter next to him and raced toward the guest bathroom. I plunged his phone into the toilet and flushed. The phone started spinning around in the bowl. I just stood there and watched it swirl, tears rolling down my face. I turned around to find him just behind me. He grabbed my hand and led me to the back patio where he sat me down. We sat there together as I sobbed. It took me a few minutes to gain enough composure to speak.

"You have hurt me so badly, Seth. I don't know who you are and

I miss my husband. I'm completely heartbroken. I don't know how to cope with all of this pain," I told him.

"I'm right here. And I love you. But you can't be acting crazy like that," he said.

I just looked at him. I was astonished.

"You need to leave," I demanded.

Then I stood up, went inside the house, and lay down on our bed. I could hear the front door close behind him, just after he fetched his phone from the toilet.

I did feel like I was going crazy. Actually, it was more than that. I felt like I was going insane, going mad. I couldn't differentiate north from south or up from down. I was in a constant state of cognitive turmoil. The next day, Seth sent me a text:

> *i am suffering really bad right now. i am in complete agony. every thought i have is centered around you. i am so sorry kathi. i thought how things would be if turned around and i felt this extreme pain and wanted to throw up. i miss you so much. i don't know if i can live w/o you. i would and will do anything to get you back.*

He sent another a few days later:

> *I have been thinking about you. A lot. I need you in my life. I want you in my life. I want our family to-gether again. I want our kids to be happy. i love you.*

That same week, he officially activated his Match.com account and, from what Gracie told me, was constantly texting with women. One day when I took her to a doctor appointment, she revealed to me that she looked through her dad's texts and found conversations he was having with different women. As such, his messages to me were incredibly confusing. I just couldn't understand how someone who was so-called suffering from losing me and in such agony and pain could engage, and continue engaging, in the kind of behavior he was. He wanted me, but he wanted other women and seemingly a lot of them.

Perhaps the oddest and most painful indicator of Seth's falling mask was his behavior at the kids' sporting events. Before the separation, the ballfield was a site of fun, laughter, and quality family time. If Seth wasn't coaching, he and I would sit together and bond over the kids' latest catch, throw, or score, and the kids would play with friends. We would bring food and drinks, comfy camping chairs, and plenty of sunscreen and shade to defend ourselves from the hot Texas sun. Someone always had a cooler with built-in speakers loudly jamming the latest hits pumping up the kids at whatever field we were playing on. We loved hanging out with the other parents and families and often ate meals together as a large group at some off-road restaurant after a game or tournament.

After the intense pain of my husband's betrayal, the ballfield immediately became a place of pain, hurt, and isolation. It was incredibly difficult for me to hide how excruciatingly uncomfortable it was for me to be near him. I was so extremely heartbroken. After all, I didn't ask for a divorce because I no longer loved him. I asked for a divorce because of his extensive cheating and deceit. I missed Seth so badly, but I knew we could never be together unless I wanted a lifetime of infidelity and lies. I felt naked, exposed, and vulnerable, like I had a scarlet letter branded on my forehead and people would know just by looking at me how much the strong feminist professor had been duped. I spent most of my time at the kids' sporting practices and games holding back tears.

I distinctly recall the first game after the reveal of Seth's other life; it was one of Henry's baseball games. I arrived at College Station's Wayne Smith Athletic Complex fields in the early evening with

Gracie. Seth was coaching, and he and Henry had arrived early. It was extraordinarily bizarre how casual Seth was. You'd hardly know his marriage was falling apart; he seemed like his normal self the way he interacted with the kids and other coaches. Me, not so much. I was a total wreck. I could only hold it together for about 10 minutes at a time before I would have to get up during the game and go bawl in the restroom. It continued this way for me for months. In fact, I think going to the ballfield was the most difficult thing I had to do during the divorce. I did not want to see, talk to, or coordinate with my husband. I wanted him out of my life. Eventually, we agreed to trade the kids each week (he would have them one week, and I would have them the next, and so on), which helped but was by no means a panacea.

Because being around him was so distressing for me, I asked Seth for a temporary favor. I requested that, just for a while, he not attend the kids' activities during my weeks with the kids unless he had to as a coach or it was an important game so I could begin to heal and get in a better headspace. He never did cease attending the kids' activities on my weeks, however. Although it was tormenting, I learned to live with it. During his weeks, I mostly stayed home and focused on healing and self-care unless the kids had a big game or specifically asked me to attend. Although I hated to miss many of their games, it was absolutely necessary for my mental health and well-being. I had to lessen my interactions with Seth if I was ever going to make it through the hell I was experiencing. I had to find a way to be strong and refuse him. Christina Perri's "Jar of Hearts" became my constant companion.

THE PARK HUDSON PLACE APARTMENT

To strengthen the boundary between Seth and myself and cat- apult my healing, I decided to move out of the family home a few months after I learned about Seth's other life. Apartment hunting was a strange experience. I was crying half the time and told every apartment manager my story if they gave me their ear. It was also sort of exciting. I made enough money for something really nice, which made me feel relieved and, at times, even hopeful. Even though my marriage was ending and my world crumbling around me, I was taking baby steps toward the future. I settled on the Park Hudson Place Apartments in Bryan, the city adjacent to College Station. I loved my apartment. I felt so free but was still so incredibly brokenhearted. I was also tremendously grateful that I was financially able to get my own place; I thought often about the so many other women trapped in relationships with bad husbands but didn't have the funds to leave and get a place of their own. I decided I would emphasize the importance of financial independence for women in my Psychology of Women class.

My new place was a three-bedroom, two-bath apartment with all the bells and whistles: stainless steel appliances, granite countertops, and large walk-in closets. It felt good to be able to give the kids their own rooms like they had in the family home. I took the furniture from the den (the smell of those leather couches made me sick) and the big farmhouse table; they looked great in the apartment. I purchased new bedroom furniture and bedding sets for me and the kids and let them bring over whatever toys and personal items they wanted. I so badly wanted them to be happy in my apartment. I was competing with the big house in the "we made it" neighborhood where they had friends and their school within walking distance to compete with. My favorite thing about that apartment—and thankfully a big draw for the kids— was the resort-style pool. It was gorgeous! I loved going for a dip after work like I was on vacation. And it was wonderful to take the kids out to the pool and grill and hang out when they were with me. I began to smile, occasionally.

But I missed Gracie and Henry when they were with their dad. I also really missed the dogs, Penny and Frosty. I thought about bringing the dogs with me to the apartment but decided they would be much happier at the house. So, there I was, all alone. I was in a beautiful apartment but still by myself a lot of the time. I decided I needed a companion. I heard about a dog adoption event at the local PetCo and decided the kids and I would go and check it out.

I was very clear with the kids: "We are *not* getting a dog today; we are only looking."

And then we saw an angelic six-week-old beige mini poodle in one of the cages. We asked to see him. He snuggled up with Gracie and was so sweet and adorable. He just lay on her lap sleeping.

"Please, Mom, please. We have to adopt him," Gracie said.

Of course, I caved, and we brought that little puppy to his new home at the apartment. We threw around some names and finally decided on a name that fit him perfectly: Peanut. We were so happy to have our little Peanut! And I was no longer alone when the kids were with their dad. I felt so bad, though, when I had to go to work and leave our little Peanut. I decided he needed a buddy. I scoured Petfinder.com for our perfect match. I liked that Peanut was small and, as a poodle, didn't shed. I decided to look for a pup with similar characteristics. I found him almost instantly. His name was Cooper, and he was a one-year-old Maltipoo. The next day, the kids and I drove an hour to where he was sheltered. We brought Peanut too. Cooper was running around with about twenty or so other dogs in a big concrete room when we arrived. They brought him out to see us. What a doll! Sweet, friendly, and loveable. We took him home. We decided the name Cooper fit him perfectly, so we kept it.

Little did I know in that moment how important those pint-sized loves would become to me and my healing. I was excited to have two little furballs to keep me company, but I had no idea how curative Peanut and Cooper would be for me over the next decade. We became inseparable, and I took them nearly everywhere, including to classes on campus. They brought me such joy, such unconditional love, such happiness. I started to mend, in large part, because of Peanut and Cooper.

LEAVE ME ALONE, BUT NOT REALLY

After a few weeks in the apartment, I realized that, if I was going to really move on and rebuild, I needed to continue severing my connection with Seth. Even though I had less contact with him now that we were trading off weeks with the kids, he continued to lovingly contact me trying to reconcile. So, I demanded he completely leave me alone. He, to my surprise, instantly complied. He stopped calling, texting, and emailing me. And it seemed like it was easy for him. Similar to when we immediately separated, I would see him at the kids' sporting and school events, and he seemed content and happy. He would be laughing and carrying on with the other coaches or parents; you would never know his marriage and family had only recently disintegrated. This took my heartbreak to an entirely new level. He just didn't seem to even care. It was especially difficult when I knew he was traveling and, in my mind, having a great time flirting with women. I broke down when he went to the same conference where he had cheated on me with Carly the prior year. It was extremely likely she was there; it was the yearly conference for their industry. I imagined them drinking cocktails and giggling at the hotel bar and eventually having passionate sex. It made me sick. I cried the entire time he was at that conference.

It didn't help that I agreed to go by the family home to take care of Penny and Frosty while he was away. I would feed and walk the dogs and then sit on the leather loveseat and cry. I missed my husband. At one point, I began walking around the house, memories flooding my mind: helping the kids with their homework, cooking dinner in the kitchen, reading bedtime stories, grilling in the backyard, and having sex in our bedroom. I stared at our bed for an especially long time. I thought about the thousands of times I had slept next to Seth, snuggling and spooning. As I stood there, I noticed a worn t-shirt of his lying on the floor next to the bed. I walked over and looked down at it. I slowly bent down and picked it up. The white cotton fabric was soft between my fingers. I brought it to up my heart, clenching it tightly, like it was a long-lost dear friend I hadn't seen in years. I put my nose deep into it, my hands nearly cupping my face, and sniffed it deep and long. It smelled like him. It smelled like my beautiful, loyal, adoring husband. I missed him more than anything. Grief and pain completely overcame me. I would never see him, or feel him, or kiss him again. That husband wasn't real. He had been in my imagination. In that moment it didn't matter. Real or not, I wanted to be with him. I went over to his side of the bed, lifted up the ruffled sheets, got into the bed, and rested my head on his wrinkled pillow. I lay there for a while, still clutching his t-shirt, sobbing. I desperately wanted my (fake) life back. "You Lost Me" by Christina Aguilera repeated over and over in my mind.

I finally got the energy to sit up. I placed the t-shirt back in its original spot and sighed deeply. Then I noticed something. All of our pictures were gone. We had several pictures of us over the years, including our wedding pictures, strewn around our bedroom. Now there were none. I threw the sheets off my legs and bolted to the living room. I frantically inspected the built-in bookcase shelves, fireplace mantle, and walls. All of the pictures of he and I, the family, and me with the kids had disappeared. The only ones that remained were pictures of Seth with the kids. You wouldn't even know I once lived there. It was like I was erased, like I had died. Maybe I was dead in his mind. I felt so small, unimportant, and invisible. With my jaw dropped to the floor, I grabbed my purse and fled to my car. I cried the entire way back to my apartment, calling my sister, Jill, along the way for support. I was so grateful I had her.

After that day, going back to the family home became rare for me because it was so anxiety provoking. I hated it when I had to go there because I would flash back to when all the pain and heartache of my husband's toxic secrets began. But alas, the kids would forget some homework, their bat, or their backpack, or our schedules would conflict in such a way that I couldn't pick them up directly from school. It was always a horrible experience. One time, I was picking up the kids from the family home at a scheduled time, but they never came out. I just sat there in my car, waiting. I texted them several times and still nothing. Dammit. I had to go to the door to claim them—*my* door, the door to *my* home, the door to the home where so many wonderful memories were made. I tried repeatedly to explain to the kids how hard it was for me to be even near the house, but they didn't get it. They just couldn't fathom what the big deal was to go by the house for a second to pick them or something up. For me, though, it was a devastatingly visceral experience that always left me driving away in tears while the lyrics to the Smiths' "Back to the Old House" played in my head.

I know I insisted Seth stop communicating with me, but this was like night and day. I was bombarded with love messages one day and then heard crickets the next. I would constantly check my phone or stare at it like I was a curious Martian who had come upon some fascinating human device. I so badly wanted a text to come through from him but then would pray one wouldn't come. It was exhausting. Did he really get over me that quickly? Clearly, this was a breeze for him. He didn't miss me. He didn't care. He didn't and probably never loved me. Maybe he didn't even have the capacity to really love. This realization was agonizing; the pain was too much. Every ounce of my heart felt like it was ripping in pieces, dark and lifeless. Still, I found myself struggling not to reach out to him. I would begin to question my sanity as thoughts would whirl around my mind urging me to contact him. *What is wrong with me? Am I the sick one? Do I enjoy being mistreated? Am I a masochist? Why can't I let go?*

One evening, it was my week and the kids were each at a friend's house for a sleepover. I made a big pot of potato soup, opened a bottle of cabernet, and lit some candles. I was determined to have a relaxing evening, just me, Peanut, and Cooper, in my beautiful new apartment. I felt strong and resilient. After a few glasses of wine, though, I broke. I had to contact him. I had to hear that he still loved me. And I wanted to tell him, again and again, how much he had hurt me. I texted him. No word. An hour later, still no word. I texted him again, this time with tears streaming down my face. Still, nothing. After another hour, I was fuming. I started obsessively calling him. I couldn't stop. Finally, he picked up.

"Hello," he answered.

"Why haven't you responded to my messages? I am sitting here crying my eyes out, missing my husband who I loved with all my heart and who has hurt me beyond repair and you wait all this time to answer? For someone who supposedly loved me, you sure have moved on quickly. Tell me: Was any of it real? Or did you just use me to have your cake and eat it, too?" I screamed through my tears.

"That's not it. I have been given advice to set boundaries with you and I'm trying to do that," he responded. "Can I come over?" he asked.

I was shocked and puzzled by his announcement that he was trying to establish limits on our relationship while at the same time asking to spend time with me. Why was he constantly messing with my head? Was this a game to him?

"Set boundaries with me? What does that mean? You're the one that wouldn't stop contacting me until I demanded you leave me alone. And hell no, you cannot come over. I do not want to see you. I just want you to know how devasted and heartbroken I am.

I want you to hear my sobs and experience the depths of my pain. I want you to know that you have hurt me so badly that I can't even function!"

"I'm so sorry, Kathi. I do love you and I am so sorry for hurting you. I have been in a really dark and lonely place lately. I have brought this all on myself and I miss you so badly. I hate myself, and I wish there was something I could do to go back and change the things I have done. I wish I hadn't been so selfish."

"Oh, fuck off! I'm glad you're hurting, you asshole!" My head crashed down on the pillow next to me.

The next thing I knew, it was morning and my phone was ringing. It was my sister, Jill.

"Hey, Kath. Check your email. I just forwarded you a message that Seth sent last night. You won't believe it!"

"Really? Ok. Let me check!" I reached for my laptop.

I went directly to my email account. Jill had forwarded to me a message Seth had sent to her, my dad, and my stepmom the evening before. This is his email:

You all are the closest people in Kathi's life and I owe you all an apology for things I have done to Kathi to end our 15-year relationship. Any excuse or reason I can give you will not justify the things I did. Please know I love Kathi with all of my heart. I am ashamed and disgusted of the person I have become. I have justifiably been branded as a liar and a cheater, two things I never wanted to become. I have lost my integrity and honor with my selfish behavior. I am now in a lonely dark place hurting without the person whom I care for and love the most. I know I have lost her (and my precious family) and I hate myself for treating her the way I did. Kathi is an amazing beautiful thoughtful giving person who never deserved this or the pain she has endured. I just wanted you all to know that I am driven to change from the person who I have become. I am totally remorseful for my actions. I hope that one day when I have become the man I want to be you will find it in your heart to forgive me. I want to be the best father to our children and I know someday I will have to sit down with them and look them in their eyes and tell them why our family was torn apart. I have been in constant agony and pain since we have been separated. I would do anything to get her back, but I know that I don't deserve her. Again, please know that I love her very much and I wish I could do some-thing to take away her pain and get her back. I spend countless hours every night crying and lying awake in turmoil thinking of how badly I hurt her. I miss her and wish I could take back all the bad things that have happened. I hope one day you will find it in your hearts to forgive me. Again, please know that I truly love her and always will.

I felt conflicted reading Seth's message to my family. It killed me to think of him crying in bed. I wanted to go to him and make him feel better. I wanted to hold him, kiss his face, and convince him it was all going to be ok. But then I remembered all the betrayal and manipulation. My empathy quickly turned to disgust. I was happy he was suffering. I wanted him to sob day and night, not be able to sleep or eat, vomit even. I wanted him to regret, with every cell of his being, what he had done to me and our family. I wanted this to be the biggest mistake of his life.

Mostly, though, his email to my family made me feel really, real-ly good. It proved that, in his own fucked-up way, he did love me and he wanted to be with me. Still, the guy had major problems, problems I wasn't willing to tackle. His issues weren't just about deceit and infidelity. They were much deeper than that. I began to see that my love for him was more profound than his love was for me, but not in a way that if you were to measure our love with a ruler my love measured ten inches and his measured five inches. It was that our rulers were different sizes; they weren't equal. His ruler only went to five inches; he wasn't capable of more. That was where his measurement instrument stopped. We simply had different capacities to love.

This was a huge realization for me, and it helped me understand myself, and Seth, a tiny bit better. He didn't love me to the same extent that I loved him because he wasn't able to. He had a double life of chasing women. He lied and cheated and made my friends feel uncomfortable by his sexual innuendos. I did none of those things. I was faithful, loyal, and committed, all because I loved him deeply and authentically. And although he said it with words, his actions showed that he was not experiencing the same kind of hurt and grief that I was. He said he was in tortured agony because of losing me yet continued to talk to, and date, other women. He was happy and laughing during the kids' games and activities. He picked a blond bombshell for an attorney. He went weeks without contacting me. Yet he was in excruciating agony? I don't think so.

WAS HE ALWAYS CHEATING?

I started to wonder how long Seth may have been disloyal to me. I always believed he was faithful, but the revelation of his cheating suggested he was capable of behavior I couldn't even comprehend. It seemed unlikely that Carly, the woman he had sex with at a work conference and whose texts I had discovered after our family trip to Mexico, was the first. I began to think back to when I first met Seth, a decade earlier, at my restaurant coworker Jenna's Halloween party. I decided to reach out to some of those old friends and seek the truth. What I found repulsed me. Not only was Seth regularly having sex with Jenna when we started dating, but he had slept with my other coworker, Sidney, the night I met him. She was the one who kept approaching him that night at the Lizard Lounge and whom I erroneously assumed he wasn't interested in because he asked for my phone number. Clearly, he had been interested in both of us. Her mortification at me bringing him to the restaurant for the Christmas party suddenly made much more sense when I found out they had hooked up. He had sex with her the night of that Halloween party and never spoke to her again. He had called me instead. Although Seth and I were not exclusive at that point, it sickened me that he was sleeping with my coworkers while courting me—juvenile, repulsive, and misogynistic, not to mention dangerous.

I then began to speculate about Seth's relationship with Angela, his coworker at the juvenile detention center where he worked while we were in Michigan. Seth's best friend Gus's wife Nikki had revealed to me that she thought that Seth and Angela might be having an affair. Seth, however, had thoroughly swayed me, as did both Angela and Gus, that Seth and Angela were not having an affair and that Seth was unquestionably devoted to me. I believed them and never further questioned Seth's faithfulness. Until now that is. Did Seth (and Angela and Gus) lie to me all those years back when he so authentically and persuasively denied having an affair with her? Did he really, when we were still newlyweds and trying to have a baby, have sex with another woman in our own home? The possibility that he had so convincingly lied to me about being a monogamous and loyal husband those two devastating weeks with my sister Jill in California, in therapy when I returned, and over the course of our marriage made my stomach twist in knots. Was he capable of that kind of sustained deceit?

I needed to find out for sure whether or not Seth had an affair with Angela during the first year of our marriage. To find out the truth, I had to come up with a lie of my own. I phoned him and told him that I wanted to have a serious talk. I told him that I now trusted how genuinely sorry he was and how much he wanted to save our marriage. Then came the big hitter. I told him that I would consider reconciliation if, and only if, he came clean about any other extramarital affairs that he had engaged in during the course of our relationship and that I was aware of one. I told him that this was the condition under which he could get me back. He agreed, and after a deep breath and a long silent pause, he confessed.

"I slept with Angela."

My head thumped to my chest, and my eyes glazed over. I was so overcome with astonishment and pain that I couldn't even cry. I could hear Seth's voice coming from my phone, which was now on the floor next to me, saying, "Kathi, are you there?" I slowly picked up the phone and brought it to my ear. But I had nothing to say. I had no words. I simply hung up the phone.

Although his confession was perhaps the most crushing and traumatic blow of all, hearing him say it did bring me some closure; I finally knew the truth about Angela. He did have an affair with her during the first year of marriage, and he did have sex with her in our home. He had been unfaithful since the very beginning. This admission also meant that my husband was having an affair with Angela while I was pregnant with Gracie. That broke my heart for me and for her. I was grateful that I was strong enough to leave him. Oh, and one last thing—remember how Seth stayed with our friend Tim in Kentucky when the kids and I moved to Texas? Well, I learned through the grapevine that Seth never really stayed with Tim during those six months before he joined us. I still have no idea whose bed he shared while the kids and I were pining over his return.

Even with all this, Seth's worst behavior was yet to come.

CHAPTER 4: THE BACKLASH

I was healing at a turtle's pace. The road was crooked and steep, slippery and rocky. It felt like every time I was making some headway, I would stumble and fall again. I would then force myself to get back up with metaphoric blood dripping from my knees and elbows, and gravel stuck in my wounds. I kept working at it, hour by hour and inch by inch. It was the most turbulent ride of my life, but I was making progress. I began to have a deep sense of hope that I would overcome the traumatic jolt to my reality and loss of my marriage and family. Although I still cried regularly and continued to miss my husband terribly, I remained strong in my decision not to reconcile. I was hopeful that maybe I could even date again, make new friends and memories, and begin having fun and enjoying life.

THE I.T. GUY

A few months into the separation, I sat at my desk in my university office thinking about my husband's horrible infidelities. *I wish I had someone to talk to*, I thought. I felt lonely. I paused for a moment. *Do I know anyone? Even one man I might be interested in spending time with?* I am monogamous by nature so rarely, if ever, thought about being with someone other than my husband. The prospect of dating seemed really strange, but also kind of exciting. A first kiss, getting nervous with butterflies, romance by moonlight—it definitely appealed to me. I thought about it a bit longer, and it hit me. There was this one I.T. guy at work, Jaime. I wondered what he might be up to.

Jaime was *incredibly* handsome; in fact, he was probably one of the most good-looking men I had ever seen in person. He was a few years younger than me, super sweet and polite, and a little bit shy. I still remember exactly the first time I met him. My women's and gender studies colleague, Nia, and I started our jobs at the university the same year and quickly became friends. One morning a few months into our first year, she popped her head into my office.

"Kathi! Have you seen the I.T. guy?"

"No. Why?" I casually looked up from my computer.

"Just make an appointment for him to come and install that new software. You'll see!" she teased mischievously as she walked away.

The next week, Jaime came by to complete the software installation. He walked into my office, and my jaw dropped to the floor. I was speechless.

"Hi, Dr. Miner. I'm Jaime. I'm here to install some software on your desktop."

"Oh, okay, sure. No problem. Here you go," I said as I got up from my office chair while motioning toward the computer monitor.

We chatted a little bit while he worked though I'm sure I wasn't very articulate; all I could think about was how gorgeous he was.

"Here's my cell number if you need anything. Have a nice day."

Not two seconds later, Nia plopped down in the chair across my desk.

"What did I tell you!" she exclaimed.

"Oh my! He is one of the most attractive men I have ever seen in my life! I could barely talk!" I waved my hand up and down near my face as to cool myself down.

We started laughing and joking about how we would have to feign problems with our computers so Jaime would have to come by our offices. (I know—horrible for two women's and gender studies professors to treat a man like a sex object!) Our colleague, Dave, whose office was next door to mine, walked into my office.

"You know Jaime was just in my office and heard *every* word you two just said," Dave loudly whispered. "But he just laughed. Don't worry about it."

Nia and I were utterly embarrassed and appalled. And then we laughed and laughed. Of course, this first interaction I had with Jaime occurred when I was still with my husband, so I never gave Jaime a second thought as someone I could possibly date. But now, I was separated and headed toward divorce. I decided to send Jaime a text.

"Hey there. How're you?" I wrote nervously.

"I'm fine. Who is this?" His response was instant.

"Oh sorry, it's Kathi, from Women's and Gender Studies."

"Hi Kathi! Nice to hear from you. What's up?" He was just as friendly as when I first met him.

"Just seeing what you're up to. Any interest in going to happy hour after work?" I think it was the first time I had ever asked a man out and could feel my stomach turn.

"Sorry, I can't tonight. I have plans with my daughter. But thanks for the invite! Some other time?"

"Sure, sounds great!" I acted like I wasn't disappointed.

Ugh. Rejected! But he was super sweet, so it felt like no big deal. Later that evening, I was back at my apartment playing on my laptop while waiting for my favorite pizza delivery when I received a friend request on Facebook. It was from Jaime! My mouth opened wide and smiled with happy surprise. *Um yeah. Accept!* Not long after, he sent me an instant message:

"Hi Kathi. How's your evening going?"

I waited a few minutes to reply as to not seem too eager.

"I'm great. What're you up to?"

And that was it—I was now officially talking to the most beautiful man in the world; well, in College Station, anyway. For the next several months, Jaime and I spent hours and hours messaging back and forth on Facebook. We talked about our favorite music, sent each other funny videos and memes, and constantly liked and commented on each other's posts. He was so fun to talk to, and he made me laugh. He was smart and vulnerable and asked me questions about my life and about my day. What was especially wonderful about Jaime was that he was so supportive. I told him all about the demise of my marriage and what my husband had done. And Jaime was there for me. He genuinely was.

We even started calling each other "babe" and "honey" and signing our messages with "love you." But our relationship was mostly confined to our computer screens. I saw Jaime in person only once (he came by my apartment to help with a computer issue on my laptop) even though I really, really wanted to see him more seriously. He wasn't interested in taking it farther than friendship. He said he was afraid that starting any dating relationship would hurt his chances of getting joint custody of his eight-year-old daughter (I realize it was also possible that he just wasn't interested in dating me). He too was on his way toward divorce, and that bonded us even more. Jaime talked at length with me about his and his wife's issues and whether divorcing was the right decision. I think we were both just grateful we had someone to confide in about our failed marriages. I felt a strong bond with Jaime; he became one of my best friends. He helped me start feeling like someone who deserved love, attention, loyalty, and honesty and to smile, laugh, and have fun. I stopped crying all the time, and I stopped constantly pining for my husband. I decided to take a trip!

DUBAI

The timing couldn't have been better! I received a grant from the university to conduct some research in Amsterdam, The Netherlands, in the summer of 2011. I was so excited to get out of Texas and away from my soon-to-be ex-husband and all the toxic bullshit. My friend and colleague, Nia, had a fantastic idea. Her research area took her to the Middle East regularly and she would be in Qatar over the summer.

"Why don't you come to Dubai before your Netherlands trip? It's only an hour flight from Qatar to Dubai, so I could get there easily. We'd have such a great time!" she said convincingly.

"That would be fun," I said hesitantly. "Fuck it. I'm in! I'll spend a week in Dubai with you before heading to Amsterdam for work," I announced excitedly.

It was the most hedonistic trip of my life. We stayed in a beautiful resort hotel, ate fabulous food, drank lots of high-end cocktails, relaxed by the pool, played in the ocean, and slept in. Because Nia took regular trips to Dubai, she had a lot of friends that we met up with for dinner, barhopping, and clubbing. There was a lot of flirting (and sometimes more) with handsome men and beautiful women. This was new behavior for me. Growing up, I had internalized the societal expectation of being a "good girl." I always had a serious boyfriend and never slept around. I was loyal in all my relationships, not even a kiss, not even one time. While my husband was with who knows who, I was a devoted wife. And where did that get me? It was time to explore! I was single in Dubai with a broken heart and an ending marriage. I could do whatever I wanted! I gave myself permission to do anything my heart desired. I committed to doing what felt good in the moment. It was amazingly liberating.

Our last night in Dubai, Nia and I went to a chic bar near the club we would later go dancing. The bar donned gorgeous semicircle dark leather booths and shimmering candles and crystal chandeliers. The vibe was cool, and the music was smooth. We each got a fancy cocktail and then grabbed a booth. A few moments later, a woman and two men asked if they could share the booth with us. We nodded yes and motioned to have a seat. We started chatting with them and instantly became chummy. The woman, Janny, was from London but now lived in Dubai. She had straight blond hair and pale white skin. She wore all-black clothing and had thick black eyeliner; her look reminded me of my Goth friends in the 1980s. She was extraordinarily outgoing and had a sarcastic sense of humor. Her two friends, Ahmed and Omar, were both from Dubai. They were a bit quieter than Janny but welcoming and sociable. We had conversation over a few drinks before heading to the club.

The club did not disappoint. The place was packed with beautiful twenty- and thirty-year-olds laughing, drinking, and dancing. The music was loud and exhilarating, the kind that your body automatically starts swaying to and you can feel pulsating deep within your body. A disco ball and colorful strobe lights darted and danced around the room like laser beams. We ordered a drink and took in the atmosphere. It felt amazing; I felt happy and free. I watched the people on the crammed dancefloor, body to body, moving together to the music like one giant organism. We decided to join them. We walked to the middle of the dancefloor and immediately became one with the group. We stayed there for hours, until our faces were drenched in sweat and our hair stuck to our face and neck. We danced with our friends and we danced with strangers, whoever shared our space. That's when I met him.

Samar was an extremely good-looking Middle Eastern twenty-nine-year-old who lived in Dubai; he was the definition of tall, dark, and handsome. Once we started dancing together, we didn't stop. We didn't talk—we couldn't over the music—so we just danced. It became more and more obvious that we were extremely attracted to each other. We dripped with sweat as we moved closer and closer together and our eyes locked with an I-want-you-so-bad look. At one point, he grabbed my hand and slid his fingers into mine until our hands were tightly locked together. Our bodies moved in perfect unison. We were in a world all our own, in an impenetrable bubble, yet surrounded by a festival of people. Although I was a decade older than him, that seemed not to matter. Our connection was profound.

Before I knew it, it was closing time and bright lights came on. I couldn't wait to learn the name of the hot guy with whom I'd been dancing the night away. We introduced ourselves and began chatting. He asked if my friends and I wanted to go to an after club. Right when I was about to say "Hell yes," Nia quickly grabbed my hand, pulled me toward the door, and announced that we had to leave immediately to get a taxi. It was one of those moments when you're being pulled away from the love of your life, arm stretched out, and a swarm of people envelopes your one true love. Such a bummer! I grinned the entire taxi ride back to the hotel thinking about how much I enjoyed dancing with that dazzling man. I still had a smile on my face when my head hit the pillow.

Nia woke me up around noon. "C'mon get up. We're going to brunch!"

I was definitely tired, but I pulled myself together. I love brunch! We arrived at a trendy upscale restaurant and were brought to our table set for six people. We were the first to arrive and ordered some prosecco.

"Who else is coming?" I was so curious.

"Just a few friends of mine," said Nia playfully.

A few minutes later, the rest of our party arrived. It was Janny, Ahmed, and Omar, the friends we had met from the night before! So fun! They were followed by two other men. *OMFG. Samar!* Janny got his contact information the night before and invited him to surprise me. I just about died. I started getting really nervous but really excited at the same time. This was going to be an amazing brunch! We all sat there for hours eating and drinking and laughing. Conversation between Samar and me started off very matter-of-factly but turned very flirty very quickly. I felt sexy, attractive, and confident—

feelings I hadn't felt in a while, especially after my husband's incredulous deceit and adultery.

After brunch, Samar offered to drive Nia and me back to our hotel in his beautiful black BMW. I sat in the front seat, and Nia sat in the back. He turned up the music and put on his sleek black sunglasses. I just sat there and stared at him. I couldn't believe where I was and who I was with. He was so handsome! When we got to the hotel, Nia announced that she was going over to a friend's house for the night. That meant Samar and I would have the hotel room to ourselves. My stomach fluttered with anticipation. I hadn't been in this situation—single and alone with a gorgeous man—in over fifteen years. I was ready!

Samar walked me up to my room while holding my hand. Once in, we closed the door and immediately started kissing as we made our way to the bed, clothes flinging left and right as they came off. We made incredible love for hours and hours. In fact, we didn't even go to sleep. I went straight from Samar to the airport. I was beaming the entire way. It was wonderfully exhilarating to be with someone other than my asshole husband. I listened to Liz Phair's "Rock Me" the entire flight to Amsterdam where I switched gears and donned my professor cap to conduct the research that had taken me out of the U.S. in the first place. I chronicled all of my adventures in Facebook messages to my sister Jill during the trip. She couldn't believe all the crazy fun I was having and agreed I had earned the right to totally let loose. This was a new chapter in my life where I made the decisions and choices. There were new experiences to be had, and I didn't have to answer to anyone.

Perhaps not surprisingly, Seth resumed regularly sending "I'm sorry" and "I love you" messages right when I left for Dubai, likely because he wanted to rope me back in and have me pine over him while I was overseas:

I really hate that things are so negative b/n us. I do care and love you. I worry about you. I'm sorry. Just know I will continue to attempt to repair the damage. I wish u didn't hate me. I will do what I can for that to change.

I want to official raise the white flag and declare peace. I will do whatever it takes to accomplish that. I want us to have trust in each other as co-parents and we both want what is not only best for our kids, but for each other. My future behaviors will show that. I do love you and I hope you do love and care for me.

His messages definitely had a saddening effect on me, but my escapades lessened their blow. It felt good to be getting better, and my yearning for Seth to contact me lessened. More than anything, I just wanted him to leave me alone so I could get over him.

YOUR GUARDIAN ANGEL

Although I had such a wonderful time on my trip, it was nice to be home. I missed the kids tremendously while I was away, and I was excited to see them. I was also eager to resume talking with my favorite IT guy, Jaime. He and I picked up right where we left off chatting on Facebook. He missed his "honey" and I missed my "babe." Seth's desire for peace and redemption changed on a dime, however. One night when he was dropping the kids off at my apartment, I got distracted by something in my bedroom and left him standing there in the front doorway, in direct view of my open laptop where I was messaging with Jaime.

"Who is Jaime Sims?" he demanded to know when I returned to the living room.

"A friend from work," I responded warily.

"A friend? According to your messages you're a lot more than friends. Or do you call all your male friends from work 'babe'?"

"It is absolutely none of your business who I talk to or what I call them."

"Well, whatever. Talk to whoever you want," he said sarcastically.

"Oh, I will. Time for you to go." I firmly closed my laptop.

"Yep!" he replied as he left.

Later that evening, he sent me a text:

> *I looked up your friend Jaime Sims on Facebook. He's married. So, you're seeing a married man? Maybe his wife would like to know!*

Then he sent me another text, then another, then another, each more furious than the last. He called me selfish and a hypocrite and dubbed me a lying homewrecker. He threatened to contact Jaime to have a "man-to-man talk with him" and to contact Jaime's wife to let her know her husband was cheating on her. I explained to him that Jaime and I were just friends and demanded that he keep out of my life. I reminded him that he had no right to be in my business, especially given everything he had done.

The next morning, I received a Facebook friend request from "Your Guardian Angel." Curious, I went to the profile page. I quickly glanced at the profile picture; it was a family. And whoever it was, they only had one friend: Jaime Sims. I looked closer at the profile picture. It was a picture of Jaime and his family. That was weird. Did Jaime create a new Facebook page but was a friend on the page? It didn't make sense. *Oh, no, no, no way*, I thought. *Seth?* Could Seth have created the page? In that moment, I received an email from Jaime. He confirmed that it was indeed Seth that had created the Facebook page; Seth was Your Guardian Angel.

Apparently right when Jaime accepted the friend request (obviously without thinking), Seth sent him an email. Jaime forwarded me the email and his reply back. In the email, Seth told Jaime that he knew about Jaime and my relationship and was going to contact Jaime's wife unless we stopped seeing each other. (Of course, Jaime and I weren't in a "real" relationship but rather in a close cyber friendship. Seth interpreted our relationship to be much more than it really was. And, oh, by the way, it was none of his business!) Seth also gave Jaime some advice; he told Jaime that he had been there, that he himself had lied to and been unfaithful to his wife and that he enormously regretted his choice. He said that he had lost his family as a result, and he didn't want the same thing to happen to Jaime. Jaime, in his reply, apologized to Seth, thanked him for his email, and assured him he would no longer be talking to me. Seth agreed to remove the Facebook page and not contact Jaime's wife.

Jaime was completely freaked out, not only because Seth threatened to tell Jaime's wife about our "affair" but that he had contacted Jaime at work to do so. He was so distressed by Seth's behavior that he absolutely refused to talk to me. Jaime sent me a very simple message: "I'm sorry but I can't talk to you anymore." And he held to his word. Seth scared the shit out of him. Jaime unfriended me on Facebook, and I never heard from him again. My relationship with Jaime ended that abruptly. Months later, I sent Jaime an instant message on Facebook: "Hey, how are you? I miss our friendship." He read it and did not (and never did) respond. I missed Jaime terribly. Although we were nothing more than really good friends, it felt like a breakup. On top of the loss of my husband, it hit me hard. I listened to Damien Rice's "Cannonball" for weeks after receiving Jaime's last message. Perhaps I was in love with Jaime all along. (By the way, Jaime did separate and divorce his wife shortly thereafter and has since remarried.)

Although Jaime told Seth he was going to end our relationship immediately (and he did), Seth really didn't know for sure. He assumed Jaime and I were (still in Seth's mind) romantically involved and continued to threaten to contact Jaime and his wife and accuse me of being with married men. He was relentless. I finally responded:

> *You make me so uncomfortable with all of these judgmental angry emails you are sending. You have NO idea what you are talking about. Please do not contact Jaime again. He and I aren't even talking and you contacting him makes you look crazy and me stupid. I AM NOT TALKING TO HIM ANYMORE. Leave him alone. He is still a work colleague and you are embarrassing me!!! Stop!*

He responded a few hours later:

> *Glad to know you all are not Facebook friends anymore. In the future I request that you do not bring prospect or current paramours to your residence while you are caring for my kids [he was referring to the time Jaime came to my apartment to help me with my work computer; the kids must have mentioned it to Seth].*

Even though Seth's ridiculous accusations of Jaime being my "paramour" and threats of contacting Jaime and his wife waned over time, Seth's toxic behavior became worse. Now when he contacted me, he was full of irate degradation. He called me crazy and pitiful and put me down as a wife and a mother. He began to deny all that he had done, minimize the toll it had on me, and blame me for his adultery, calling me abusive and cunning. His maltreatment was persistent and made me incredibly unnerved. It was shocking how quickly he went from loving me to hating me. I decided to keep track and document how many times he contacted me, venom spewing, so

I could show my attorney. This was the daily count for a two-week period:

Day 1: 18 texts

Day 2: 69 texts

Day 3: 67 texts

Day 4: 5 texts

Day 5: 29 texts

Day 6: 36 texts

Day 7: 51 texts

Day 8: 1 text, 3 calls

Day 9: 2 texts, 1 call

Day 10: 5 texts, 3 calls

Day 11: 19 texts, 2 calls

Day 12: 7 texts, 4 calls

Day 13: 4 texts, 10 calls

Day 14: 2 texts, 21 calls

My renegade attorney, Lyle, finally sent an email to Seth's attorney, Chelsea, to help calm Seth down:

Dear Ms. Lord:

My client informed me today that your client repeatedly contacts her by phone, text, or whatever. If I remember right, she said he called her 21 times already today. This has been a continuing pattern on his part. While she is more than willing to take and respond to his calls or other communications relating to the children, the couple is divorcing and she has no interest in other communications with him. Rather than expend court room time on this issue, will you see if you can

calm him down? Thanks for your attention to this time sensitive matter.
Very Truly Yours,
Lyle Lexington

Thankfully, Seth decreased the extent to which he contacted me after Lyle's email. I continued to be extremely wary of his behavior, however. I began to wonder what else he might be capable of. He had already engaged in extensive cheating, lying, accusations, harassment, and threats, none of which I would have thought in a million years he would ever do to me. What would come next? Where from the dark shadows would he unexpectedly rear his monstrous head? And indeed, although Seth went silent for a few weeks after my attorney's intervention, he began infiltrating my life once again. This time, he began stalking me, mostly by creating fake profiles on Facebook.

MULTIPLE IDENTITIES

Seth's first few bogus Facebook profiles impersonated men from Dubai. He sent me friend requests from two different men who said they lived in Dubai and met me while on my trip. I didn't recognize either of them, so it seemed really strange. I didn't accept either of the requests, but Janny, the woman I had so much fun clubbing with in Dubai, did. She began talking with one of them, Roni Salibi, about me. Roni was especially interested in how I spent my time in Dubai and if I was with any men. When Janny, in passing, mentioned this to me when we were chatting about our trip, a blaring siren went off in my head.

"Wait! Do you know this guy? Have you met him before?" I was completely freaked out.

"No, never, but he's cute," she replied coquettishly.

I immediately interrogated Roni Salibi's Facebook page. There were only two profile pictures, but they were of different people and he only had three friends (one was Janny). It was obviously a phony account. I knew instantly it had to be Seth. Janny immediately unfriended him and the other unknown man from Dubai. But she had already provided details of my hedonistic time there. How could Janny be so gullible? Seth was good at bringing on the charm, though, and as a result, she had been easily manipulated by him to spill the beans. Good thing was now I was onto him and his new strategy of pretending to be someone else to find information about me. So, when I received the email below from a person and email address I didn't recognize and couldn't find online, I knew exactly who it was from: Seth.

> *Dearest Kathi,*
>
> *It is me. I have thought of you since we met at the club. You are very beautiful and the memory of your body is still in my mind. Do you think of me? Did you enjoy me? I am at work and think of our time together. I saw your English friend Janny at the market yesterday. We live very close to each other. She said you had a wild 72 hours. I looked you up at your university and wanted to chat with you. I hope not to offend you. What did you all do after we slept together? She said you and Nia were very active and sexy. That night was very nice and thrilling for me. I never been with American girl. Please let me know how you doing.*

The message didn't make sense and was clearly drawing at straws. My first thought was that it was Samar, my hunky hookup, but he and I had exchanged phone numbers and he had already checked that I had made it safely back to the U.S. Plus, not one person I met in Dubai talked like the person in the email. It was just weird all around. I never responded and never heard from the sender again. Phony Roni Salibi did try several more times to friend me on Facebook, however. I finally blocked him, as I did fake Shane Robbins, Jon Wallace, Jason Nansen, Sylvia Trahan, and Samir Michael. I also warned my friends and family that Seth was creating sham profiles and trying to friend people in my life to find out information about me. Sure enough, my sister Jill had also received friend requests from Jon Wallace and Jason Nansen. *Sorry, ex, I'm onto you!*

Seth engaged in several other stalking tactics as well, ones that were downright disturbing. My friend Nia went to a work conference for a week and asked if I would go to dinner with her husband Eric while she was away. Nia and Eric had been a big support to me from the beginning of the separation, and we had become good friends. I was happy to go to dinner with Eric. We went to a little Italian restaurant in town one evening. We had some Cajun pasta and chatted about our lives and my divorce. I really appreciated Eric's company given everything I was going through.

About a week later, my daughter Gracie asked, "Mommy, why do you go out with married men? Daddy said you were out with Eric on a date the other night."

I was floored. "Eric is married, yes, to Nia, but we weren't on a date. Eric and I are just good friends," I reassured her trying to maintain my cool.

I had absolutely no idea how Seth knew I went to dinner with Eric. Seth also knew details about my other whereabouts and who I was with that he should not have known unless, that is, he had been following me or somehow hacking my personal devices.

Along these lines, Gracie said to me during that time, "Daddy has some device where he can see all of your messages and emails. I heard him telling Grandma."

At the beginning of all this, Seth was an asshole cheater, but now he had taken it to a whole new level. I felt like I was constantly looking over my shoulder, hunted like a weak fawn. One day, I drove with Gracie to the family home to pick up some school supplies. I dreaded interacting with Seth, so I took her when I knew he wasn't home. He was driving out of the neighborhood, though, and saw me driving in. He quickly turned around so I drove off in a different direction, sweat dripping from my brow. He followed me in and out of streets until I lost him. It scared the crap out of me. I even began to have nightmares of someone chasing and trying to murder me. My friends and family became concerned, too. At their urging, I searched my apartment for listening devices and installed extra security on my laptop computer and phone. One of my friends bought me a self-defense key chain, "cat ears," that became glued to my right hand. Nia and Eric also became apprehensive.

"We are really worried about your safety. Does Seth have guns?" she asked me one day.

They, like Jaime the IT guy, began to withdraw from our friendship.

Then, I got another friend request from Roni Salibi (yes, even after I had blocked him), and it was an entirely new picture. *That's it. I'm done*, I thought. I reached out to Lyle, my attorney, for help. He again contacted Chelsea, Seth's attorney, this time making it clear that, if Seth did not stop his behavior, we would seek a restraining order:

> *Dear Ms. Lord:*
> *My client has informed me that your client is engaging in threatening behavior towards her and taking multiple actions that are clearly meant to harass and distress her thereby causing emotional damage. Please advise your client to immediately cease and desist from any such actions or I will file an emergency restraining order on my client's behalf. Please be advised that if your*

*client's behavior persists there will be no further warn-
ing given prior to the filing of the restraining order.
Thanks for your attention to this time sensitive matter.
Very Truly Yours,
Lyle Lexington*

The next morning, my intuition told me that Seth's behavior was
not going to stop and I shouldn't wait on the restraining order. But
when I went to gather Seth's threatening messages to start building
my case, I realized they had almost all been deleted. Seth had hacked
my accounts. He had deleted his harassing messages, even texts on
my phone (I later learned about a form of spyware called keylogging,
which, once installed, records every keystroke made on a keyboard
without the user's knowledge or consent. I assume he used this, or
something similar, to get access to my accounts). He also forwarded
emails to himself between me and my attorney, Lyle, some of which
included confidential divorce documents, as well as the Facebook
messages I had sent to my sister Jill describing my wild, self-indul-
gent trip to Dubai. How could I get a restraining order now? I had
no evidence! I was fuming. How could he get away with this? As was
now a regular occurrence, I sobbed myself to sleep in defeat.

The next morning when I woke, I felt like I had been beaten
up during the night. I felt drained and hopeless. It kept me in bed
most of the day. The pouring rain didn't help. I probably would have
stayed in bed all day had there not been a knock on my door. I
looked through the peephole and saw a woman holding a black um-
brella. I opened the door.

"Can I help you?" I asked exhaustingly.

"Kathi Miner?"

"Yes," I answered.

"You've been served," she said as she handed me a document.

"What? What is this?" I inquired confusingly.

"It's a restraining order. That's all I can say. Sorry," she said as she left.

I could not believe it! Seth had issued a temporary restraining order *against me*. The crux of the order concerned the children. He maintained that I was an unstable, violent, alcoholic mother who routinely put her children in danger. Seth's "evidence" included complete falsehoods and events taken out of context. It was clear that Seth was using the court system as a way to punish me. And it was crystal clear why I was being chastised: I was beginning to take baby steps toward having my own life on my own terms, and Seth was losing control. The restraining order had nothing to do with the kids and keeping them safe and had everything to do with him castigating and dominating me. Distancing me from the kids was simply a byproduct of this penance.

Seth's acquisition of a restraining order was the first clear indication that things had taken a totally different direction. While Seth had certainly engaged in some bizarre behavior up to this point, he now was in full-fledged coercive control mode. *Coercive Control* refers to non-physical, hard–to-detect, and nearly invisible conduct that seeks to restrict a target's ability to participate in everyday behavior. The primary objective of this abuse mechanism is to reduce the target to an almost hostage-like state, commonly resulting in a loss of dignity and safety and a heightened sense of powerlessness and entrapment. In this case, Seth had restricted my ability to mother my children. There was nothing I could do and I was at his whim.

During the time period of the restraining order, I was unable to see the kids unless supervised, and when I tried to set up times to see them, Seth refused, saying he was uncomfortable with the people I suggested supervise the visit. In addition, the kids were starting school in a few weeks and there was a meet-the-teacher event, an occasion I looked forward to every year yet, because of the restraining order, I was not permitted to attend. The kids were upset and hurt, too, that I couldn't be there. Thankfully, there was a court hearing scheduled two weeks from when I was served the restraining order. During that hearing, I would have the opportunity to state my case, and the judge would decide if the order should go into full effect or if it should be dropped for lack of evidence. It felt like it would be the longest two weeks of my life. I couldn't sleep, felt constantly sick to my stomach, and cried a lot. I was terrified that the judge would side with Seth and make the order permanent even though I knew he was being deceptive and controlling.

MEDIATION

During the two-week period prior to the hearing about the restraining order, Seth and I were required to go to mediation as part of the divorce process. Divorce mediation is the use of a supposedly neutral third party to negotiate a resolution between the spouses on various issues, such as child custody and separation of assets and debts. The assumption is that both spouses will engage in such negotiations in good faith, but I had zero expectation that Seth would use it as such. Rather, I felt like Seth would take advantage of mediation to gain power and control me, especially given his leverage of the restraining order. But it was mandated by the court, so I had to go.

The mediator, Jim Delano, was a gentle older man in his mid-sixties. I felt safe and comfortable with him, so that eased some of my nervousness. I was in one room with my attorney, Lyle, and Seth was in another with his attorney, Chelsea. Mediator Jim went from room to room, back and forth, trying to help us come up with a deal that satisfied us both. Seth wanted full custody (you know, because I'm such a horrible mother) and for me to pay the house mortgage (in addition to my apartment rent), half of the credit card debt, and half of the kids' extracurricular activities. I wanted 50/50 custody, him to pay the mortgage to the house, him to pay all of the credit card debt, and us each to pay for the kids' activities that we enrolled them in. I also wanted him to pay all of my attorney fees and part of my student loans, which I had taken out solely to support the family (not for my tuition and books, which the university had paid for) while we were in Michigan. Finally, I requested that all of us—me, him, and the kids—each separately attend psychological counseling sessions on Seth's dime to deal with the causes and consequences of the divorce.

Here was my logic for my requests. Both my current attorney, Lyle, and the one I fired, Harry, strongly encouraged me *not* to seek full custody of Gracie and Henry given the prevailing norms in family law regarding child custody. Currently, most judges believe that what is best for children is to have both parents equally involved in their lives via joint custody and view parents who want full custody as being "unfriendly" to the other parent, potentially negatively interfering, or even damaging, their relationship with the children. This is especially true for mothers in heterosexual marriages, who are often stereotyped as wanting to limit fathers' access to their children and even sever the bond between them. These norms meant that it was critical that I be perceived as a friendly parent who cheerfully wanted to share custody of Gracie and Henry with Seth. Otherwise, I might risk losing them altogether. As such, I agreed to ask for joint custody even if I truly believed the kids were better off full time with me.

In addition, because Seth was living in the family home, I felt he should be the one to pay the mortgage. I didn't live there anymore, and if he couldn't afford it, then we should sell the house. (By the way, Seth later decided to rent the extra bedroom in the "we made it" house to a male coworker, Ryan, to help with the mortgage. The fact that he let a male live in the home with two young children, including our daughter Gracie, without knowing this man's history was completely unacceptable to me. I was furious, but there was absolutely nothing I could do about it.) I also believed that Seth should pay all of our credit card debt, my attorney fees, and a portion of my student loans. It was his adulterous behavior that led to the divorce, so he should be financially culpable for all of it. Plus, because he handled our finances, it was unclear to me what purchases were on the credit cards. I knew partly, of course, because I used our cards for the grocery store, travel to conferences, meals out, etc. But what I didn't know was the extent to which Seth may have used the cards for expenses related to infidelity. Did he use those cards to take women out, buy them gifts, pay their bills? I just didn't know, and I was damned if I was going to pay for his extramarital pursuits.

Regarding the kids' activities, Seth, I felt, always wanted the kids involved in way too much. The kids always had at least three forms of extracurriculars happening and it was, in my opinion, detrimental to their well-being. Seth also wanted them involved in elite tournament sports teams which were unbelievably pricey, especially when there was travel involved. My wallet just couldn't handle it. I wanted them to have hobbies beyond school as well but not to the same extent. From my perspective, if he wanted them to be over-committed and over-involved in expensive sports teams and other activities, he should have to pay for it.

Finally, I believed that Seth needed to see a professional about his behavior, I needed to see a professional about the trauma associated with his behavior, and the kids needed to see a professional to help them cope with all the changes—again, all on Seth's dime. All of these asks were fair to me then, and they are fair to me now.

After hours and hours of mediation, neither of us would budge, and it was nearing the end of our five-hour time slot. Seth's attorney, Chelsea, even had to leave to go pick up her son from school. Then, mediator Delano came in from over an hour with Seth with an announcement.

"Your husband has a deal for you. He said that, if you agree to his requests, he will drop the restraining order and you will be able to see your kids again. What do you think?"

My jaw dropped to the ground, and my eyes started frenetically twitching. I was so incensed! What a prick! I knew that dumb-ass restraining order was always about power and control and never about the welfare of Gracie and Henry. If he was so fraught about the kids spending time with me because of my negligent tendencies, then why would he agree to drop the order? I declined his bullshit offer.

"Ok, I'll let him know," Delano said as he left the room.

He returned with a new proposal a few minutes later:

"Seth said that, because it is getting so late and we are all ready to have this over with, he would like set up another mediation to discuss the outstanding issues [we never did, actually, and it wasn't until our day in divorce court that the other items were decided]. He also said he is willing to drop the restraining order if you agree to have a court-appointed social worker do an in-depth investigation, called a social study, into who, you or him, should be the custodial parent. I know of someone who is very good, May Hazelwood, who I could recommend to the court to conduct the study."

"Ok," I replied. "I agree to that."

And, *poof*, just like that, the restraining order disappeared. I was glad the day was over and was thrilled I could resume my mommy role.

As we were leaving mediation, Seth tauntingly yelled across to me in the parking lot:

"So, your attorney, Harry, fired you, huh? You're such a joke he wouldn't even work with you. How sad!" He laughed to himself as he got into his truck.

He was wrong, of course. I had fired Harry. But it still got my goat. I felt like a bomb ready to explode, teeth clenched and smoke coming from my ears, as I drove down the highway, enough, in fact, for me to turn my car around and head directly to the police station.

THE INVESTIGATION

I was at the College Station Police Department in less than ten minutes. I described to an officer Seth's stalking, harassment, and intimidation. Trying to reassure me, the officer said that Seth's behavior was common in a divorce and that it should decrease in frequency. He told me to come back if the behavior didn't cease in the coming weeks. I was not comforted. Nothing suggested that Seth was going to stop. The officer also encouraged me to go the Texas A&M University Police Department given that Seth, who also worked for the university, likely used his work computer to stalk me and hack my accounts. It never occurred to me that evidence could be on his work computer, but I thought it was definitely worth looking into. I went to the campus police department the next day.

I met with Officer Kekoa when I arrived. I repeated everything I had told the previous officer. I also brought and showed him whatever text and email documentation of Seth's abuse I still had. The officer took notes and made copies. At the end of our visit, he told me what he thought about my case.

"Based on what you have given me, I think there is enough evidence to move forward and investigate. Of course, I will have to corroborate your accusations before I can bring it before a judge," he explained. "We will likely have to confiscate his work computer."

"Yes, of course, whatever you need to do. Thank you so much."

I felt just a bit of hope. This was great news! Seth was now officially under investigation by the Texas A&M University Police Department and was hopefully going to be punished for his abusive, malicious, and unnerving actions, especially given those behaviors violated university code of conduct and computer use protocols. I was so relieved and optimistic.

Three days later, Officer Kekoa called to report that two officers had gone to Seth's work to seize his computer. They caused quite a scene, apparently, with Seth's coworkers watching and whispering as the officers whisked his workstation away. They did indeed find information on the fake profiles as well as other "inappropriate" content on his computer. Woohoo! We got him! I played Lily Allen's "Smile" over and over that night.

Officer Kekoa and I talked regularly as he kept me abreast of the case and how it was unfolding. One day he called with some interesting news.

"Hello?"

"Hi there, Kathi. This is Officer Kekoa. Do you have a minute?"

"Of course!" I responded.

"That last Facebook friend request you received from so-called Roni Salibi, you said it was an entirely new profile picture, is that correct?" he inquired.

"Yes, the most recent friend request was the name Roni Salibi, but the profile picture was of someone totally different. Why do you ask?"

"Do you know who that is a picture of?" he replied with a little laugh.

"No. Who?" I asked curiously.

"It's a picture of Tommy Puicci. Tommy works for a local radio station that covers Texas A&M sports. He's sort of a celebrity." He was surprised I didn't know.

"Really?" I was astonished.

"Yeah. I contacted Tommy and told him that someone was using his picture on a fake Facebook profile and asked him if he wanted to press charges. He doesn't want to, but I just wanted you to know about it."

"That's crazy! Thanks for letting me know. Any other news?" I was so intrigued and hoped there was more to bring Seth down.

"Not at this time, but I'll keep you posted."

"Yes, please do. Thank you so much!" I finally felt like someone had my back.

"You're very welcome, Kathi," he responded supportively. We hung up the phone.

A week later I got a call from Officer Kekoa.

"Kathi, we need to talk about how to proceed. Although your husband did create fake profiles and have porn on his work computer, those behaviors aren't illegal. The only thing that your husband has done that is clearly in violation of the law is hacking your accounts. The issue is that, before your separation, you hacked his accounts. I realize your goals were very different: you were trying to discover whether or not he was cheating, and he sought to delete evidence of his harassment and to get ammunition against you to use in the divorce, but the court will see it as the same. You hacked his accounts, and he hacked your accounts. It's tit for tat."

I was crushed.

"But, Officer Kekoa, yes, I accessed his accounts, but I knew the password. As his wife, he had given his password to me. Well, I guess there was one instance I had to figure out the answers to his security questions to enter his Yahoo! account, but still. I know him so well that it was easy. When he accessed my accounts, he clearly used other tactics, like putting some kind of software on my devices. Won't the court see the difference?"

He paused for a moment, like he was empathizing with my situation, then continued.

"My supervisor doesn't think so and believes that this is a case you likely won't win. It could also be very costly. My advice is to drop the charges and move on with your life," he concluded.

To say I was disappointed is an understatement. I didn't have the money to hire a criminal attorney (in addition to my divorce attorney whom I already couldn't afford) for some long, drawn-out court case where I was unlikely to triumph. I took Officer Kekoa's advice and dropped the charges. Seth was off the hook, again. I lay in bed and started to sob, Peanut and Cooper simultaneously licking the tears off my face. I was completely overcome with defeat and exhaustion. A *ding* came from my phone. It was Seth.

Ha-ha nice try. You're so fucking pathetic! his text read, accompanied by laugh emojis.

"I hate you!" I screamed as I threw the phone across the room and dug my face into the pillow.

Then, Seth went silent.

CHAPTER 5: THE NEW FRIENDS

I was so relieved that the temporary restraining order against me was dropped just in time for the new school year. It was my week with Gracie and Henry, so I was the parent who got the privilege of taking them to their first day of second and fifth grade. I got up early that morning, put on a pot of coffee, and started a batch of French toast. The kids were easy to wake up. They came from their bedrooms each wrapped in a blanket and relaxedly sat at the farmhouse table in the apartment. They quietly ate their breakfast while glancing over at the TV that, like every morning, was playing the *Today* show. I started making their lunches as they went back to their rooms to get ready for the big day. They each looked great in their pristine back-to-school outfits. They grabbed their new backpacks brimming with new school supplies and their lunch boxes. We were off!

The first day of school excitement was palpable. I first took Gracie to her classroom and then Henry to his. They were both thrilled to see their friends, their new classrooms, and their new teachers. They were smiling and happy. Although I felt heavy because it was the first time I was taking the kids to the first day of school without Seth, I felt optimistic. Thankfully, Seth had been pretty quiet since the investigation by the Texas A&M Police Department. Although it didn't result in a conviction, I hoped it relayed to Seth that I was serious about ending his egregious behavior and would get law enforcement involved if needed. I welcomed the sense of peace I felt.

When the kids were both settled in their classrooms, I began walking the hall toward the school parking lot and ran into my friend Wanda. We started chatting about innocuous topics like the weather and the fruit on sale at the HEB grocery store down the street when another mom approached us. Her name was Sheri. Sheri was a forty-something curvy woman with long dark straight hair, piercing blue eyes, and the biggest Roman nose I had ever seen on a woman. Her clothes were colorful and stylish, and she wore lots of bracelets and big hoop earrings. I was in workout clothes.

"Hey, y'all!" Sheri was incredibly outgoing.

"Hey, Sheri. How are you? Do you know Kathi?" Wanda asked motioning in my direction.

"Oh yeah," Sheri said. "I've met Kathi a few times before."

"Hi, um, we have?" I had no clue where I had met her before.

"Yeah, you dropped Henry off at my son Carter's birthday party a few months ago. We live just a few streets down from you. The boys played army in the trees across the street from my house. Carter and I also came to Henry's last birthday party at Mr. Gatti's Pizza."

"Oh, yeah, sure. Of course." I still had no recollection.

I instantly realized why I didn't remember meeting Sheri. Both of the events she described occurred at the start of my separation from Seth when I could barely function and sobbed constantly. I did recall how difficult it was for me to host Henry's birthday party at Mr. Gatti's Pizza, however. I was teary-eyed the entire time while trying to put on a happy face for Henry and his guests. Plus, I knew Seth would be arriving, and it devastated me to be around him. I was on pins and needles the entire time just waiting for him to walk through the door. He never did, though. He never showed up to Henry's birthday party.

"How's everything else going?" Wanda asked empathetically looking in my direction.

I knew she was asking about the divorce. "Honestly, it's been horrible. It's really tough. It's the hardest thing I've ever been through. The last six months have been brutal." I was never good at faking pleasantry. I turned to Sheri to fill her in. "I'm going through a divorce. It really sucks."

"I'm so sorry to hear that. I'm sure it is. Well, if you ever want to get together and chat about it, I'm your girl!" she said with a warm smile. "Here, put your number in my phone."

"Ok, sure. Thanks. I appreciate that." I could tell she and I would become good friends.

"Alright, ladies, I'm off to the gym. Have a good day," I said as I grabbed my keys out of my purse and brought down my sunglasses from the top of my head.

About a week later, Sheri texted me and invited me to happy hour at the Republic Steakhouse. It was one of the nicest restaurants in College Station, and I drove by it every day but had never been inside. I loved their slogan and often whispered it while driving past: "Steak. Wine. Whiskey." Definitely my kind of place. I accepted her invitation and met her the next day at the bar around five. The ambience was just my style. Dark wood hues, dark leather booths and chairs, flickering candles, and upbeat jazz filled the entire area. Sheri had already arrived and was sitting at the bar. She waved hello to make sure I saw her, and I headed to the empty bar stool next to her.

"Hey, girl!" She welcomed me with a big hug.

"Hey, hi. I'm so happy to be here! What are you drinking?" I asked.

"Oh, just starting out with a Miller Lite," she answered.

"Glass of red for me please!" I bellowed as Sheri handed me the drink menu.

Sheri was one of the kindest, friendliest people I had ever met in my life. She was dynamic, energetic, and silly. She laughed loud and hard and was a virtuoso at making perfectly timed salty, sarcastic jokes and remarks. In a word, she was fun! And she was exactly what I needed in my life. We sat there for hours chatting, laughing, and telling our life stories. I shared the death of my mom, my close relationships with my sisters, my hard work through graduate school as a feminist academic, and, of course, the demise of my marriage to Seth. She disclosed the difficult relationships she had with her divorced parents, what it was like to grow up as an only child, her job as a stay-at-home-mom, and the problems she was having with her husband, Kenny. Kenny, she disclosed, was both emotionally and physically abusive. Sheri revealed to me that she had been considering divorcing Kenny for a long time.

Sheri and I connected instantly and on a soulmate level, like we had known each other for years or in a previous life. We both felt it and knew we were on to something really special. After that day, Sheri and I were inseparable and became each other's main source of social support. She decided to leave Kenny and file for divorce (which, to this day, Kenny blames me for), and we helped each other through the process of leaving and divorcing our abusive husbands. Our families blended, too, and her daughter and two sons became instant siblings to my Gracie and Henry. We ate dinners together, grilled in the backyard, went on weekend and tubing trips, had sleepovers, movie, and game nights, and laughed and sang together. We even went "t-ping" (toilet papering houses), and Sheri and I joined in. I still remember the delight we felt as divorcing women in our forties side by side with the kids throwing toilet paper rolls over trees and bushes while trying to hold in bursts of laughter. On one of our t-ping adventures, we may have even put a dab of dishwashing liquid in the water feature at the neighborhood community entrance. So many bubbles! It was a joy to feel like a kid again! We spent countless hours belting in the car or dancing in the living room to "Get Lucky" by Daft Punk or whatever jam felt like gold. Even now, when I hear "songs of Sheri," I am instantly brought back to those wonderful memories we made together during one of the most difficult and painful times of our lives. We became so close as a family that Henry even told Sheri he wished she and I would get married so she could be his other mom!

Not only did Sheri and I have loads of fun together, but we shielded and protected each other from our exes when we had to interact with them. We would root for each other from behind the scenes, making reassuring "You've got this!" or "You can do this!" proclamations. Or we might flip off or make silly faces at the phone if the other was texting or having a phone conversation with her ex-asshole. If we knew a face-to-face interaction was coming with Seth or Kenny, we did our best to actually be present for the other, simply standing in the background as a witness and support. The men got used to this and hated it. We loved it. It made us feel strong and powerful to protect each other from malevolent men who wanted nothing more than to see us squirm and suffer. We quickly learned, too, that the presence of each other in those interactions thwarted the amount of abuse we received.

It was common, for example, for Sheri to accompany me to the kids' games and practices or if Seth and I had to swap the kids outside our normal exchange times. In a clear bullshit attempt to demonstrate I was full of shit and he was being portrayed as a bad guy, Seth would be overly friendly to Sheri ("Hi, Sheri! It's nice to see you. I hope you're doing well!" or "You look really pretty without makeup, Sheri.") and at one point even tried to warn her about me and my "manipulativeness." Sheri and I would just roll our eyes. She had seen and heard the detailed evidence against him and had experienced an abuser firsthand. She saw right through him.

Seth could usually keep his composure in these instances, but there were times he would lash out at me right in front of Sheri. For example, one evening Sheri and I took her son Carter and my son Henry to the school fair. Henry had been with Seth earlier that day and Seth was set to drop him off to me at the local Subway sandwich restaurant where Sheri, her son Carter, and I were getting a bite before the fair. We saw through the restaurant windows when Seth and Henry arrived. My body had a visceral reaction of apprehension, like it usually did, when Seth was in close proximity. Henry got out of Seth's van and headed into the restaurant. Seth stayed in the driver's seat but was clearly incensed; it was written all over his face. His lip was furrowed, his eyebrows came together in a letter V, and he was slowly nodding his head side to side as to be relaying an air of disgust. I saw him reach for the door handle like he wanted to come in and scream at me but then checked himself and paused. He did this several times, Sheri and me wondering what the hell he was doing. He finally got out of the van, slammed the door, and entered the restaurant. He started intimidatingly yelling at me about something I couldn't even understand, his finger pointing at my face as to reprimand me.

"Leave!" I shouted at him. "Leave me alone!"

He laughed under his breath and said, "You're such a joke," as he left the restaurant.

He got into his van and drove off, his tires screeching along the way. I believe that interaction would have been a lot worse if Sheri hadn't been with me. Sheri helped me feel like I could get through the agony of my divorce and is one of the best friends I have ever had. But she wasn't the only new friend to come into the picture.

MEET SETH'S NEW FRIEND, JESSICA

It was no surprise that Seth was dating and meeting women during the divorce; he was simply carrying on as usual. What I didn't expect, though, was for him to enter into an "exclusive" relationship with a woman while we were still separated. Although I was committed to healing from my shattered reality and extreme sorrow, I was nowhere near forming a romantic relationship with someone. In fact, I didn't know if I would ever be able to love that way again. I was deeply and profoundly broken, and Seth seemed to have moved on with lightning speed.

Roughly six months into the separation, the kids told me that a woman named Jessica had been coming to the family home and would sometimes stay the night in their dad's bed. They also revealed that they had started going to Austin, where she lived, and would stay the weekend. Apparently, my husband and Jessica had gone to high school together and had reconnected over Facebook. As far as I know, she was not one of the women my husband cheated on me with during our marriage. That made me feel at least a little bit better.

The kids seemed to really like Jessica. They said she was nice and, in fact, reminded them a lot of me. I immediately looked her up on Facebook. She was very liberal, feminist, and concerned about social justice issues. She was expressly interested in dog rescues and routinely fostered and adopted dogs. She had a lot of tattoos (which I found interesting because Seth would often say he didn't like tattoos on women) and was heavier than me (which was also noteworthy because he would frequently comment about my weight if I had gained a few pounds). I found her pretty, with a warm smile and beautiful green eyes. Like me, she was educated, independent, and had a successful career. She also seemed to have a close and active female friendship group. She was someone I could imagine I would have been friends with under different circumstances.

I didn't break down into tears or anything when I found out Seth was seeing someone seriously. I more felt sorry for her. I knew he had likely lied to her about the reasons surrounding our divorce and portrayed me as a terrible wife and mother. I also knew that, for him, she was simply a new ego supply. He likely loved the challenge of getting another intelligent, independent woman to fall in love with him. I'm sure if Jessica knew the real truth about Seth, she would have run for the hills. He was good, though, at pretending to be a progressive, liberal, sensitive man who loved strong, confident, feminist women, so it was no surprise she had fallen for him. I did, after all. And he had made it very easy.

Shortly after the kids told me about Jessica, she unexpectedly appeared at one of Gracie's softball tournaments. I was sitting on the hard metal bleachers when Gracie, who had a break between games, came and sat next to me. She pointed to a woman to the left of me a few seats down.

"Mom, that's Jessica. I'm gonna go say hi."

I immediately felt my throat fall to my stomach; I was on the verge of throwing up. It was one thing to know about Jessica, but to actually see her in person was different. That it was at one of my kids' games made it even worse. Yep, I definitely felt like I was going to puke, but I kept my cool. I just very nonchalantly kept watching the game. But then I would look over at her and then back at the game. Good thing I could only see the back of her, or she would have noticed me repeatedly glancing at her.

Then, in a matter of seconds, grief overcame me and tears began to flood my eyes. I was going to lose it. I had to get up and leave the area. I went to one of the empty fields nearby and hid in the dugout and sobbed. I was leveled like a punch that takes you to your knees in a boxing match. My husband had a girlfriend, and she was now attending my kids' sporting events. I was still mourning the loss of my marriage and experiencing overwhelming heartbreak, and he was dating and seemingly falling in love. The lying, cheating asshole husband had a girlfriend, and his loving, loyal estranged wife was losing it in a dusty ballfield dugout. I sat there for probably twenty minutes just bawling. Then, I decided to get it together. I decided to introduce myself to her. I walked directly up to her.

"Hi. I'm sure you know who I am, and I also know who you are. I thought I should come and introduce myself. I'm Kathi, the kids' mom." I sounded calm and cool but was shaking on the inside.

"Nice to meet you. I'm Jessica," she replied amicably.

Then I said something I'm sure she was not expecting.

"I want you to know that I think it's really great that you have come here today and want to support the kids. But to be honest with you, it is really, really difficult for me to have you here. I am still grieving the end of my marriage. Would you please consider only coming to the kids' events on Seth's weeks and not on my weeks? When it's Seth's weeks you can knock yourself out and attend everything you want. But when it's my week, can you just let me enjoy my kids? It would mean a lot."

At that moment, Seth walked up and interrupted me. He had heard the last bit of my request.

"Oh God," he said. "She's not going to do that. She is going to come whenever…"

Jessica cut him off by turning toward him and holding her palm up as to stay stop. "Yes, I am willing to do that. I will only come to the kids' events on Seth's weeks," she agreed empathetically.

"Thank you so much. I really appreciate it," I said with a sigh of relief.

Seth rolled his eyes and angrily put his hands on his hips.

"Come walk me out," she said to him.

He walked her toward the parking lot, and when they were far enough away but close enough for me to still see, they hugged and kissed for a few minutes before she left. It tore me apart. It felt like he was parading her and their new love right in front of me, rubbing their relationship in my face. He seemed happy, content, and light, and I felt insecure, distressed, and heavy. I resumed watching the game but felt nauseated and demoralized.

I had an irresistible need to warn Jessica about Seth's duplicitous, abusive ways. Later that night, I sent her a message on Facebook detailing the reasons for the end of our marriage and his treatment of me to that point in our separation. I told her, woman to woman, that Seth was not a man she wanted to get involved with. Not surprisingly, I never heard back from her. I now know it's common for targets of betrayal and abuse to want to warn other potential victims but those attempts almost always prove futile and end up making the ex-partner look irrational and jealous. Indeed, the crazy ex-girlfriend/wife trope was invented by men so they don't have to take accountability for the ways they traumatize women. This was just another incidence of that. I also now understood why Seth had been so noiseless for a bout: he was grooming Jessica.

MR. HYDE

Shortly after I had reached out to Jessica to warn her about Seth, he began to again rear his ugly head, especially at the kids' sporting events. At nearly every game or practice, he would leer at me from a distance with an air of hostility and intimidation. There were also dozens of times that he would stand near me with his chest puffed out, chin up, and fists clenched and look me up and down with a face of disgust while slowly shaking his head back and forth as to shame me. I could feel the terrifying rage emanating from his body. Sometimes, this in-person abuse occurred in front of the kids. Usually, though, he would be cruel in a way that the kids (and others) couldn't see. He would look at the kids (who might be sitting several feet way) to make sure they weren't paying attention and then turn to me; his face would change from calm and relaxed to sadistic and spiteful. His dog-whistle behavior was so under the radar that it seemed that only I could "hear" it. It was a form of intimate terrorism that he started to engage in regularly.

If Seth wasn't bullying me from a distance, he would approach me to have an ostensibly innocuous conversation but end up degrading, insulting, or yelling at me. With venom spewing from his mouth, he would call me a horrible mother, an alcoholic, a fraud, an embarrassment, or a liar. He would tell me how happy he was that he no longer had to deal with my so-called craziness or how thrilled he was that he finally escaped my purported abuse and manipulation. His near-constant projection would go on and on and grind me further and further down. Usually, it would be in a place where there were not a lot of people around, like if I had to get something out of my car, went to get a snack at the concession stand, or use the restroom. That way, no one would be privy to his maltreatment.

I just couldn't wrap my mind around how Seth could have so much contempt for me, someone he said he loved, had been married to, had children with, and who was visibly hurting from his own abhorrent actions. Even if he was pissed off for my contacting Jessica, his reaction was disproportionately callous, hostile, and unnerving. It was completely unparallel to my protective gesture toward Jessica, and moreover, it never stopped. It was a continuous stream of hate and malice every time I was in his vicinity. He had absolutely no remorse or concern for how malevolently he was treating me, let alone his numerous lies and betrayals during the marriage. Even worse, he seemed to get off on emotionally tormenting me. He was cold and cunning and wanted to inflict the maximum level of harm on me.

Although I was completely astonished by his behavior, I also knew from teaching courses on gender oppression and interpersonal gender dynamics that marital separation and divorce are frequently the catalyst for such family violence and almost always by husbands toward wives. The U.S. Department of Justice's Office of Violence Against Women defines family violence as follows:

> *physical, sexual, emotional, economic, psychological,*
> *or technological actions or threats of actions or other*
> *patterns of coercive behavior that influence another*

person within an intimate partner relationship. This includes any behaviors that intimidate, manipulate, humiliate, isolate, frighten, terrorize, coerce, threaten, blame, hurt, injure, or wound someone.

I never, ever thought Seth would get to that point. The person I was married to was not the same person I was divorcing; they were drastically different people. I was now not simply divorcing my husband, but dealing with an intensely abusive situation. And just like so many other women ending relationships with abusive men, I was constantly wondering what he would do next. My personal lived experience began to substantiate that separation/divorce is a distinctly gendered phenomenon and can be deeply threatening for women.

Although it took everything I had in me, I got pretty good at being a gray rock. That is, I would become completely emotionless, boring, and indifferent so that he would lose any interest in trying to communicate with me. After all, he could only enjoy abusing me if he could see me distressed, and when I didn't respond, it lost its luster. The first instance I used this strategy made him absolutely furious. He had found a family therapist for himself and the kids, which I was thrilled about and had been vocally advocating. When I told him I was not comfortable signing the agreement forms until I spoke with my colleagues in the Psychology Department at the university about the chosen therapist, he harassed me for days to sign the forms. At one point, he came to my car window as I was sitting in the car watching Gracie's softball practice and demanded I sign. I calmly asked him to leave me alone and rolled up my window. He stood there for several minutes more yelling at me, calling me names, and banging on the closed window. Although I was horrified, I didn't show it. I finally just started the car and drove to another parking area to end the interaction. It was a win because I stayed calm and collected, just like a dull beach pebble.

A few times, though, it was more than I could tolerate, and I would heatedly demand he stop looking at and talking to me so maliciously. Of course, that was exactly what he wanted. He would prod and goad me, trying to get me to react. And ultimately, I did. The first time was when we were at one of Gracie's softball tournaments. Gracie was between games, and I was coming out of the restroom. Seth approached and began roaring at me in my face, his body tall and towering over mine. No one could see what was happening, but Gracie and Henry were nearby playing and saw us interacting. Seth stood there insulting me and calling me names. My face reddened, my lips clenched firmly together, and my heart started hammering. I went in self-protection mode.

"Stop talking to me like that!" I shouted as I struck the paper towel I was still drying my hands on from the restroom across his shoulder.

"Oh, you're going to hit me now?" he seemed proud to have provoked me so easily.

"I'm so sick of you talking to me like that! Just leave me alone!" I asserted.

Just then, Gracie got up from where she and Henry were playing and frantically ran off. "Stop fighting!" she screamed to Seth and me as she bolted.

Seth and I both immediately started going after her. He pushed me aside as to get to her first.

"Nice job, Kathi. You've upset Gracie. You are such a joke of a mother!" he said with a smirk.

"Seth! This is my week with the kids; I will go after Gracie. You need to leave. Please leave!" I pointed toward the parking lot.

"You are so pathetic! You don't love her! You don't care about her! Go away. I will take care of her. If you don't go away, I will call the police!" he warned.

"Great! Call the police; please call the police. You are the abusive one here!" I shouted as I took off to find Gracie.

I found Gracie almost instantly, and she and I returned to where Henry was still playing. I told her I was sorry for arguing with her dad and gave her a big hug. I saw Seth walking toward the parking lot, get in his van, and take off. I was so distraught by the whole incident that I had trouble enjoying the rest of the tournament.

Another time, it was Seth's week with the kids, and he and Henry were at Henry's football practice. Seth was coaching. I was happily napping in bed with Peanut and Cooper. Henry called me, his voiced stressed and frantic.

"Mom! I need my cleats. I left them at your house. I need them for practice. Can you bring them to the practice fields?"

I responded sleepily, "Hi honey. Um, where are they? Are you sure they're here?"

"Yes, I know they are. Look in my closet," he directed.

I started to sit up. "Ok, let me get up and get dressed. I'm in bed."

"Hurry!" he demanded as he hung up the phone.

I got up out of bed and started to put my jeans on that were lying on the floor by the side of the bed. I walked to his closet and slid open the door. I had to look around for a second but found them quickly. They were pretty easy to spot given they were pink, Henry's favorite color. I must say I really appreciated that he chose the color pink for his cleats. I didn't know the game of football, except for what a touchdown was, so I was always looking for his pink cleats or jersey number to easily locate him during his games. I never really cared about the actual game; I just wanted to watch and cheer for my kid! He was an amazing player, so it was usually when he was running toward the goal (is it a goal in football?), ball clenched in his arm and me screaming, "Go, Henry! Go, Henry!"

My phone rang as I grabbed the cleats and then my purse. "Hello?" I answered with the phone nestled between my cheek and shoulder.

"Mom! Where are you? Are you coming?" Henry asked anxiously.

"Yes, Henry, I'm coming. I just got my pants on and found your cleats. I'm on my way. Calm down," I assured him.

In that moment, I heard Seth in the background.

"You know you can't count on your mom, Henry! You know how unreliable she is!"

That pissed me off! I had the damn shoes in my hand and was walking out the door. No wonder Henry was freaking out. He had Seth in his ear telling him he couldn't count on me. I hung up the phone and drove off to the fields, my blood boiling! When I arrived, some ten minutes later, I slammed my car door shut and started walking toward the fields. Seth was doing drills with the boys. Both he and Henry glanced over at me. I held up the cleats in my right hand and looked squarely in Seth's face. He was standing probably ten yards away from me.

"Unreliable? Unreliable?" I heatedly yelled out holding Henry's cleats high in the air, probably louder than I should have.

Henry ran up to me, grabbed the cleats, and was off to join the other boys. At the same time, Seth began gathering the team and told them to move over to the next field. Seth then proceeded to walk angrily toward me, his feet stomping on the grass. He stopped within a few inches of me, only a waist-high chain-link fence separating us. Then he moved his face slowly to mine, so close I could smell his repellant breath. He looked directly into my eyes and loathsomely spoke to me with a whisper. His voice was slow, calm, and cold.

"You're such a fucking idiot. You're a pathetic joke. You disgust me. Such an embarrassment. Get over it, Kathi. Stop living in the past. You need help."

A drop of his spit landed on my lip, which I quickly wiped off with the back of my right hand. The detestation he had for me was oozing from his pores. It was tangible. And it was scary.

"Get away from me!" I demanded as I raised my hand to push his face away from mine.

He quickly moved out of the way, though, and I pushed his ballcap slightly off his head instead.

He backed up a foot or so, then slowly moved back in as if to inspect me.

"Are you having a mental breakdown?" he asked accusingly with a sadistic sneer.

I instantly turned toward the parking lot and marched directly to my car, slamming the door as I got in. I made sure the windows were securely shut and then screamed at the top of my lungs. It took me hours to calm down, and I was in bed the rest of the day. I hated him. He baited me, and just like a fish, I took the bait. He provoked, and I reacted. Moreover, he once again seemed to actually gain pleasure from inflicting fear and emotional pain on me. His cruel indifference toward me was mind-blowing. He wasn't even a modicum of the man I had married.

A few days after that event, I was walking out of the lecture hall where I had just wrapped up a lecture in my Psychology of Women course when my cell phone rang.

"Hello?" I answered with my hands full of lecture notes.

"Kathi Miner?" the voice inquired.

"Yes. Who is this?" I used my shoulder to keep the phone steady on my ear.

"This is Officer Cedro Cervantes from the police department's Family Violence Unit. I'm calling about a recent incident that occurred between you and your husband, Seth. Seth has filed a police report accusing you of physical assault against him. I wanted to get your side of the story."

"What? Are you kidding me?" I was shocked.

"No, I am not kidding. This is very serious. Did you assault your husband at the ballfield a few days ago? He said you hit him in the face. That is physical assault, Miss Miner," he scolded.

"I did not assault him," I countered, my mouth practically frothing with anger as I threw my things down on a nearby bench. "Let me tell you about my ex. He is extremely emotionally abusive. That day at the ballfield he came right up to me, right up to my face, and started calling me names. He called me an idiot, a pathetic joke, disgusting, and an embarrassment. He was so close to me I could smell his breath. This kind of abuse is common for him, and I'm sick of it. I went to push him out of my face telling him to leave me alone, and he quickly backed up. My palm caught his baseball cap instead. I did it to protect myself from his verbal abuse."

I started pacing nervously back and forth. Was the officer going to believe me? Certainly, someone working in the Family Violence Unit would be able to see through an abuser like Seth, right?

"So, you assaulted him!"

I was stunned by the officer's accusatory tone. "No!" I responded, now yelling and passersby looking my direction. "Look. I am the victim here, not him. This is just another one of his tactics to harass me."

I was annoyed that I had to defend myself and my actions against Seth's abuse. I wondered if perhaps Seth and the officer were friends or maybe coached together. It was unbelievable how much he was on Seth's side, like two peas in a patriarchal fucking pod.

"Sounds like physical assault to me, Miss Miner!" He sounded like a real misogynistic prick.

"This is ridiculous. This is just another example of the system siding with the abuser. You should be supporting me, and instead you are making me feel anxious and unsafe. What's your name again?"

"Officer Cedro Cervantes. I'm with the Family Violence Unit.

CHAPTER 5: THE NEW FRIENDS

And from what I can tell, you engaged in violence toward your husband."

"Are you joking? How is it that you work for the Family Violence Unit yet seem to know nothing about family violence, Cedro? This case is textbook. You are making this situation worse for me as his target. You are protecting the abuser here."

Tears were now running down my face.

"Well, you can tell it to the judge. I am putting this case forward. You will receive a letter from me in the next few days about how to proceed," he said unempathetically. "Good day, Miss Miner."

He staunchly hung up. Stunned, I looked at my phone.

"It's Dr. Miner, asshole!"

I felt like I was going to detonate! I was enraged at the injustice! I gathered my stuff from the bench and sped to my office in the Psychology building. I couldn't get the door unlocked fast enough. Immediately when I entered, I buckled to the small brown leather sofa where I sometimes took a nap during the workday and sobbed. How was this happening again? How was Seth getting away with his abuse? How was a police officer from a family violence unit so uneducated about men's abuse toward women and the tactics abusive men use to coercively control their female partner? Seth was once again using the system to punish, degrade, and control me, just like he had done with the stupid restraining order. I felt completely retraumatized by my interaction with Officer Cervantes. Feelings of helplessness and panic began to resurface. And on top of it, I had to find a criminal law attorney.

I asked around and settled on a bad-ass feminist criminal attorney, April Valdez. When I met April, I knew immediately that she was a boss. I was thrilled to have her in my corner. A few months later, I, accompanied by April, went to the courthouse to plead my case. I was so nervous. I was so over Seth getting away with his vicious behavior and could hardly handle him winning the case and being able to claim that *I* was the abuser, especially to Gracie and Henry whom he told I was likely going to jail over the incident.

Seth showed up at the courthouse, sans an attorney, shortly after April and I arrived. He was so smug, just sure I would lose. He just couldn't wait to see me go down. I'm sure he had prayed that they would issue me a hefty fine and take me off in handcuffs. We all sat in the reception area just outside the courtroom for what seemed like forever. Then, April was called to talk to the prosecutor who apparently was in a small room off the courtroom looking over the docket of cases to be heard that day. April was gone for thirty minutes or so when she came out and sat back next to me.

"What's going on?" I asked impatiently.

"Oh, you're good, girl. The prosecutor wanted more information about the case and your relationship with Seth. I described to him Seth's abuse and how this was just another way to hurt you. He said he imagined so and that it was clear to him that Seth had a vendetta. He threw out the case. You're off the hook!" she said excitedly.

"What? Really? That's great!" I said with relief. "So, no fine, no jail time, no nothing?" I asked hopefully.

"Nope. Nothing. He saw right through Seth. You owe nothing, and nothing will be on your record," she confirmed. "The best part, though, is that Seth is gonna be so pissed. Go and enjoy your day!" she laughed.

"Can I hug you?" I asked.

She giggled. "You sure can."

I gave April a big hug, and we said our goodbyes. I was so grateful for that small win! *Fuck you, Officer Cervantes*, I thought to myself. *Fuck you!*

To this day, Seth insists that I assaulted him in both of the above incidents by hitting him with a paper towel and tipping his hat even though both were in response to him sadistically inciting me with his hateful words and actions. He would deliberately cause chaos and then act like the victim in the chaos he created. I was simply reacting to his abuse and trying to get him out of my lane. He wanted to distress me to the point where I would react. And he did get me to react but not to the extent he wanted. He wanted me to completely fucking lose it. He just had to try a little harder. So, he did.

THE TRIANGLE

When Seth's hateful words didn't get the unhinged reaction from me that he longed for, he tried another tactic to mess with me during one of Gracie's softball games. As I pulled into the parking lot of the ballpark, I noticed Seth getting out of his van and that someone was with him. Up to that point, Seth had attended the kids' games solo on my weeks with the kids because his new girlfriend Jessica agreed to only come on Seth's weeks. But this time he wasn't alone. This time, Jessica was with him. I was fuming! Now, I realize that on the face of it Jessica attending the game might not seem like a big deal. But coupled with Seth's frequent verbal abuse at the ballpark, her presence was just too much for me to handle. I had a visceral reaction to seeing her and wanted to pounce. The ferocity of my response was unlike me; it surprised me how irrational and out of control I felt.

The kids and I got out of the car, and they immediately ran off to join their friends near the field. I opened the trunk of my car to get out my camping chair and started walking toward the field, as did Seth and Jessica. Soon, Jessica and I were side by side. I looked over at her, then confronted her.

"I thought we had an agreement. I thought you agreed you would not attend the kids' events on my weeks," I said indignantly.

She looked back at me with arrogance and disdain.

"You know what, Kathi? You need to think about your daughter and do what's right for her. The more people here at her game to support her, the better. You need to do what's right for your kids and stop thinking about yourself."

She seemed pleased to educate me on what a good mother should be like even though she had no personal experience. Her comments about my kids and me as a mother evoked the mother bear in me. I was overcome with rage. There was an immediate surge of adrenaline in my body.

"Do what's right for my daughter, what's right for my kids? Are you fucking kidding me? Like Seth did when he fucked all those women? Like that? Like when he broke up our family? Is that what I should do Jessica? You need to leave—now."

We were still walking side by side, but my head was contorted so I was looking directly at her. Seth was still on the other side of her, quietly and happily taking it all in. He had Jessica and me arguing, nearly brawling, and that was exactly what he wanted. He was practically shooting up he was so high.

"No. I'm not leaving. This is public property," she huffed.

"I don't give a fuck. You need to leave!" I ordered.

Seth then interrupted us.

"Leave us alone! She can be here if she wants to. She acts more like a mother than you do anyway!" His countenance was characteristic.

In that moment I realized that Jessica had officially become a flying monkey—she had been manipulated and fooled by Seth to believe that he was the victim and that I was the abusive, insalubrious one. As his flying monkey, she would likely now engage in abuse by proxy, assisting Seth in his torment and harassment of me. Jessica and Seth walked directly to the bleachers and sat down together. I sat down right next to Jessica, our thighs touching. I repeated myself.

"You need to leave!"

"No, this is public property, and I'm not leaving." Her voice was firm and serious, but I could tell she was in way deeper than she had expected or wanted to be.

"Well, then, I guess I'll just sit right here next to you the entire game," I warned caustically.

I pushed my thigh firmly into hers.

"Fine. Do whatever you want. Go, Gracie!" she shouted to Gracie who was now out in the field.

Clearly my message wasn't coming across strong enough. I was done with the bullshit and trying to stay calm and in control. I was in full fight mode—a complete amygdala hijack. I stood up, moved up the bleachers in between and separating Jessica and Seth, and stepped up to the next bleacher. I then sat down directly behind Jessica, my knees against her back. I pressed my knees forward into her back as hard as I possibly could. Her back arched, and she moaned uncomfortably. After a few seconds, she started to stand. She just stood there silently for a few moments with her back to me. Then she made her way down the bleachers and headed toward Seth's van. Seth immediately got up and went after her. A few minutes later, they drove off. I finished the game, then went home, called my sister Jill, and cried in her figurative arms.

I regret treating Jessica that way, and I wish I hadn't. Looking back, it's clear to me that I was once again goaded and simply reacted—a scenario I would learn is common for abusers and their victims. Abusers are adept at manufacturing such love triangles where they actively incite feelings of anxiety, rejection, and jealousy in their victim by bringing another person into the dynamic. They do so as a tactic to have power and control over the victim as they paint them as deranged when they negatively respond. The abuser, in turn, reaps the benefits of multiple sources of attention and ego strokes. Indeed, Seth seemed gloriously haughty during the incident. Moreover, he again appeared to enjoy the pain and distress I was feeling. Still, I didn't like that I completely lost my composure and gave Seth the opportunity to "prove" I was many of the things he claimed I was (e.g., crazy, spiteful), thereby solidifying his stance that *he* was the *real* victim. Not only that, but provoking such negative emotions in me likely allowed him to feel justified in engaging in further abuse toward me. Jessica didn't come to the kids' games a few times after that but at some point did come and came regularly. Before I knew it, she was there all the time.

SWEET AND MEAN

It was insurmountably difficult for me to be in the same environment as Seth and Jessica. I would catch them out of the corner of my eye, and they seemed joyfully in love. Sometimes I would even torment myself by scrutinizing her Facebook page (I had blocked Seth so couldn't see his page). She had a plethora of pictures of them affectionately smiling and laughing. I once knew that side of Seth, and I still grieved for and loved him immensely. He seemed to have returned from the dead but now into the arms of Jessica. I wondered if he had learned his lesson, changed, and was now the faithful, adoring man I always believed him to be (or that he convinced me he was). I questioned if he had ever cared for me at all. Regardless, he now treated me, the wife he had supposedly loved, as insignificant, nasty, and worthless. I was discarded like yesterday's trash. But I still missed him, even after all his horribly abusive behavior.

These thoughts caused me enormous amounts of mental anguish. What was wrong with me that I would long for (and still even cry over) someone who had hurt me so profoundly and in so many ways? Any sane or reasonable person would be thrilled to escape from someone so destructive and heartless. And how did he move on so quickly and seem so happy with his new partner while I was feeling blown to pieces? I remained hurt, devastated, and humiliated by his betrayal and the failure of our marriage. I was nowhere close to healed and only felt hopeless and lost.

Strangely, I sometimes felt an overwhelming need to contact him during these times, thinking it would somehow bring me closure. I wanted so badly to talk to the Seth that was the love of my life. I longed to have an honest heart-to-heart talk with him to figure out what went wrong with us. I sought to know if he ever did love and care for me and, if he did, why he was continuing to hurt me so badly with his vindictiveness. I think some part of me believed that his disparaging behavior would stop if I could just get through to him how incredibly unkind he was being. Sometimes I would reach out to him with a simple "I need to talk to you about something" text but would then wise up and realize that such a discussion was impossible. Seth had shown me repeatedly that he was incapable of the level of compassion, empathy, and introspection that kind of conversation required. So, when he would reply with a "Why?" or "About what?" I would just ignore the message.

Making things especially confusing, Seth would sometimes act considerate and pleasant toward me. In those instances, I felt like my sweet husband was back and I would let my guard down. I fell for this inauthentic amicability many times. The below email provides a good example.

> *Kathi,*
>
> *The following discussions are informal and intended to be used only between us, no one else, and not for court . . . I hope in the end, we still care for each other and want what's best for each other . . .*
>
> *I know you want to do a strict 50/50 on physical custody . . . but please keep in mind your physical proximity [my apartment] and daily travel . . . I am not saying it can't be done. I am just worried about the daily grind. Traffic has to be perfect. The hustle and bustle of*

getting the kids up in the morning. The stress of getting them dressed, fed, and the final last corrections and review of homework. It will be hard enough for me to do it and I am here [near their school]. That is why I was thinking of a 4-3 schedule [with him having the kids during the week and me on the weekends; sounds to me like he's trying to set up a custodial/noncustodial parent arrangement but I didn't catch it at the time].

I know your work will pick up as well. Especially, during the week. I know your pubs [publications] and time given to them will need to increase and time devoted to your grants will increase too. Also, the kids have their practices that will tie up additional time in the evenings and take away from what you need to get done at home. I know it is crunch time for you at work and you need to be productive. I want to help you in that. The kids will only benefit from your professional success.

I am just saying we could keep this temporary until Henry gets out of [his current school]. Then your travel will decrease. Just think about it. Keep an open unbiased mind about the suggestion. This is one of the issues that has been weighing on my mind. None of these suggestions or comments are threats or intended to be ugly. Just my thoughts. The kids need BOTH of us in their daily lives. We both are good parents and care tremendously for Gracie and Henry. I don't care about winning or losing the battles we are having. The lawyers are more worried about that. I just want what's best for the kids and I know you do too. Again, please

keep this email only between us. We need to start the
road of healing and co-parenting.
-Seth

These communications would completely catch me off guard and throw me off balance. He would be so cooperative, accommodating, sincere, and even sweet. He seemed to be looking out for us as family and even looking out for *me*. It made me think back to all the times we had successfully worked together as a team to build a life and raise our family. The amnesia of his abuse would set in, and I would start to question whether he was the evil horror he appeared to be. Maybe he never meant to hurt me and really did care for me and my well-being. Perhaps he had finally seen the error of his ways and turned a corner toward us having respectful, healthy interactions. I so badly wanted to believe he was a good person and that at least one ounce of the love I felt for him was reciprocated. But his sweetness never lasted for long. His viciousness always resurfaced.

This cycle—of him being sweet one moment, then mean the next—became one of the most common strategies he used to mess with me over the course of the divorce. His feigning concern, consideration, and like he wanted to work together (e.g., "I hope in the end we still care for each other," "We are good parents," "We need to start the road to healing") to reopen the lines of communication and get me to question my perception of him as abusive or gain control over a situation worked like a charm. It always ended the same way, though: I would open the door an inch for him to communicate with me, and then he would sneakily burst through the door and pounce, again engaging in some kind of threatening or malicious behavior. It would once more be clear that he wanted me in pain. I would once again be walking on eggshells knowing that a hostile look, gesture, or comment would be coming my way. I also learned that anything I disclosed to him, no matter how minor, would later be used against me, especially if I had shown any vulnerability. His momentary sweetness was always just another manipulative ploy to suck me back in. And each time the traumatic cycle completed itself, the more I was bonded to him. I knew the pull to Seth was bizarre and illogical, but I just couldn't seem to release myself from the rotation. The back-and-forth good and bad behavior had taken over and locked me in. My psychological well-being continued to plummet.

PURSUING AN ORDER

After many talks with my family and therapist, we decided that, for the sake of my mental health, it was time to go completely no contact with Seth and get a restraining order (about time, huh?) to bolster the boundaries between us. I set aside an afternoon and drove to the Brazos County Courthouse to request the order. Usually this was something Lyle, my attorney, would do on my behalf, but I was already breaking the bank from paying him so much in legal fees and I didn't want to add to my bill. Moreover, he was super busy with other cases and I just felt like I couldn't wait. I wanted the order immediately. And I felt like it was something I could handle on my own.

I quickly found the correct office to request a restraining order. The officer behind the counter handed me some forms and asked me to complete them. I sat down on a dark wooden chair directly behind me and got to work. I wrote about the emotional abuse I had endured over the course of the separation. I described how he would approach me at children's events in an aggressive and intimidating manner. I explained his stalking over social media and while I was out with friends. I described how he followed me in and out of streets in our old neighborhood until I lost him. I told of his threatening tone, demeanor, and body language. I made clear that his behavior had escalated to the point where I was fearful and anxious in his presence, always felt like I had to be vigilantly looking over my shoulder, and was concerned about my safety and mental health.

As I sat there recording the details of Seth's abuse, I became more and more distraught. It began to feel like I was actually reliving the events and the horrendous emotions associated with them. When I finally finished my narrative, I was sobbing and nearly hyperventilating.

"Are you ok?" asked the officer.

"Yeah, he has just put me through a lot," I said through my tears, barely able to catch my breath. I stood up and handed him the forms.

"Give me a few minutes to look these over."

Those few minutes felt like forever. Finally, he got up from the desk where he was sitting and came over the counter.

"Do you have any evidence, like maybe a police report against him or maybe a video of his behavior? Do you have any witnesses?" he asked with his head tilted to the side and with one eye squinted.

I thought for a second.

"So much of what he does is under the radar," I explained while sniffling. "I do have some text messages and emails showing his name-calling. I can show you on my phone; I didn't bring any hard copies. I don't have a video of him; he's much too smart for that. I did file a police report after he was stalking me. Maybe you can find that in the record system."

"What was the outcome of that police report? Was there an investigation?" he inquired.

"Yes, but it was dropped."

My head plummeted in defeat.

"I'm sorry, sweetheart, but there's just not enough evidence here to issue a restraining order against him, especially because there wasn't any real, well um, physical abuse," he muttered condescendingly.

"What? How is that possible? I am telling you that my ex is

abusive and that I feel unsafe. I need a restraining order to protect myself!"

My eyes began to swell like water balloons.

"I'm sorry, but it's just not gonna happen. I'll put it in the system that you asked for one but will also note that there is insufficient evidence. There is nothing we can do to help you based on what you have reported."

I stood there recalling how easy it was for Seth to get a restraining order against me even though it was completely based on fabrications and without evidence.

"This is bullshit! This is so unfair! I am asking for your help!" I started to panic. "I need help! I need a restraining order today!"

"You need to calm down, ma'am. Please don't be so emotional," commanded the officer.

"I can't calm down! My ex is an abusive asshole, and he keeps getting away with his abuse! I just can't stand this anymore."

I sat back on the chair where I completed the forms. I put my head in my hands and bawled, trying desperately to regain my composure.

"I swear I'm gonna kill myself," I quietly muttered to myself.

A few minutes later another officer walked into the office and knelt down in front of me.

"Miss, my name is Officer Downey. Are you ok? You mentioned that you wanted to kill yourself," he said empathetically.

I realized the officer behind the counter must have made a phone call about a woman in his office freaking out and saying she was going to unalive herself.

"I'm not going to kill myself," I replied. "But I feel totally defeated. I'm going through an awful divorce, and my ex will not stop his psychological abuse no matter what I do. I came here for help. I thought that, if I got a restraining order, I would at least have something official demanding he leave me alone."

"I'm so sorry. I know that must be very difficult. Please call me anytime," he said as he handed me his card. "Let me see if I can get something from the judge that you can provide your ex to show that he should refrain from any negative behavior toward you. You wait here."

"Ok," I replied sniffling.

Officer Downey came back roughly fifteen minutes later with a very official-looking document—one that looked very similar to the restraining order I received from Seth. I was confused when he handed it to me. Did he get me a restraining order against Seth after all? I started to perk up.

"Is this a . . . restraining order?" I asked curiously.

"Well, not exactly. But it is something you can give your husband to remind him of respectful behavior during a divorce. There's nothing enforceable, but it's a good reminder . . . for both of you."

"Great, thanks," I said sarcastically.

Then I gathered my things and left the courthouse, fucked over by the double-standard gender-biased law enforcement and court systems once again.

I HATE BALLPARKS

For the most part, the ballpark continued to be a place of intense negativity for me. With no consequences for his abuse or a restraining order to protect me, it was easy for Seth to continue his malicious treatment. My reactions seemed to change over time, though. At the start of the separation, I was despondent when attending the kids' practices and games. Later, I became either angry, intimidated, or a gray rock because of Seth's behavior. Ultimately, I became an empty, detached shell just counting down the minutes when I could leave. I would bring my camping chair and sit as far away from Seth (and now, also Jessica) as I could. I had to for my psychological survival. If I found myself near them, especially him, my body would react as if I was in a warzone, in a near-constant state of hypervigilance and hyperarousal. Or I would become completely disassociated, like I was in a movie, watching myself and everyone around me acting a role and following a script. I also began to question and distrust my own perceptions, experiences, and sanity. Maybe I was the horrible, crazy, pathetic person Seth said I was. Maybe I was a bad, selfish person. Maybe it was *me* who didn't deserve *him* and I had been lucky to have him. Maybe I was the root cause of all the problems between us. Why else would Seth come out of this nightmare completely unscathed—and even supported by police agencies and a cool new girlfriend—while I was repeatedly kicked while I was down? I felt powerless and corroded and had lost my zest and exuberance for life. I didn't even feel like a real person, just a numb body going through the motions. I stared getting worried because thoughts of suicide began entering my mind. I didn't actually have a plan to commit the act (consistent with what I told Officer Downey), but I did think about it. I just wanted a way out; I wanted the pain, hurt, and helplessness to stop. I wanted to get better, and I wanted to move on. It just wasn't happening.

Making things worse, because he was usually coaching, Seth would sit with the coaches and Jessica with the coaches' wives and I would, as always, sit by myself. This was true for the other single moms as well so there was usually a main group of married coaches' wives and couples and then a few single mom stragglers. Interestingly, the single dads, if there were any, didn't seem to be outcasted in the same way as the single moms. It sucked to not be part of the group, but what I hated more was that Jessica had stealthily slipped right in to take over the role as the kids' "mom," at least at the ballpark. I would sometimes think to myself, *Fuck it, Kathi. Just go over and sit with the married moms and couples. You are the kids' mom, not Jessica, and you have every right to be there*, but I just couldn't. Physical and mental paralysis would take over, and I could only seem to just stare ahead. I absolutely could not be around or interact with Seth and Jessica. And even if Seth wasn't coaching, he still had enough connection with the coaches that he and Jessica were part of the group of married couples. I would see Seth and Jessica sitting with the other parent couples laughing, cheering, and carrying on and think about how that used to be me. I would ponder why Seth got to have this aspect of the kids' lives. He was the one who cheated, lied, and broke up the family. He was the abuser, and I was the aggrieved. It was just another instance of Seth having zero repercussions for his abuse and harassment. I spent many lonely hours at the ballpark under these circumstances. But I did it anyway, for the kids.

I'm not sure many of the other moms even knew who I was or even cared. If they did, it was likely that Seth (and perhaps Jessica) had said negative things about me, making the other moms have little interest in mingling with me. In fact, this was once actually confirmed to me. Linda, one of the moms on one of Henry's baseball teams (the *only* team in the years the kids played ball where I felt truly included by both the parents and the coaches), would often chat with me during games, and we became friends. She revealed to me that Seth had indeed said many undesirable things about me (e.g., that I was crazy, didn't care about the kids' sports, was an uninvolved parent, was a liar) but, once she got to know me, realized it was simply a smear campaign and those things didn't represent me at all.

Interestingly, one of the few relationships I made at the ballpark was a woman named Lara who had divorced her abusive husband years before. We would swap stories about the continued injustices we endured from our exes and from the system. Her story terrified me about what was to come for me in my own divorce. Lara had experienced psychological and physical abuse from her ex-pro-football-player husband. She had ample proof of the abuse and was even represented in court by the Domestic Violence Clinic from the University of Texas, Austin's School of Law. Because her ex had copious amounts of money, he was able to bring in the very best and most expensive attorneys in the country to represent him. Ultimately, Lara lost her case and her ex received full custody of their four children. She also came away from the divorce nearly destitute. Her case was so unfair and explosive that it even appeared in the local papers. Hers is a perfect example of how moms can no longer assume they will be awarded custody in a divorce, especially if their husband has greater power and resources.

Today, ballparks are a major trigger for me. They were a place where I was distressed, harassed, intimidated, and ostracized. Although I do have many good and fond memories of my kids playing ball, I am more than content to never set foot on a battlefield—uh-um, I mean ball field, ever again. A play on words, yes, but I did feel like I was in a war, a war that I was constantly and bloodily losing. Then, completely out of the blue, I had an aha moment. I realized I had been in combat all along.

CHAPTER 6: THE EPIPHANY

I was in my Park Hudson Place apartment kitchen cutting up some vegetables for a big dinner salad and wiping away the tears that were running down my face when it hit me like a freight train. I swiftly put down the knife, grabbed my glass of cabernet that was on the counter next to me, and headed toward my laptop that was sitting on the couch. I sat down, picked up my computer, and went directly to the folder marked "My Classes." I opened the folder to my Psychology of Women class and started manically searching for my PowerPoint lecture on violence against women. I had given that lecture dozens and dozens of times, but it never rang as true for me personally as it did now. How did I miss it all this time and for so many years?

It took me only seconds to find the lecture. I stared at one slide in the deck for what felt like hours—the slide depicting Dr. Clare Murphy's power and control wheel. The original power and control wheel was developed by the Domestic Abuse Intervention Programs (DAIP) of Duluth, Minnesota, in the 1980s. DIAP conducted interviews with battered women to understand the strategies their physically violent male partners used to achieve and maintain dominance and control over them. In an extension of this work, Dr. Murphy developed an additional wheel focusing less on men who physically abuse their female partners and more on men who psychologically abuse them. She created her wheel after researching and interviewing women who had experienced psychological abuse by their male partners. Dr. Murphy's wheel not only captures more of the non-physical coercive control tactics used by abusive men toward their female partners, but also highlights the critical role living in a patriarchal society plays in reinforcing those behaviors. As with the DAIP wheel, the center of Dr. Murphy's wheel is labeled "power and control," which is the goal, or effect, of the abuse tactics. One of sixteen tactics is depicted in each spoke of the wheel, each of which give it strength and help hold it together.

I sat there sipping my cabernet, inspecting each tactic, only just then grasping the extent to which they were indicative of my husband, our marriage, and how he treated me, even before the separation. I had taught my students about both wheels for years, but the tactics just didn't seem personally relevant to me until now. Putting the dots together was now suddenly painfully easy. Instances of Seth's abuse were there all along, since the very beginning. How had I not made the connection sooner, especially as a feminist psychology professor who taught about the violence and abuse of women on a regular basis? Had Seth been that good at his craft? Or was I just incredibly stupid? Perhaps what made his behavior so difficult to label as abusive all those years was that it consisted of low-level non-physical mistreatment. Individually, each negative act may have seemed like no big deal, especially when they occurred months or years apart, but together they told a story of Seth's subtle and longstanding abuse. Memories of his maltreatment started inundating my mind, and I couldn't make them stop. It was like I was mentally throwing up all of his disparaging comments and actions I had buried deep to keep up the narrative of my progressive, respectful, happy marriage. That narrative was now crumbling as the abusive, patriarchal norms within our marriage and family became more and more evident.

The first two abuse tactics on Dr. Murphy's power and control wheel—"economic abuse" and "one-sided power games"—definitely described Seth's behavior throughout our marriage. Seth made all the major financial decisions including, for example, what cars, furniture, and house we would purchase. Even if we would look at options together and discuss possibilities, we always did what he wanted in the end. He also controlled our finances and how the money was spent. He would get angry with me if he felt I was spending too much money. This is typical for heterosexual couples, but what is interesting is that he could purchase whatever he wanted and I was to hold my purse. I recall one time, in particular, when he made me promise to buy only essentials like food and gas, but then, when he returned from Disney World for a conference a few days later, showered the kids with Disney clothes and toys worth several hundred dollars. I was pissed about his double standard but kept my mouth shut because the kids were so excited about their gifts. Keep in mind that this would occur even though I was the primary breadwinner in the family and took out substantial student loans to support the family while we were in Michigan.

Seth also made most of the other major decisions, which gave him nearly all the power in the family. For example, he would decide if, when, and where we would vacation (it was rare that we ever did; he would rather buy a big screen TV than a trip to the coast) and how to raise and discipline the kids (he was more authoritarian than I), including what sports and activities they would be involved in and how many (this was always a point of contention because I thought the kids were over-involved, being on numerous sports teams, music lessons, etc. at the same time). In fact, he made most of the smaller decisions as well, like if we were to eat out or at home and what TV shows we would watch. If I wanted to watch a show, I would have to go in our bedroom to watch it, or he would "let" me have the family room and he would go watch what he wanted in our bedroom. I always sought to be together, so I yielded.

As I continued to study the power and control wheel, two more tactics resonated: "using restrictions" and "isolation." It wasn't like Seth would lock me in the house and not let me talk to anyone, but he did engage in indirect behavior that restricted and isolated me. For example, if one my sisters came to visit, he would limit our time together, calling and texting repeatedly to ask my whereabouts or when I was coming home. One year when my sister Jill came from California to Kentucky to visit, we went out shopping shortly after she arrived and Seth kept blowing up my phone demanding to know when we would be back. I hadn't seen my sister for over a year and we were so excited to spend some good sissy time together. But I felt pressured to return, so I cut our shopping trip short. Another time, when Seth and I were living in Texas, Jill again came to visit from California and she and I drove down to Houston to see Lucinda Williams (one of our favorite artists) perform, and he again kept calling and texting to see when we would be returning. He was also really rude to my sisters when they would visit. One time, Jill made dinner for us, and Seth made it clear he didn't care for her cooking ("This is horrible!" he said indignantly), and another time he was so discourteous when my sister Kenzie visited that she vowed never to visit me again if he was there, and she didn't. My sisters didn't reveal to me until the separation that these occurrences really bothered them. He was also mean and unpleasant for a few days when I would return from traveling to visit family or for work; I always chalked it up to him missing me because that was what he told me ("Sorry I'm being so cold and moody. I just really missed you."). In reality, I think I was being punished for having a good time or leaving him alone with the kids, making me question whether it was ever worth the repercussions of going out or traveling on my own.

Seth also engaged in "emotional unkindness," "degradation," "using the children," "threats and intimidation," and "denying, minimizing, and blaming." For example, Seth often made me feel stupid by calling attention to my lack of knowledge about something no matter how minor; one of his most common comportments was to smirkingly laugh at me in front of others and say, "You didn't know that?" It might have been something so simple as the exact location of Myanmar, how many yards there are in a football field, or, what he found completely hilarious, the difference between a fiddle and violin (there aren't any). He laughed for days about the fact that I didn't know a fiddle and violin are the same instrument. When I would talk to him about it and tell him it hurt my feelings, he would just tell me I was overreacting and that he was just making a joke. He would also belittle me when we would play games with others, like Pictionary or Taboo, because, he would say, I would supply dumb clues or not get his clues quick enough. It was not uncommon for me to get up from the table and walk away while playing a game with him because he was so condescending. After several years, I stopped playing group games with him altogether and would just suggest another activity. That was so unfortunate because anyone who knows me knows I love a good game night!

His emotional unkindness and degradation seemed to coincide with the times in which my career was going especially well. For example, I recall when I had just graduated with my PhD in psychology and women's studies from the University of Michigan and begun a tenure-track position at Western Kentucky University (WKU), my first job out of graduate school. It was a thrilling time for me, not only because I had attained my doctoral degree and secured a coveted academic position (my lifelong goal), but because I was able to increase our family's quality of life. I began making substantially more money, and we bought our first home. Seth was angry and bitter during this time; we agreed it was because of the difficulties of him being a "trailing spouse," but I think it was more than that. I think he felt threatened and emasculated by my accomplishments and success. In fact, two of my saddest memories of that time were during my graduation weekend and the weekend I moved into my office at WKU. He was incredibly callous during both; the entire time I was walking on eggshells trying to make him happy and combat his coldness. Needless to say, two important events in my life that should have been joyous I remember mostly as negative. His disparaging treatment continued for at least six months after we moved to Kentucky. I even began therapy because I was so depressed about the situation.

I began to recollect other instances of his mistreatment as well, such as verbal derogation. Seth's type of verbal abuse during the marriage was more about tone and volume than words, and it built up slowly over the years. In fact, the most egregious verbal abuse didn't come until after we had kids. It was also more often coupled with hostile facial gestures and threatening body stances.

Sometimes he would talk to me so contemptuously, usually in front of the kids, that I would have to ask him into another room and demand to him, "You cannot talk to me that way, especially in front of the children. You are being mean and disrespectful, and I don't want the kids to think it's okay for you to treat me that way!"

At one point, he began to talk to our daughter Gracie in the same way—but with an even more humiliating tone and, if he was really angry, pulling her ear—and I would have to again ask him into another room to staunchly remind him of how we, his wife and daughter, should be treated. It usually fell on deaf ears. The more I tried to stand up for myself and the kids, the louder and more menacing he became. I would have to completely stop talking, not one more word, and lower my head for him to stop. Using one's voice is at the core of personal empowerment, and he would literally eradicate mine. I became passive, weak, and silent in those moments. He would psychologically punish me into acquiescing. In short, he would become an intimidating dictator who, through angry outbursts and a profound sense of entitlement, demanded power over me, the children, and the home. But it didn't happen routinely, so I let it go and chalked it up to just a shitty part of marriage.

He would also often use the children to make me feel bad about myself, insinuating I was a bad mother because, in his words, I could not "control" the children. He was constantly on me to be harder on them, discipline them more, or instill fear in them as a means to regulate their behavior. Authoritarian parenting just isn't my style, though. I tended to use warnings, time-outs, and the withdrawal of privileges as forms of discipline. Whenever possible, I would try to guide the children's behavior by allowing natural consequences to occur so they could learn on their own. As such, sometimes I may not have intervened in a situation or demand a certain behavior. For example, if I knew it will be a chilly day but the kids didn't want to dress warmly (within reason), I would ask them to change or wear a jacket. If they insisted that they will be fine, I would let the issue rest and let them experience the natural consequence of their choice (being cold). Another example was if they were asked on a school assignment to write neatly but they rushed through the assignment resulting in a sloppy product. I would point out the directions and suggest they do it over. However, I would not make them sit there and do it over and over until I was satisfied, yell at them for being lazy, or send them to their room, as would be typical for Seth. Instead, I would let them experience the natural consequence of their behavior (getting a poor grade or reprimanded by the teacher). I believe this strategy teaches kids to be responsible for themselves and make better future choices. Although this strategy did not always work perfectly or as I intended—and let's be honest, sometimes I totally flipped my lid because the kids wouldn't listen or drove me crazy—I always tried to be a good parent. But it was never good enough for Seth who routinely disparaged me for not being the hard-core disciplinarian that he was and blamed me when Gracie and Henry didn't fall in line.

One day while living in College Station, roughly two years prior to the dissolution of the marriage, I was going to Kroger grocery store and Seth said he wanted to go and bring the kids to spend some time together. I didn't think it was the best idea, and I told him so. At five and seven years old, I hated taking the kids to the store, especially when they were overtired and cranky, which they were this particular day. But I agreed, and we all went. Not long after we entered the store, the kids started misbehaving.

"This is why I didn't want to bring the kids," I said to Seth.

He completely exploded and began yelling and demeaning me, and to a lesser extent the kids, in the store. His vicious attack came out of nowhere and was humiliating, cruel, and wrong. I recalled an email exchange we had the next day and was able to retrieve it in my email files. Although he took some responsibility, he minimized his egregious actions and ultimately made me culpable for his behavior, stating that my full plate caused him to lash out. Below is our actual email exchange. I initiated the conversation.

> Seth, I do not understand what's going on. Why are you so angry and why am I the target? I feel like I am being punished. Is it because I went out of town? Spent money without consulting you first? You feel I undermined your authority with the kids? You are not getting enough of my attention? You are in a job you do not like? I'm thinking that your behavior yesterday is probably a combination of all of these things. You have behaved in a way that has caused me to completely shut down. You belittled me and yelled at me to the point that I could no longer speak. You literally caused me to stop speaking - because if I tried to say anything you got louder, more intimidating, and more belittling. I had to stop in order for Gracie and Henry to not see this side of you, and us. Your behavior was inappro-

priate to me and damaging to the kids and our family. You are not a patriarch. You do not have the right to belittle, humiliate, or laugh at any of us. It is hurtful, unforgettable, and will have long term effects on all of us. It was completely inexcusable. I hope that you will consider doing a little soul-searching to figure out why you felt so negatively about me and hostile toward me yesterday and why you feel it is appropriate and warranted to publicly humiliate me and the kids. I also think that you/we should consider talking with a professional about it. I saw a side of you I do not like - a hostile, mean, angry side. This has happened before and I'm not sure what your triggers are, but you need to figure them out. You are being borderline abusive. I don't know what else to say other than let you know that I cannot believe how you treated me (and to a lesser extent Gracie and Henry) yesterday. You have really hurt me with this one. I will never, ever forget the look on your face when you laughed at me when I was so upset.

He responded almost immediately.

It might be a combination of all. all i know is that when you said the comments in the store and in the parking i mentally "snapped". i missed you A LOT when you were gone, actually, I have missed you A LOT lately. i know you were busy, and you will continue to busy w/ work and what not, i have been feeling neglected and feel like i have to compete for your attention, not w/ the kids, but the other i.e., work. i don't want to put another burden on you. i just wanted so badly to have some family time and be w/ you, that when you said the comments (and i know you didn't mean it that way) i took it as a form of rejection and i felt insulted and angry and i felt belittled and thus i acted inappropriately and i am sorry for that. i am also sorry for laughing at you that way i did, it was the only thing i could think of doing w/o acting hostile back at you. if these points of angry continue i will considered talking to someone. i was thinking it was just a bad phase or something. i should talk to you about it but i sometimes have a hard time going to you w/ my troubles, especially when you are happy doing what your doing. Please forgive me.

Me: *It's ok to be unhappy, angry, hate your job, feel neglected. You have a right to feel what you feel. You do not have a right to take it out on me.*

Seth: *You are right, i got angry w/ the comment you made and should of handled myself better. sorry*

Me: *So, what am I supposed to do now? Just forget it? I am really pissed and hurt. And what exactly was the comment that started all this?*

Seth: *of course not, take all the time you need. what got me going was when you were saying something like, 'this is the reason i didn't want to bring the kids' i felt it was a unwarranted jab. all i wanted was to be together, as a matter of fact, i think i said to you when we were at home that i wanted us to be together. that comment just really made me mad or sad. just mad me snap. and that is when i began to lash out.*

> Me: *This is a perfect example of how your reaction didn't match the event. Not even close. Kids are kids sometimes, and they are generally not fun to take to grocery stores. I think most people feel that way; it does not mean I do not love my kids, or my family, or family time together. I would have rather run to the store alone and have family time at home, not in Kroger. I also feel you need to get over wanting to have perfectly behaved kids. They're kids; and my letting them be kids, with arguing and being cranky and touching things in stores, does not mean I am not disciplining them.*

Seth also sometimes hounded me for sex and would get angry, sulk, or give me the silent treatment when I wouldn't comply, which made me feel guilty for being a bad spouse. Although I did enjoy having sex with him and made it my motto to always say yes, occasionally I just didn't feel like it, especially if I was exhausted from home and work responsibilities or if he had recently been emotional abusive. In those moments, he reacted incredibly negatively. According to Dr. Murphy, this is a form of "sexual abuse."

I took a deep sigh. Out of the sixteen different abuse tactics on Dr. Murphy's power and control wheel, I could identify at least half my husband had engaged in during the course of our relationship. There were many times during our marriage that I felt demeaned, controlled, and intimidated. An insulting or condescending comment here, some anger and guilt there, and yet, I would just try to ignore or explain it away even when I knew it was wrong. Or I would quite literally "forget" the abuse and the circumstances surrounding it or remember it as less stressful and degrading than it was. I tried to focus more on the times when he was kind and caring. I wanted to give him the benefit of the doubt. That's what you're supposed to do for the sake of the marriage, right? I guess I felt like there were aspects of our relationship—the fact that we shared housework and childcare equally, for example—that made up for these instances. I took a blind eye to his maltreatment to preserve our marriage, just like a "good" wife should do.

There were several abuse tactics Seth never demonstrated. The first, "domestic slavery," is when men demand their female partner engage in traditional gender roles surrounding housework and childcare, nearly treating her like a servant. Such behavior was unheard of for Seth. I think I let his progressiveness in this area overshadow the other ways in which he was an abusive patriarch. Seth also never engaged in "physical violence." He still likes to announce this fact and claims that he was never abusive toward me because he never hit me, as if he should win some award or something. True, he never hit me with his fists, but he did assault me psychologically. Abusers don't have to punch you, choke you, or slam your head into a wall in order for it to be abuse. They can denigrate you, humiliate you, blame you, yell at you, laugh at you, and try to control you. It was still abuse even though he never laid a hand on me.

After spending hours studying Dr. Murphy's power and control wheel, I decided not to criticize and blame myself for overlooking and mislabeling Seth's abusive behavior over the course of our relationship. Indeed, it's not uncommon for victims of abuse to rationalize, diminish, and rebuff the abuse; such mental distortions serve as survival mechanisms in order to reduce the cognitive dissonance that forms when the person who claims to love and care for you mistreats you. Victims of abuse may convince themselves that the abuse is really not that bad, that there are situational reasons why the abuser is behaving negatively, or that they may have done something to cause the abuse.

But there was no more denying or ignoring Seth's behavior, no more seeing the beauteous aromatic flowers apart from the painful blood-seeking thorns. If I had any chance of getting through this new hell I was in, I had to admit it to myself. It was so difficult to say, but I made myself say it out loud and with conviction: I had been in an abusive marriage. The professor of psychology and women's and gender studies, the strong, confident, independent role model for thousands of college women, and the woman who had for over a decade pronounced her marriage as progressive, egalitarian, and respectful was married to a man who was a psychologically abusive asshole. The womanizing, cheating, and lying—the actions that catapulted my seeing my marriage for what it really was—were simply an additional form of the mistreatment I had already endured for years.

Sadly, just as Dr. Murphy depicts in her power and control wheel, many of the abuse tactics Seth employed during our marriage intensified and became more frequent after I left him. Dr. Murphy terms the escalation of abuse tactics when the marriage begins to dissolve "separation abuse." Seth even added a few new ones: "mind games" (leading the target to question her judgment and reality), "cyber abuse" (online stalking and bullying), and "using social institutions" (using the legal system with the aim of maintaining power and control). This latter from of abuse by men toward their female partners has also been termed "legal and administrative aggression" and "paper abuse." Specific examples include filing false restraining orders, making fabricated claims of assault, claiming that the mother is an unfit parent, and manipulating the court system to obtain sole custody of the children. My husband was like a walking textbook of abuse. What a shitty epiphany!

Just then, I noticed my stomach growling. I was so distracted by the power and control wheel that I had completely forgotten about the salad I had been making. I was completely nauseated by my purge of memories but knew I had to eat. I was starving. I got up, finished cutting the vegetables, and put them in the bowl. I topped it off with some shredded cheddar cheese, fresh-ground black pepper, and blue cheese dressing. I poured another glass of red and walked back toward the couch. I instantly put on my professor cap and decided I needed to do some in-depth research about the how to deal with abusive men during a divorce. I needed to prepare myself for what was to come. As I began researching, I immediately came across information on narcissistic abuse and the divorce process. I read for several more hours, diligently taking notes as I went along. What I found was completely in line with what I was experiencing, from the examples to the actual terms used in the narcissistic abuse literature. Here's a synopsis.

NARCISSISM AND NARCISSISTIC ABUSE

Individuals with narcissistic tendencies (typically men—go figure) have a grandiose sense of self-importance, fantasies about unlimited success and power, a belief that they are special and unique, and a constant need for attention, admiration, and praise. They also have a propensity to use others for their own needs or wants, lack empathy and feelings of guilt, and are unable to recognize and honor the needs and feelings of others. It is the desire for complete adoration that they engage in sadistic behavior at whatever the cost or whomever it may harm. Some people may even become victims of full-fledged narcissistic abuse, which involves manipulation, vindictiveness, vengefulness, contempt, rage, deceit, ridicule, derogation, harassment, stalking, invalidation, and dehumanization as the narcissist seeks to break down their victim. A subset of narcissists, termed "malignant narcissists," seems to actually enjoy the pain, distress, and suffering the cause in their victim as it provides a high of power and control.

The cycle of narcissistic abuse is known as "idealize, devalue, and discard." In the early stages of forming relationships, narcissists tend to come on really strong, completely idealizing potential victims. They are especially drawn to victims who can make them look good and boost their ego, whether it is through status, resources, or reputation. Individuals who are trusting, kind, caring, conscientious, educated, intelligent, and generous are particularly appealing. This is the period in which narcissists "love bomb" with excessive positive attention and affection, often mirroring positive characteristics of the target so as to make the target feel they have similar goals, values, and proclivities. Once the victim is hooked, they use the victim's adulation to boost their own ego, which fills their "narcissistic supply." But their extravagant love-bombing behavior wanes, and they slowly begin to devalue and mistreat the victim as a means to chip away at their self-esteem in order to keep them under control. When the victim begins to question and point out their abusive behavior, the narcissist may engage in "gaslighting" by twisting and spinning information in a way that makes the victim doubt their own reality and experiences. It is also common for narcissists to engage in "projection" by trying to convince the victim that they are the one who is the actual abuser. The narcissist may begin to love bomb their target once again, especially if they think the victim might end the relationship. The idea of the victim leaving triggers the narcissist's fear of losing their much-needed ego-boosting supply, and they will do whatever it takes to reconcile and keep the relationship going. This cycle continues until the victim is completely confused, mired in self-doubt, and wondering what they may have done to cause the narcissist's erratic behavior. Often, narcissistic abuse goes full circle, and the narcissist completely discards the victim they had seemingly previously loved and cherished by treating them as insignificant, worthless, and invisible.

Narcissist also engage in "hot-and-cold" or "sweet-and-mean" cycles where they periodically engage in loving behavior to keep the victim hooked, then, in the blink of an eye, turn cold and uncaring. This up-and-down, positive-negative sequence is a psychological device known as intermittent reinforcement. In some cases, the intermittent reinforcement of these cycles creates an emotional bond to the narcissist, known as "trauma bonding." If trauma bonding occurs, it becomes nearly impossible for the victim to leave the narcissist and end the relationship. If, however, the victim is able to muster the strength to leave, two options will likely occur. Either the narcissist will react as if the victim never existed (the discard part of the cycle), which usually means they have moved on to their next narcissistic supply, or they escalate their abuse. In the latter case, the narcissist may try making the victim look bad and engage in a "smear campaign" against them in order to keep earning admiration from others.

Narcissists often call their victims crazy, diagnose them with mental health issues, or tell them they need psychological help. In so doing, the narcissist seeks to have the target question their own sanity about the manipulative tactics used by them. Diagnosing their victims with mental health problems is also a way for narcissists to pathologize their victims in order to undermine their credibility. This is especially effective when they provoke, or "bait," strong emotional reactions in their victims to "prove" they have mental health issues or are themselves abusive; this is termed "reactive abuse." Narcissists might then threaten to use these instances as proof of mental instability or maltreatment to use against victims with legal authorities.

Narcissists are especially adept at manufacturing "love triangles," also known as "triangulation," where they actively provoke jealousy in their partner by bringing another person into the dynamic. They do so as a tactic to have power and control over the victim as they paint them as unhinged when they negatively react. The narcissist, in turn, reaps the benefits of multiple sources of attention, praise, and ego strokes for their narcissistic supply. Narcissists thrive on eliciting reactions and emotions from others, whether they are negative or positive, because it gives them the glorious narcissistic high they seek.

There is also a strong correlation between having narcissistic traits and infidelity. That's because, for a narcissist, staying faithful pales in comparison to the rush they get from being revered and desired by other sexual or romantic partners as they seek to replenish their narcissistic supply. Moreover, because narcissists lack empathy and feelings of guilt, they will rarely have remorse for their adulterous behavior, though they may pretend to if they get caught. They may begin to once again love bomb their partner so that they don't lose their partner's supply. If the love bombing doesn't seem to work, they'll revert to abusive behavior to crush their victim.

This research made it clear to me that, not only was Seth an abuser, but a narcissist as well. And I was his chosen victim. I could give multiple examples of each and every narcissistically abusive behavior Seth engaged in during the separation, including the way he initially idealized me and our marriage, then completely devalued and discarded me, gaslighted me into questioning my own experiences and reality, projected me as the real abuser in the relationship, employed sweet-and-mean cycles that ultimately left me trauma bonded, created situations that provoked me to uncharacteristically engage in negative behavior, triangulated me and his girlfriend Jessica against each other, seemed to enjoy watching me in pain—the list goes on and on.

I also learned why I may have been targeted in the first place. I recalled how impressed Seth was when I told him I planned to earn my doctorate and become a college professor; both are very prestigious accomplishments that bring status and, likely in his mind, a very comfortable income. Narcissists crave such status indicators. I also have many qualities narcissists are drawn to, some almost to a fault. For example, I am incredibly trusting and generous. At the same time, I am strong and independent, which also appeals to narcissists. I thought back to our fifth date when Seth pretended to forget his wallet and I told him I didn't want to see him again. He probably loved that about me, seeing me as the perfect challenge. He also stated early on that he too embraced the ideals of egalitarianism and mutual respect that were so important to me in a relationship. He affirmed he wasn't hung up on "wearing the pants" in a marriage or being the patriarch of the family. He claimed that he didn't care if I was more educated than him, if I made more money than him, or if we moved to help build my career as long as we did what was best for us as a couple and our family. But I think he really did care and cared a lot; he was just telling me what I wanted to hear to win me over. He became my perfect mirrored reflection. I had fallen in love with a con artist. We were once again a fucking textbook case.

My research also helped me recognize why Seth cheated during our marriage. As a narcissist, he had an insatiable need for attention and adoration from women. It was so obvious to me now; he cheated to boost his narcissistic supply. I thought back on our entire relationship and again around the time we had first met. This need for adulation from women had been present way back then. He was well known as a "player" and for having sexual relationships with many women, often simultaneously. Moreover, I realized that infidelity itself is a form of interpersonal abuse and, therefore, like other forms of abusive behavior, very much a feminist issue. As feminist academic and author Truus van de Berg described in her own meaning-making about her husband's infidelity,

> *Infidelity is about power relations . . . and about injustice and oppression . . . [T]here is nothing feminist or empowering about being betrayed. I felt disempowered, small, humiliated, denigrated and blamed. I felt made irrelevant, unworthy, hurtfully silenced, victimized; I felt abused.*

In other words, the very personal experience of being cheated on represents a larger social issue of power and control in that it subjugates and demeans the person who was betrayed, particularly when men cheat on women.

Well, would you look at that. I, as a feminist professor, was actually living the 1970s women's movement slogan I lectured on every semester: "The personal is political." I now fully appreciated that my husband's abuse stemmed not only from who he was as a person, but from living in a misogynistic society as well. And it was not a situation that I was uniquely experiencing but one that millions of women also encountered. I had taught about the connection between patriarchy and the abuse of women in my classes for years, yet I couldn't see it when it was happening in my own marriage. My husband was a narcissistic abuser whose patriarchal habituation made him feel entitled to coercively control me, and when he couldn't, the fury began. He simply could not tolerate any sign of independence from his best supply.

WINTER IS COMING

Seth's ire wasn't even close to over. According to everything I read, his abuse wasn't going to stop until he felt like he had won and won big. What would his ultimate revenge against me be? What would drop my chin immediately and unequivocally to the floor in one punch? The prize, I instantly understood, was the children. He wanted Gracie and Henry. Perhaps that was the point all along; constantly breaking me down was simply a means toward that end. What better way to get back at me for leaving him than if I lost my kids? Then, I remembered something Seth had said to me more than once during the marriage.

He would look me directly in the eyes and say, "If we ever divorce, I will fight you 'til the end for my kids. I will take you down."

He wasn't exaggerating.

CHAPTER 7: THE "UNFIT" MOTHER

Perhaps I shouldn't have been so surprised that Seth would use Gracie and Henry to get back at me for leaving him; it was a common technique for narcissistic abusers, after all. Moreover, Seth had already begun his crusade to portray me as a neglectful, incompetent, mentally unstable, and downright dangerous mother and utilize social institutions to do so (e.g., the restraining order and physical assault charge that were both dropped), his ultimate goal unclear to me up until now. Now, it was crystal clear that Seth's plan all along was to use the family law system to demonstrate I was an unfit mother so he would be awarded full custody of the children. Indeed, research shows that abusive men are twice as likely to petition for sole custody of their children as non-abusive men. In his mind, the social study he requested in mediation was just another mechanism toward this end.

Even so, I felt pretty confident that the social worker assigned to conduct the social study, May Hazelwood, would deem me a fit parent and recommend a 50/50 custody split, at the very least. I had also now read numerous books and articles about narcissistic abusers so I felt I had a good idea of the strategies Seth would use to gain custody and how I could address them head on during the course of the study. The study itself was conducted over ten anxiety-provoking months and involved in-depth questionnaires, home visits, repeated questioning and interviews with myself, the children, family members, friends, and colleagues, and frequent requests for information and documents. I spent at least 100 hours just completing the initial questionnaires. The process was like a full-time job, demanding hundreds of hours of work.

I was on track for tenure at Texas A&M University, and because the situation was so time-consuming, the university provided me a tenure-clock extension. The tenure process usually occurs like this: when you enter a tenure-track position, you are an assistant professor and have roughly six years to prove you have the potential to be a leading scholar, contributor, and teacher in your field and university. If you are successful, you are promoted to associate professor and granted tenure. In essence, tenure means job security for life and is something most academics decidedly seek. It is a symbol of status and respect in the academic world and highly coveted. Sometime after that, usually after four to six more years, you can be promoted to full professor, but you need to have gained "rock star" status in your field. When my marriage fell apart, I was smack in the middle of my six years as an assistant professor trying to establish myself as worthy of tenure and promotion.

Tenure-clock extensions were developed to allow assistant professor faculty to add time to their tenure and promotion process when they experience time-consuming events or situations that may make working full time toward tenure difficult. For example, some faculty, usually women, extend their tenure clock because of the birth or adoption of a child. Other common situations include caring for an ill parent or when the university is unable to provide an adequate laboratory for the faculty member to conduct their research. Seeking a tenure-clock extension because of a divorce and custody battle is rare. In fact, to this day, I have not heard of anyone being granted an extension under these circumstances. But my colleague, Wendy, encouraged me to try. I wrote a letter to the university provost explaining my situation and request. Not long after, I was awarded an extension. What's more, because my divorce was so long, contentious, and full of anguish, I received a second tenure extension. I will forever be grateful to Texas A&M for those decisions. I received tenure in 2017 and was promoted to an associate professor—a long, grueling haul, especially while in the throes of a bitter and devasting divorce.

The first thing I realized Seth did to demonstrate my deficiency as a mother was bad-mouth me to the children. Every time the kids would return from being with him, I would be shocked by the things they would say and would have to spend time addressing their comments. I think he may have done this so that when May, the social worker, talked to the kids about me, they would repeat the things he said and make it seem like I was unfit to mother them. I started keeping track of the things the kids would say to me. Here are some examples:

- *"Why do you have married boyfriends?"*
- *"You are a bad mother!"*
- *"Daddy cares more about us than you do."*
- *"I don't want to be with you. I want to live with Daddy all the time."*
- *"I don't want to see you."*
- *"Don't call me your daughter. I don't break my promises like you."*
- *"Shut up, Mom! You're a liar."*

Seth also bad-mouthed me by repeatedly telling the children during the divorce (and for many years thereafter) that I did not want them to play sports as a way to get back at him. He told them I would purposely not take them to practices and games and, if I did take them, would intentionally be late. He would also imply that I did not care about their involvement with sports because I did not attend every game (which was actually because of his intimidation and abuse). His stance on this was always perplexing to me. Perhaps he thought this because I was adamant that they only be involved in one sport at a time (which never, ever happened), but beyond that I just don't get it. Why would I not want my kids to reap all the benefits of being involved in sports? I would often teach in my psychology courses about the importance of sports for kids' well-being and development, especially girls, so I was well aware of all the positive outcomes of sports involvement (exercise, fun, teamwork, healthy competition, working toward a goal, etc.). So not only was his standpoint completely wrong, but it suggested to the kids that I was deliberately trying to sabotage their happiness and success.

Moreover, the kids would often confide in me about feeling over-scheduled, that they were tired of playing this or that sport, that they felt pressured to play, or that they didn't have enough time to do school work or hang out with friends because they were so busy with practices and games. Sometimes, they just wanted a break. I would listen, try to be compassionate, and encourage them to talk to their dad and tell him how they were feeling. Every time, the kids would say that was just not possible and that they didn't want to hurt their dad's feelings because he loved them playing sports so much. The few times I reached out to Seth to explain that they had disclosed to me that they wished to take a pause with sports or try something different, it would simply fall on deaf ears and he would accuse me of trying to sabotage the kids or get revenge on him. It was so strange—and it wasn't just with the kids' sports—how much Seth would deny the existence of the real truth and cling to his own fabricated reality no matter how many times he was confronted with evidence to the contrary. He would literally make up irrational stories in his mind that were based on zero proof. It was futile to try and refute him, so I stopped trying.

Below is an actual conversation between Seth and Gracie that

Gracie recorded (I never asked her to record any of their conversations; she did so on her own). It is a good example of the way Seth would smear me to the kids and suggest I tried to disrupt their sports. Seth and Gracie were in his car and headed to one of Henry's games for a last-minute tournament. Henry was with me in my car, and we were also headed to the game. Seth asked to take him, but I said I wanted to because it was my weekend and I wanted to spend time with Henry because he had been spending a lot of extra time at his dad's house. I had let Gracie spend the night with Seth the night before, even though it was my weekend, because she had been spending a lot of extra time with me. During the drive, Seth was anxiously texting Henry that I would not get him to the tournament on time. Henry, in the car with me, was completely stressed out and encouraged me to drive faster. We were not late. Here is the transcript of that actual conversation:

Seth: *It gets me crazy because that's what she does to you and your brother, and I'm sorry for saying that, Gracie, but this is a perfect example. Makes me so angry . . . Henry's gonna be late.*

Gracie: *No, she's getting him . . . It's fine.*

Seth: *She's so full of crap, man. Can you do Find My iphone on her and see where her location is, Gracie?*

Gracie: *I don't know her password. You shouldn't have to track her dad, just believe she's—*

Seth cuts her off: *No, because she lies, Gracie! She lies about this stuff.*

Gracie: *No, no—*

Seth cuts her off again: *She is a liar when it comes to*

you and Henry. She lies. I don't trust her. Period . . . 'Cause when she says she's gonna do something or take you to things she doesn't! I don't trust her. I never have! She lies! She lies about being abused. She lies about all kinds of stuff. Okay? She lies! Period! And this is a perfect example! And the reason why I'm stressed is because when she says she's 5 minutes away, you know what that really means?

Gracie: *5 minutes away.*

Seth: *She's 20 minutes away!*

Gracie: *No, it doesn't.*

Seth: *Yes it does! 'Cause that's the way she does it, Gracie!*

Gracie: *She's on time a lot, for everything.*

Seth: *Not only, ya know . . . She's . . . then I'm not worried about it. She'll get there on time, but if she's 5 minutes late . . . But you see the stress that Henry's going through now, right?*

Gracie: *Yes, because he's so—*

Seth cut her off again: *No, no, no. But you see the stress that Henry's going through. You know why he's stressed? Because she's been late all the time for his stuff.*

Gracie: *Dad, I'm not saying this to start a fight or anything, but you're literally late more than she is.*

Seth: *I'm not arguing that at all. At least I show up!*

Gracie: *So does she. Literally, so does she. They weren't*

even supposed to have a tournament this weekend, like literally.

Seth: *But what does that have to do with me taking him and getting him there on time?*

Gracie: *Because it's her weekend.*

Seth: *And she tells you . . . do this and do that to your dad. Not one time have I told Henry to do anything disrespectful to his mom, not one time. What are you shaking your head for? Is that not true?*

Gracie: *No. She never has done anything like that.*

Seth: *Huh* (laughs). *Okay . . . [She will find] a perfect opportunity to get you against me and get you stop playing this and stop doing softball and stop doing that . . .*

Gracie: *She likes me playing softball.*

Seth: *She does not. She likes all the benefits of softball. She likes saying, "Oh, that's my daughter that hit the home run" or "That's my son who's so fast," but does she want to take you to practices? No. Does she want to pay for it? No. She'd rather pay for a 100-dollar bottle of wine than pay for your baseball stuff.*

Gracie: *That's not . . . No.*

Seth: *That's not true?*

Gracie: *No, it's not true at all.*

Seth: *Yes, it is.*

End of recording.

Making matters worse, Seth would frequently keep me out of the loop on information related to the kids' sports and school activities, which made it difficult for me to know exactly what was going on with them and their schedules. This was tough for me not only because I had been in charge of the kids' schedules their entire life to that point, but because it made me appear like I wasn't a fully present and involved parent, which was absolutely not the case but what was exactly what Seth wanted the kids (and others) to believe. Seth usually had information I was not privy to either because he was one of the coaches on the kids' team or because school information (letters sent home, emails, etc.) went directly to him because the home address on file for the children was the family home. One time I missed a parent-teacher conference because a letter was sent home that Seth did not tell me about. As an educator, it has always been important to me to be involved in the kids' schooling, and I was pissed that I missed meetings because he would keep information from me. I contacted the kids' school and teachers numerous times to tell them our family circumstances and request that I be included on all emails and be made aware of all issues regarding the kids. It usually went in one ear and out the other.

All I asked from Seth was that he put the information on our shared calendar for the kids. I brought my concerns about keeping me appraised of the kids' schedules up to him many times. Here is an example:

> *Seth - I am very, very frustrated that you are not putting the kids' activities into our calendar so I am aware of them . . . I don't want to go back and forth about this. Just put things on the calendar. -Kathi*

Here's another example:

Me: *Send me Henry's football game and practice schedule.*

Seth's response, with a condescending stab at the end:

I don't have his football schedule but it sounds like you have an interest in attending more games now. I think that is great!

In this next email, Seth reaches out to me to confirm I know about a change in Henry's schedule that I was previously uninformed about. It is my period of possession.

Seth: *I assume you received the email concerning the cancellation of Henry's football game. Since there is no game he should go to baseball practice tonight . . . Since I have his bag, I can meet you on his way to practice. I just need a time. If you cannot take him to practice because you made other plans, then I have no issue taking him . . .*

My frustrated response: *No, I did not receive a message. Once again, I am not made aware of Henry's sport activity schedules. I seem to be intentionally kept out of the loop. Please send me the coach's information so I can contact him to be put on the email list. And wait - aren't YOU a coach on the team? Yes, you are. As such, there is NO excuse for me not having this information. So now, once again, there is a change I am unaware of. I told Gracie I would pick her up from practice and then planned to go to Henry's football game. Now, there is no game and he took his baseball bag so now you have his bag and you want me meet up with you (something I am incredibly uncomfortable with). You also state that you "have no issue taking him" yet you actually do - because you use it against me later and say that I never take him to practice and you always have to because I'm so, in your exact words "unreliable." You keep setting me up . . . I will contact the head coach and let him know that he should expect Henry at practice.*

Seth also tried to paint me as neglectful. It didn't really matter the event or the circumstances surrounding it, he would find a way to make me look like I wasn't paying attention, didn't care, or didn't have the kids' best interest and well-being in mind. For example, he would routinely call the kids to check on them when they were in my care asking them, "Are you ok?" "Are you safe?" "I'm checking on you to make sure everything is fine." When I asked him why he did this, he replied "Because they are with you." One time he even called Gracie's school counselor and asked him to check on Gracie because it was my week. Gracie was very, very confused about this. It was entirely inappropriate but, I'm sure in Seth's mind, helped build his custody case against me.

A perfect example was one day when I took the kids roller skating. I wanted to do something fun and different, so we drove thirty minutes to the nearest roller-skating rink, the Silver Wings Ballroom, which was located in Brenham, Texas. We were having a ton of fun going around and around the rink to the disco lights and music when Henry suddenly fell. I was skating a few feet behind him and witnessed the whole thing. He tripped, flew up into the air, and landed directly on his left elbow. And I mean directly on his elbow, like it was the first thing to hit the floor. He gripped his elbow in pain (but no crying, which shocked me!), and I immediately rushed over. I gently helped him up, skaters obliviously passing us by. At the same time, one of the rink employees hurriedly skated over, scooped up Henry with two arms like a baby, and sprinted off the rink. When we stepped off the rink, they had ice ready to go and inspected the elbow. The employees and I all looked at each other. It was really bad; his bone was protruding from his stretched skin. It was clearly broken. I quickly got directions to the nearest emergency room, and we headed to the hospital.

When we arrived at the emergency room, I immediately had Gracie call Seth to let him know what was going on while I consoled Henry. I didn't want to talk to Seth. I knew he would find a way to blame my "poor mothering skills" on Henry's injury or find some other way to make me feel terrible about Henry's fall. He didn't answer, so Gracie left a message. In the meantime, I completed a slew of forms and they did some X-rays on Henry's arm. They laid him in a hospital bed and started a morphine drip while we impatiently waited for the results. A few minutes later, Henry turned to me and smiled.

"I'm feeling so much better, Mommy. I feel really good," he said.

"Yeah, I bet you do. That morphine is starting to kick in," I said with a little laugh while brushing his hair back.

The X-ray confirmed the obvious: a horrible break. Moreover, it broke in such a way that he needed to see a pediatric orthopedic surgeon. To do so, we had to go to Houston, which was about an hour-and-a-half drive away. But I couldn't drive him; he had to go in an ambulance, and I would follow. As I started getting our things together, Seth called. I hesitantly decided I would talk to him and give him the update. I walked outside for some privacy. He responded worse than I had anticipated. He completely went off on me but not for Henry's fall. Rather, he was furious because I had Gracie call him to let him know what was going on.

Seth said, yelling, "How dare you have Gracie call me and tell me Henry broke his arm! You should be the one calling me to tell me news like this! I need to have all the details of what happened, every single specific detail, and Gracie can't tell me that. I can't believe you put her in the middle of this! You're so pathetic!"

Me: "Seth! Do not yell at me! This is exactly why I had Gracie call you! This is the situation. We are in Brenham. We came to go roller skating and Henry fell. He needs to see an orthopedic surgeon in Houston. I will be following the ambulance. When I know the address of where we are going, I will have Gracie text it to you. If you have any questions in the meantime, you can speak with the doctor here at the Brenham ER. I am hanging up now."

I hung up the phone.

His screaming rattled me, and I began to sob. I was over him yelling at me, over him putting me down, and over crying. I wiped the tears from my cheeks and walked back into the emergency room as if I hadn't just been verbally assaulted by Seth. Henry was ready to go in the ambulance, so I gathered Gracie and our things and we started our trek to Houston.

Seth arrived at Texas Children's Hospital in Houston around thirty minutes after the kids and I. One of the worst things about having children with a man you're divorcing, especially when they're abusive, is having to be in the same room with him; it was awful. Not only did we have to be in the same room for hours while waiting for the surgeon, but Henry had to stay overnight for surgery, so I had to see Seth the next day too. Moreover, I had to occasionally talk to him, which made me want to throw my guts up all over the hospital. While we all sat there in the intake area, Seth would occasionally glare at me with disgust and anger. It was so uncomfortable, like I was sitting on pins and needles. I was afraid to catch eyes with him, so I limited my gaze to the floor, my phone, or the kids. At one point, Gracie even saw him doing it and asked him to stop. I think the only time I really looked at Seth was when I watched him scold Henry for going roller skating because it was football season. Seth made it clear that he would never have let Henry go skating if Henry had been in his care. That pissed me off! I wanted to scream at him to shut up and leave Henry alone, but I kept quiet. I had learned that saying anything would only bring out the beast, and that was the last thing the kids and I needed, especially injured Henry.

Once Henry was officially admitted, we went up to his private hospital room. It was large and spacious with plenty of seating. That was a huge relief. There was also a small sleeping area off in the corner were Gracie and I slept overnight, with Seth sleeping in one of the chairs, because Henry's surgery was scheduled for early the next morning and we both wanted to be there every minute to support him. I didn't interact with Seth unless absolutely necessary. It was so awkward being in the same room with him overnight; I woke every hour praying the sun was up and we could get the surgery process started. Finally, it was time for surgery. The nurses came and whisked Henry away before Gracie even opened her eyes. All went smoothly, and the check-out process was easy and efficient.

Gracie and I fetched my car in the parking structure and drove to the entrance to pick up Henry while Seth waited with him. I got out and walked around to help Henry get into the car. When Henry was comfortably buckled in, I started walking back over to my door. I could feel Seth walking indignantly behind me, his toxic energy breathing on the back of my neck. I quickly opened the car door, jumped in the driver's seat, and frantically pulled the door toward me. I just wanted to get out of there! But Seth blocked the car door as I was closing it, bent down, and said sarcastically with a menacing sneer, "Goodbye, Carly! . . . I mean Kathi!" (Carly was one of the women he cheated on me with.) He went on to scream at me calling me a joke of a mother, a loser, a fake, and that I lacked morals. He did this with both children in the car and hearing every single word. I finally got the door closed and pressed my foot forcibly on the gas pedal. I felt like I was fleeing a serial killer who almost had me in his clutches; it was that damn terrifying.

CHAPTER 7: THE "UNFIT" MOTHER

The kids were shocked at our interaction; they couldn't believe how he treated me. But it was right in front of their eyes, something that was rare. He was usually on his best behavior in view of the kids and that he had taken off his mask in their presence blew me away. Part of me was happy he did; the kids now had a sense of what he was putting me through. I explained to them how that was a perfect example of why I was not with him and why I would never get back together with him. They understood, bouncing their heads up and down in agreement. I was so relieved when the nightmare was over and Henry was resting quietly at home. Later that night, I received an email from Seth:

> *Kathi,*
> *Please give me a full update on Henry's health tonight. I have been thinking of him nonstop. Also, I still have yet to receive the full narrative of how he broke his arm while in your care. I would like that in writing for my records. Also, what safety equipment was he wearing? What skates did he wear? Rentals designed for that rink? If not, which ones did he wear? What's the brand? Are they designed for inside use? If so please forward the documentation.*
> *-Seth*

I did not respond to his message. In my view, his line of questioning was ridiculous, unnecessary, and clearly trying to find me at fault for Henry's roller-skating accident. A few days later, he sent another email.

> *Kathi,*
> *I need an explicit narrative of how Henry broke his arm while in your care . . . I want to know where you were and your proximity to him during the injury.*

How long was it before it was decided that you were going to take him to the hospital? Also, I want to know what skates he was wearing. What brand? Were they the facility approved and owned rentals or ones you purchased? If you purchased them how do you know they are designed for indoor use? Are they designed for an expert or novice? I know some brands are designed to go faster than others. Henry has not gone roller skating in a long time and is not an expert on four wheeled skates. Also, please let me know what safety equipment he was wearing. I assume the injury would have been much worse if he was not wearing anything. Thank you in advance for the information.
-Regards, Seth

He followed up the next day, this time also inquiring about Gracie coming home sick from school and suggesting that I was a negligent parent more directly. He also asked for a "narrative" about when several weeks prior Henry was playing near a creek at one of Gracie's softball games. Henry came to me running and crying that he had been bitten by a snake. I was incredibly worried, of course, and so as a precaution called 911. They came out, checked him over, and decided it was most likely a bee sting. I was embarrassed that I may have overreacted but was glad I called for professional help just in case. After the incident, I called Seth to give him a brief overview of what had happened. Apparently, my overview was unsatisfactory.

Kathi,
I understand that Gracie was ill today. The school called and asked me to pick her up. Please give me a detailed narrative of what you asked the nurse. When I talked to the nurse she implied that Gracie was OK,

but I get the impression when you arrived that was not the case. Also, did you speak to the nurse prior to arriving at the school? Where is the nurse's station? Was Gracie lying down? Was she sleeping? Did she have a temperature? If so, what was it? Do you think she will be able to go to school tomorrow? This is the second time this week that school has called me because they were unable to get a hold of you immediately. Both times I was in my vehicle en route before you texted me to inform me you were on your way. During the weeks you have the kids you probably should have your phone on you at all times. What would of happened if I was unable to text you and you did not get the message? I looked over my calendar and today was the 5th time this school year that the school called me about the kids during your week because they were unable to get a hold of you. Also, I need an explicit narrative of how Henry broke his arm while in your care. I have asked you on several occasions for this information but you have refused to do so. I also want to know where you were and your proximity to him during the injury. How long was it before it was decided that you were going to take him to the hospital? Also, I want to know what skates he was wearing. What brand? Were they the facility approved and owned rentals or ones you purchased? If you purchased them how do you know they are designed for indoor use? Are they designed for an expert or novice? I know some brands are designed to go faster than others. Henry has not gone roller skating in a long time and is not an expert on four wheeled skates. Also, please let me know what safety equipment he was wearing. I assume the injury

would have been much worse if he was not wearing anything. Also, please give me a detailed narrative the day you had to call the ambulance while he was in your care for him the time he was bitten either by the snake or bee. If I remember correctly you instructed him to stay out of a creek the day before, but he dis- obeyed you and got muddy anyway. Was this the same area? Did you witness the incident? Or was he not in your visual supervision when he was injured. If not who did you put in charge to supervise him? Who was he with? What was the prognosis? He is allergic to a lot of things. Who determined it was not necessary of him to go to the hospital to determine if he is having a reaction? Thank you in advance for the information.
-Regards, Seth

He remained obstinate in wanting me to answer all of his ques- tions, especially about Henry's roller-skating accident. He didn't bring up Gracie being sick or what my best friend Sheri and I even- tually called "bee-sting-gate" again, though. And his interrogations gave Sheri and me ample fodder to laugh the evenings away wonder- ing what questions Seth *really* wanted to ask: "And how many wom- en were there?" "Were they pretty?" "What were they wearing?" "Did they want to have sex with me?" "Did you tell them I wanted to have sex with them?" "Why won't you let me control and abuse you?"

I did finally respond to him, telling him that I had already de- scribed what had happened and that his line of questioning was in- appropriate. I also sent him copies of the medical bills for Henry's elbow surgery so he could reimburse me for his half, which I paid on my own and totaled over $4,000. But he just continued wanting "the narrative" and now with questions about exactly how I paid for Henry's medical bills:

Kathi,

I am still awaiting the narrative of you had to obtain emergency care for Henry. Also, how much out of pocket have you paid. You never consulted me when you paid his bills. Never gave me a chance. Now that being said, did you pay $ out of pocket. Or did you make minimum payments to your credit cards?

-Seth

I had had enough and finally contacted Lyle, my attorney, for advice:

Hi Lyle,

Seth keeps asking for "narratives" before he will pay for Henry's medical bills. Do I really need to get him this info for him to pay me? I already told him exactly what happened and I feel he is using this as another way to control me and try to show me as a "bad mother." It also seems irrelevant to me exactly how (out of pocket, on a credit card, etc.) I paid Henry's medical bills. Do you agree this is irrelevant for him to pay me back? I have even suggested to him in an earlier email that he could pay me back a little at a time if his lump sum is too much.

-Kathi

Lyle confirmed that I did not need to provide a narrative of all the details of the roller-skating incident nor did I need to describe how I paid for Henry's medical costs to get reimbursed. As a sidenote, Seth did not pay me back until over two years later when he was formally ordered to do so by a judge. Even though he finally paid for Henry's medical expenses, his economic abuse—controlling funds until I complied with his demands—was incredibly stressful and ultimately put me in debt.

One of the most extreme examples of Seth trying to demonstrate I was a neglectful parent was when he took Henry to the doctor for a sports physical for school just after he had spent the week with me. After the appointment, Seth contacted me and told me that he was very concerned because the doctor said Henry looked hungover and Seth was worried that Henry had drank alcohol while with me. It was a preposterous suggestion and one that I had trouble believing. So, I called the doctor to find out if indeed this issue had been discussed at the appointment. I wasn't able to talk to the doctor, but I did talk to the actual nurse that was present in the room during the appointment. I told her that Henry's dad had mentioned to me that the doctor said Henry seemed hungover and that I wanted to find out more about what the doctor said. She was completely bewildered. She stated, with confidence, that nothing related to alcohol or being hungover was discussed at the appointment. I asked her if she was sure. She said she was absolutely sure; she even went and confirmed with the doctor. In short, Seth outright lied about Henry appearing hungover to make me seem like I was a poor and negligent parent. What the fuck?

Accusations of me as a pitiable mother also appeared in Seth's interviews and questionnaires as part of the social study. For example, the social worker, May, summarized Seth's words as follows:

Despite her flexible schedule being a graduate student, [Seth said] Kathi was insistent on obtaining child care for the kids. They would have a schedule where she would take them in the morning and he would pick them up after work. Many times, she would stay late at school and Seth would pick up the kids from daycare, start dinner, and put them to bed by himself. He stated, he never complained about this despite his own long work days, not to mention that he was in school as well obtaining his master's degree. In 2004, after 7 years of living in Michigan, Kathi finally graduated from Michigan and began to search for a job. She had an offer from Western Kentucky University. They had long discussions about the move. Kathi was persistent and again persuaded him to quit his promising job and uproot the family to Kentucky. Seth wanted to wait a year and see if the following year's job market was more promising, but Kathi stated that she was not and never will be a "stay at home" mom . . . She would spend every night on her computer working instead of spending time or playing with the kids. Many times, he would spend his evenings doing homework and spending time with the kids as she sat on the couch with her laptop working . . . she asked that he read and tuck the kids into bed so she could get work done. Her becoming consumed by work also affected the various activities she attended for the kids.

Seth used every outdated bullshit stereotype about the uncaring selfish career woman to paint me as a careless mother even when everyone knew that was absolutely not the case. Excuse me for wanting to have a career and a family and for thinking my husband actually supported that choice. Clearly, he didn't, though he sure made it seem like he did when we were together. Progressive, liberal, feminist man, my ass!

Seth also maintained in the social study that he should have full custody of the children because he was better at "controlling" (his word) them. He would frequently get on me during the marriage—like the time when he went off on me in the grocery store when he felt the kids were misbehaving—for not being harder on them and directing their behavior in ways he saw as ideal. His stance on my supposed inability to adequately control the children appeared throughout the social study. May summarized Seth's testimony in several different sections of the report as follows:

> *Seth stated . . . after 6 months [in Kentucky], he received a job offer and joined the family [in Texas] in January. When he joined the family things just seemed different and not the same. Kathi seemed to have an increasingly difficult time controlling the kids. It always seemed that whenever he left the room or was not home they would give her "fits" and misbehave. She would call him into the room and ask him to "handle it" for her, as they would not listen unless he was there. He slowly ended up feeling like he had to play the role of "villain" or disciplinarian to the kids. He and Kathi would argue about this. He complained that he felt like he had to be the mean parent and she always got to be the "nice" and "fun" one . . .*

> *Seth stated, other issues they had were in parenting style. She often had trouble in controlling their children's behavior. He felt like or it appeared to him that most of the time that a lot of their behavior problems happened when he was not present. She often would insist that that he not leave the kids alone with her for long periods of time because she feared they would misbehave . . .*

> *Over the years, he would try to support her struggles controlling the kids, but she would take his suggestions as criticisms. Even in times when she asked for help. Most of his behavior techniques he learned from years of training from his past work [working with juvenile*

delinquents] which he incorporated into his parenting style . . .

Seth reported, they have never seen eye to eye on the disciplining of their children. He stated, he believes the kids are in need of more structure and tight supervision. He stated, Kathi, believes it should be looser and care free. Yet, she continues to call me when she is having issues and requests me to talk to the kids when they are giving her problems.

Seth stated, others could see him as being demeaning towards Gracie, but that he would often have to tell Gracie to pay attention to where she was and what she was doing or needed to do and he would have to tell her in a commanding voice.

May wrote me an email curious about the issue of controlling the children specifically:

Kathi,
Seth has written that he is the one who can control and care better for the children and you are the one who can't control them and doesn't really want to, always getting him to do it. I don't believe this but it raises an interesting question. If what he said was true, why did the children come here to stay with you rather than staying with him in Kentucky? And why wouldn't you have insisted on this if you don't like to have them alone? Can you tell me the thought processes you all had when moving the children with you? Thanks.
-May

Seth grasped at other straws to show me as an unfit parent in other areas as well. For example, and as to be expected from a narcissist, he also maintained that I, not him, was the real abuser. Clearly, our testimonies conflicted in this regard, something May caught on to. For example, Seth wrote the following:

> *During our disagreements she would yell and scream at me in front of the kids using profanity and on occasion would throw things at me. She would then blame me for "pushing her buttons" and not apologize. Actually, I felt like that in every verbal disagreement we had it would always be my fault and she was never being accountable for her actions . . . In our 15-year relationship, I never called her a derogatory name . . . I never hit or pushed her, and never verbally threatened her. And despite my larger size and stature, I never walked up to her in a threatening manner to intimidate her physically.*

Then came a thread in the report about "finger-stabbing." May wrote:

> *Seth stated that Kathi would stab her finger at him and yell at him.*

Finger-pointing came up again when she was summarizing my testimony:

> *Kathi stated . . . he became very difficult and loud, getting in her face and stabbing his finger at her while giving her mean, angry looks and belittling and demeaning her.*

This pattern continued when Seth stated his view on Henry breaking his arm roller skating:

> *During the interview in his home, Seth further de-*

scribed the broken arm issue. He expressed that he was angry and frustrated because he felt the reason Kathi took them skating was because she was trying her best to outdo him . . . During the interview in Seth's home, when he brought up this incident, his expression and wording were that he remains very angry about this situation and he stabbed and pointed with his finger as part of his communication of his anger.

Also relevant was Sheri's testimony regarding the time Seth dropped off Henry at a Subway sandwich restaurant where Sheri, her son Carter, and I were eating before the four of us would head to the school fair. May indicated:

Seth then drove up to the Subway to drop Henry off. Sheri said, you could see Seth struggling about whether to get out of the car and come in. Seth did come in and he was angry, stabbing his finger pointedly and angrily at Kathi and talking loudly, talking over Kathi. Sheri stated, Kathi kept saying, please go, please leave me alone but he kept talking loudly over her and stabbing his finger at her. Sheri said it was as if he couldn't stop until he had had his say.

May ultimately put the pieces together, illuminating a troubling inconsistency:

Seth reported, Kathi would point and stab her finger at him in an angry manner. Kathi denied this. Kathi reported the same communication style concerning Seth. During the time I spent with Kathi, she never used pointing or stabbing her finger as part of her communication style. During the time I spent with Seth,

> *he repeatedly pointed and stabbed his finger as part of*
> *his communication style.*

May noticed another discrepancy as well:

> *Seth stated in his narrative and in his interviews that*
> *Kathi would repeatedly tell him that he was "morally*
> *flawed" because of his behavior during the marriage.*
> *Seth accused Kathi of being "morally flawed" in his*
> *narrative, when describing what he believed was her*
> *behavior after they had separated and after she had*
> *filed for divorce. In her narrative and in her inter-*
> *views, Kathi never used those words and never said*
> *that about Seth using other words.*

May was seeing Seth for who he really was: a narcissistic predator. She even once sent me an email about a resource on dealing with emotional manipulators.

> *Kathi,*
> *I just got notice of a workshop which is also avail-*
> *able as a Webcast from Cross Country Education. The*
> *Workshop is titled, "Emotional Manipulation: Under-*
> *standing Manipulators and Helping Their Victims."*
> *You can find it on their website. If you are interested,*
> *this might be helpful to you. Let me know what you*
> *think.*
> *-May*

Perhaps the most surprising straw Seth grasped for, though, was that he insinuated in a phone conversation with May that I was a lesbian, which he said worried him regarding my parenting. She phoned me about it, not because she was concerned about the possibility of me being a lesbian and how that would affect my role as a parent but to get insight into why he thought that might be problematic. I mentioned to her that he had also brought it up to me.

He approached me one day at one of the Henry's baseball games and told me, "There is a rumor going around the baseball parents that you date women. You do spend a lot of time with Sheri. I just wanted you to know."

Not only was it untrue, and for which I wouldn't care anyway, but it was strange how he made it seem like he was doing me a favor for letting me know and how he brought it up to May.

Finally, after almost a year, the social study was complete. I was incredibly relieved when it was over. Although I believed it was highly unlikely, I was worried that May would side with Seth and recommend he get full custody of the children. I was especially fearful about this possibility because Seth would taunt me throughout the process saying things like, "You're gonna lose your kids. You might as well just give up." It was horribly anxiety provoking and kept me staring at the ceiling many a night.

The final report was ninety-eight pages long and concluded with the following recommendations from May for the court:

— *Seth and Kathi be named joint managing conservators (in other words, joint custody),*
— *Kathi be named the primary parent (meaning I decide where the kids live),*
— *Periods of possession be week to week (a week-on, week-off co-parenting schedule),*
— *Each parent will be responsible for one child's medical insurance and have the Federal Tax deduction for one child,*
— *Whichever parent has possession of one of the children for an extracurricular/sports activity, the other parent can elect to have possession of the child not involved,*

- *The parent who registers a child for an extracurricular/ sports activity pay for the activity; the other parent can agree to assist with expenses but is not mandated to do so,*
- *Each child can, if they choose, participate in one extra-curricular activity per school semester,*
- *Gracie be allowed additional time with her mother, as she requests,*
- *Gracie attend therapy as recommended by her therapist until dismissed by her therapist,*
- *Neither parent pays child support.*

I was really happy with some of May's recommendations. I was especially pleased that May advocated for me as the primary parent, that we each pay for the activities we enroll the kids in, and that extracurriculars were limited to one activity per school semester. But after reading the entire report, I was surprised I wasn't recommended to get full custody of the kids given the numerous testimonies describing Seth's emotional abuse toward me and Gracie. I later learned in my readings that, even when wife abuse is detected by custody evaluators, it has little effect on custody recommendations because they tend to characterize it as a high-conflict divorce issue rather than a form of family violence; this is especially the case when the evaluator holds sexist beliefs against women. Evaluators, as well as the family court system in general, simply assume that wife abuse is separate and distinct from child abuse or that it won't affect the children or women's mothering role. In reality, when abuse toward the mother is present during the marriage or separation, co-parenting increases the likelihood of ongoing abuse and violence against mothers and their children partly because the family law court system actively enforces constant contact and communication between the parents. As a result, mothers may be unable to disengage from an abusive male partner. This situation can also harm the children, even if they are not the direct targets of the abuse, because they see their mother enduring years of coercively controlling co-parenting and contemptuous treatment by their father. In short, co-parenting can harm the mother and the children when abuse is involved. But I had no choice but to accept May's recommendation to the court. And thankfully, Seth was not recommended to get full custody. That was a huge relief.

One final gem written by May in the social study report was as follows:

> *In their original paperwork Kathi described three issues: Seth's infidelity, his verbal/emotional abuse of herself, and his verbal/emotional abuse of Gracie. Seth had the following issues with Kathi in his original paperwork: lack of intimacy, she forced him to look outside the marriage, lack of parenting skills, poor skills to maintain friends, poor skills to maintain extended family, her lack of religious beliefs, poor communication skills with him, alcohol abuse, poor skills with peers at work, poor financial management, her bullying him to drink, inability to function as a parent, his repeated sacrifices over the years with no sacrifices on her part, reports she is a charlatan, and he doesn't trust her judgment. When asked why he wanted to maintain the relationship under those circumstances, he stated he loved her.*

Seth's attempt at receiving May's recommendation for full custody of the children failed because he was unsuccessful at proving I was an unfit mother. In fact, his efforts to show me as an incompetent parent had the opposite pattern: they instead demonstrated I was a loving and committed mother. That enraged him, so much so that it terrifyingly fueled him. He would simply have to devise another plan, one that was sure not to disappoint.

CHAPTER 8: THE ALIENATION

Seth made every attempt to convince the social worker, May, that he should receive full custody of Gracie and Henry. He just knew in his egocentric narcissistic mind, and frequently condescendingly warned me, that he would prevail as the ideal and chosen parent. His attempts were futile, though, and May instead recommended joint custody. Seth was livid at the result and had agreed during mediation to accept the conclusion, but he just couldn't let it go. He still wanted revenge. He so badly wanted to see me writhe, so he formulated a new scheme. This time, it was the alienation of Henry. It started subtly, with him encouraging Henry to stay longer than scheduled during Seth's weeks. This did not seem like a problem to me at first until instances of Seth trying to distance Henry from me became more and more apparent.

For example, Seth would pick up Henry from school, sports practice, or a friend's house when it was my week with the kids and sometimes when I was actually there waiting to pick Henry up. Seth would also tell Henry that he was allowed to stay with whichever parent he chose; that is, he would tell Henry that it was his decision if he wanted to stay with me or his dad regardless of the scheduled periods of possession. This would put me in the horrible position of demanding Henry come with me and him refusing. Seth would even pick Henry up directly from my home without my consent or knowledge. Below are emails demonstrating this pattern. The first is me emailing Seth reminding him to adhere to the court order regarding possession.

> *Seth,*
>
> *I want to remind you that when it is my period of possession with the children they are to be with me unless we have made alternative arrangements. You have now twice - a few months ago and again last night - taken Henry to your residence and let him stay the night when I was there to take him and made clear that it was my period of possession and I wanted him with me. This is against court orders. I have sent Henry several text messages and called him to remind him that he is with me tonight, but I have not heard back from him. I plan to pick him up from school and take him to practice and then back home with me. He will be entirely with me until I drop him off at school Thursday morning as per our arrangement. I will not be coming by your house to pick up his things. Thus, if he has items that he needs for the next three days (items for practice or school, etc.) please drop them off with him at school or we can arrange a public place to meet. If you are communicating with Henry, please let him know the plan.*
>
> *-Kathi*

Then, only a week later, he again picked up Henry from my home without my approval but tried to suggest he meant no harm:

> *Kathi,*
>
> *Yesterday Henry exited your apartment with his school bag and baseball uniform. I asked him if you knew*

he was leaving and had the intention to stay at my residence. He said yes. He then went back inside your apartment to get more of his belongings and your car keys. He opened the trunk of your vehicle and took his baseball bag and put it into my vehicle. He again entered your apartment to return your car keys. He then walked back and entered my vehicle. You did not leave your apartment or come outside to protest or confirm this… Therefore, I assume you had no issues.
-Seth

My response:

Seth,
Let me be clear: Unless you have written approval from me you should not assume that I have approved a change of the schedule. I heavily protested to Henry so he knows that I strongly disapproved of him going with you. I did not come out because I refuse to interact with you, especially when a third party is not present to witness the interaction.
-Kathi

Before long, Henry would hardly acknowledge me when I went to his games, never wanted to see me, and would outright reject coming with me during my periods of possession. It seemed like every time he had a game, even if it was my week, he would sit with his dad (and Jessica), talk only with his dad, and want to go home with his dad.

The conversation below is a good example. I was waiting for Henry to gather his things after his football game. He was scheduled to stay with me and spend the weekend (Seth and I had exchanged weekends and I had it in writing) because Sheri and I and all the kids were having a special weekend slumber party with pizza, movies, games, and smores so it was extra important for Henry to leave with me. He was to grab all his gear and meet me outside the stadium. He didn't though. Instead, he headed toward Seth's van. I drove up next to the van and just waited, making it clear that I was there and he was to come with me. Before Henry was in close-enough range to hear, Seth rolled down his window and started yelling at me that Henry did not want to come with me but wanted to go home with him instead. His face was full of ire and repugnance. I wondered if he would spit in my direction. I kept my window up and tried to ignore him. When Henry was close enough to hear me, I rolled down and leaned out the window and clearly told him that he needed to come with me. He walked up to my car window and replied that he needed to go with his dad because his baseball bag, which he needed the next day, was at his dad's house. I again told him he needed to come with me and that his dad would get the bag to him some other way. Because I could tell Seth was starting to get really angry and might lash out, I hit Record on my phone. Here's what I recorded:

> Me sternly talking to Henry: *You need to come with me. He'll get the bag to you how he sees fit. It's my night. You're coming with me.*

> Henry, thinking he gets to decide who he goes home with: *It's not your night.*

> Me: *That's not for you to decide and I can't have a conversation with him about it right now. I can't talk to your dad right now because he's being abusive to me, okay?*

> Henry, questioning my use of the word: *Abusive?*

Seth: *Hey Kathi, you stay right here, me and Henry will go get his bag and we'll come right back.*

Me talking to Henry: *You need to come with me.*

Henry to me: *No, I don't like your house. And I'm also sorry for calling you an idiot* [which he had called me earlier that day]. *I'm going with dad.*

Me, starting to get irritated: *No, you are not!*

Me to Seth: *It is my night with Henry. He needs to come with me!*

Seth, insinuating there are problems between Henry and I because of what had happened at the field when Seth pressed faulty assault charges: *Why does he want to come home with me tonight? What's going on? I thought we were gonna get his bag . . .* (Henry gets in Seth's car).

Me: *It is my night with my son, he needs to come home with me. You can bring his bag or you can drop it off at school. I don't feel safe around you. I don't feel comfortable.*

Henry in the background, now sitting in the passenger seat of his dad's van, to me: *If you don't feel safe then go away!*

Seth, talking to me: *You can stay right here and I'll get the bag.*

Me: *No, I'm not staying here for 30 minutes.*

Seth: *And I'm not gonna drive across town.*

Me: *Then he'll have to get his bag tomorrow. And I'm not comfortable interacting with you now!*

Henry: *Dad! Please go!*

Seth: *He doesn't want to be with you right now. I'm not gonna make him go with you right now. This whole ordeal you just did is upsetting him.*

Henry, visibly upset: *Come on Dad, just go! Please, Dad, go!*

Seth: *He doesn't want to be with you right now. I'll talk to him. Please stay here and I'll go get his bag.*

Me to Seth: *Okay, alright, then, I guess I'll contact my attorney.*

We both drove off, Henry still in the passenger seat of Seth's van.

I was so angry when I got home and was thankful that Sheri was there to support me. She encouraged me to call the police and file a complaint, which I did. But that didn't seem like enough, so I called the police once again and told them I was going to Seth's residence to (try and) get Henry. Because I feared verbal abuse and Seth not allowing Henry to come with me, I requested a police escort. They agreed. We met at the Exxon gas station down the street from Seth's house. Sheri told her kids we would be back soon, put on a movie for them, and she and I immediately got in the car and headed toward the gas station.

Three police officers met me at the gas station and escorted me to Seth's house. I took a deep breath, and I went up and knocked on the door, my phone in my hand recording. The officers were standing in the yard behind me but close enough to hear. Both Seth and Henry came to the door.

Me: *I'm here to get Henry.*

Seth: *Okay. Um . . .*

Me, pointing to the officers: *I've got some . . .*

Seth, with an air of arrogance: *He is choosing to be here. Okay? If you want, I mean, who you got? Okay, that's fine. Invite 'em up.*

Me, already starting to get flustered and not making sense: *I'm here we—*

Seth: *You are providing an unsafe abusive environment for him. The way you portrayed yourself at the stadium.*

Me: *It's my period of possession.*

Seth: *You do not have a—*

Me, talking to Henry: *Henry, I have the police here and you need to come with me.*

Seth continuing: *You do not have . . . Listen to me. You don't have a bed for him to stay in. You're trying to provide him an environment that has seven people.* [He is referring to Sheri and her kids spending the night.] *According to the decree, kids can offer to stay with the other parent when it's not the other parent's week. This is my week . . .*

Me: *So, are you refusing to . . .*

Seth: *No, no, no. This is my weekend. Officially, this is my weekend. Okay?*

Me: *And I have written* [documentation that we had

made a change in the schedule and Henry was to be with me], *I can show you where you agreed to it.*

Seth: *Well, you can show me anything you want. But the thing is . . .*

Me: *You agreed to it.*

Seth: *Listen to me, listen to me. Officially this is my weekend. We did agree to switch and everything. Henry has said that he doesn't want to stay at your place, so . . .*

Me: *Did you—*

Seth condescendingly interrupts me: *So please invite them up here and we can start working it out. Okay? Please.*

Me to the officers: *He would like you to come up here.*

An officer started walking up.

Seth: *Because he doesn't want to go. And . . . kids can decide where they want to go.*

Me: *The decree does not say that the kids get to choose where they go.*

Seth: *Let me finish please. The decree says that the kids can go to the other parent's . . . Kids have the autonomy to decide which house they want to go to.*

Me: *No they don't . . . No they don't get to decide when it's the other parent's period of possession. The kids don't decide.*

Seth: *Now, now that being said, Henry has told me he doesn't want to go there.*

Me: *It's my period of possession.*

Seth: *I'm not forcing him or anything. Officially to the schedule, yes, this is my weekend. A couple weeks ago, when you were sick you asked can you watch him and trade over this weekend and I said that's fine, no problem because we had a history of doing that.*

Me: *So then it's my period of possession.*

Seth: *We had a history of doing that. Now, you've told Henry, well, I'd let you stay there but since your dad is being mean I'm not gonna let you stay there now.*

Me: *That's irrelevant.*

Seth: *And going back and forth and having different rules from week to week.*

Me, getting frustrated because he's taking the conversation off track and trying to regain focus on the issue at hand: *I'm here to pick up Henry because it's my period of possession.*

Seth: *Now that being said Kathi, three, two days ago, Thursday night . . .*

Me, to the officers: *This is what I deal with constantly, every time.*

Seth: *You're following your rules when you want to . . .*

Me: *All of these details are not relevant to this situation right now. The situation right now is that it is my night with Henry and I'm here to pick up Henry.*

Seth sighs: *Okay, alright, Henry doesn't want to go there.*

Me: *That is not for Henry to decide.*

Seth: *According to the decree the kids . . .*

Me: *The decree does not say that it is up to the kid's discretion. We are the parents; we decide where they go.*

Seth tries to interrupt me: *Okay, well . . .*

Me: *Let me finish now. We made an arrangement via written email that I have possession of Henry tonight. Henry does not get to decide. I am the parent; you are the parent. He is in my possession this evening.*

Seth to Henry: *What do you want to do, Henry?*

Me to Henry: *Henry, you need to gather your things. You need to come with me. It is my night with you. You do not get to decide. You are a child and I am your parent and your father and I agreed that you would be with me tonight and you need to come with me tonight, so please gather your things and come now.*

Henry: *Mom, can I please stay with Dad?*

Me: *No. It is my night with you. It is my period of possession. You do not get to choose.*

Henry: *Mom, can I please stay? I want to stay with Dad.*

Me: *No.*

Henry: *Why?*

Me: *Because it's my night of possession and you need to be with me.*

Seth: *But what does that have to do with him wanting*

to tell you how he feels? What does it have to do with that?

Henry: *Mom, there's seven people staying the night at your house.*

Me, disapprovingly, because Henry knows Sheri and her kids are over for a slumber party: *Henry.*

Seth: *Henry, do you have a bed at your mom's house?*

Henry: *No.*

Me: *That's also irrelevant. I have houseguests tonight. I mean—*

The officer, now standing to the right side of me, interrupts us: *Ok, guys, look. It's horrible to put him in the middle of it.*

Officer to Seth: *Do you want him to go?*

Seth: *No, I want him to stay here. I don't want him to be at his mom's . . .*

Officer: *Does she have possession of him this weekend? Yes or no?*

Seth: *Theoretically . . . By law this is my weekend. By law.*

Officer: *Yes or no?*

Seth: *We made arrangements for something else to go on and, by law, if she's going by letter of the law, this is my weekend.*

Officer: *Okay.*

Seth: *If she has documentation saying that that can happen . . .*

Officer talking to Seth but looking at me: *Does she have that?*

Me: *Yes, I do.*

Seth: *She has the documentation.*

Officer to Seth: *Okay, are you crawfishin' and don't want to do it anymore?* [Gotta love the officer's Texas slang.]

Seth: *What I'm doing is that I'm going off the decree . . .*

Officer: *Okay look . . .*

Seth: *I'm letting my son decide where he wants to go.*

Officer: *Okay, well, it's not up to him.*

Me, feeling validated that the officer agrees with me: *Right.*

Seth: *According to the decree it is though.*

Me: *No, it's not.*

Seth: *I mean, can we talk about the decree?*

Officer: *We can talk about . . . I know all about it and making decisions with the judge. Okay, do you want to go by the court order or do you want to go by the written agreement that y'all dealt with?*

Seth: *I want to go by the court order because the written agreement.*

Officer: *Okay, let's go. We're done with this.*

The police officers started walking to their cars, and Seth followed them. I headed to my car where Sheri was waiting.

> Seth to officer: *Tomorrow he has a baseball tournament . . . I'm worried about harassment, I'm worried about the public harassment and the embarrassment because she's made a scene, a public scene, physically assaulted me in front of Henry and in front of other people and so I don't want a repeat of that because there's a history of violent behavior.*
>
> Me: *Okay, that's not true.*
>
> Officer to me: *Okay, just go back to your car. I'm gonna finish up with him.*
>
> Me: *Okay.*
>
> I got in the car.
>
> Me to Sheri, shaking my head in disbelief of Seth's accusation: *He's telling him he's scared of me because my violence.*

We drove away.

Even though the police officer told Seth that Henry did not get to choose, Seth still refused and Henry did not come with me. Interestingly, Seth's rationale for Henry not staying with me was because I was unsafe and abusive yet he allowed Henry to come the next night to stay with me and never had problems with Gracie staying. And he says I make up different rules. Yeah, right.

A few weeks later, it was my week with the kids and Gracie was staying at a friend's house. I brought Henry to his baseball tournament, and he was supposed to come home with me after the tournament. He sat with his dad and Jessica in between games and hardly talked to me for the hours we were there. This was now the norm. When it was time to go, Henry stood with his baseball bag just outside the field where he played his last game. It was at the very back of the baseball complex. Seth and Jessica started walking together toward the parking lot, both looking down at their phones. Jessica was carrying her chair and a bag on her shoulder. I was about five feet ahead of them and video recording. I felt so bad that Henry had to see me record his dad—and he would voice his dislike of it—but I really felt I had no choice. I had learned it was a good way to protect myself and keep Seth's abuse at bay. And it provided me hard evidence of his abuse if I needed it.

> Henry to Seth: *Dad. Dad. Dad. Dad. Am I going with you?*

Seth stopped and turned to talk to Henry. Jessica walked around Seth and continued toward the parking lot.

> Seth: *What? You tell me Henry. What'd she say? She said no? You get one day a month. Okay, if she said no she said no. You can go from there. But you got unlimited . . . ah, you can ask as many times as you want.*

This time, Seth did not tell Henry that he could choose which parent he wanted to stay with but instead referred to the court order, which stated that the kids could ask for one extra day a month to spend with the same-sex parent but that the other parent needed to approve and confirm which day. Henry had asked me earlier in the day if he could go home with Seth, and I had told him no because it was my week.

> Henry, speaking to Seth: *I don't know what to do!*

Seth started to walk away, leaving Henry standing

there: *So you discuss it with her and go from there. Okay?*

Henry lifted his arms up as if to say, "I give up." Seth continued walking.

Henry: *So I have to go with her?*

Seth stopped and turned around to talk to Henry.

Well, I mean, she has rights and stuff. You have to be respectful. The last thing you want to do is be disrespectful.

Seth then turned back around and resumed walking toward the parking lot. He walked past me. He was still looking down at his phone. I saw Jessica walking way ahead of him.

Me to Henry: *Ready, babe?*

Seth walked for about twenty seconds, then turned around and started walking toward Henry and me.

Seth to himself: *Forgot my chair.*

Seth approached Henry, who was still in his original spot but now sitting down on a wooden log drinking a Gatorade.

Seth to Henry: *I forgot my chair, buddy.*

Me to Henry: *Henry, let's start walking please. Why are we standing here? Let's go.*

Seth headed toward the bleachers at the back end of the field. Henry followed him, and I stayed put. I saw they were talking along the way. Seth grabbed his chair, and they headed back to where I was standing. I started to decipher what they were talking about as they got closer.

> Seth: *So, at minimum, you're gonna put one day a month and you should be able to get that. And it's the rules that you can request . . . It's known that that's the minimum. In other words, in other words . . .*
>
> Henry: *It's annoying.*
>
> Seth: *No, no she has to give you minimum if it says minimum. But, um, the only reason that, you know, if she wants to spend time it's her right and everything else, bud. But um, if you request as many times as you . . . If she says no, she says no.*

They began walking together and passed me by a few feet. I was completely invisible to them.

> Me to Henry: *Henry, can you please walk with me? Henry!"*

Henry turned around to look at me.

> Me to Henry: *Can you walk with me? I mean, you're with me.*

Henry ignored me, stopped walking, and put down his bag as if to look for something.

> Henry to Seth: *Where's my black shirt and my white pants?*
>
> Seth: *I don't know.*
>
> Henry: *I put it on top of my bag.*

Seth: *Then I put it in your bag. I don't know because you got here before I got here. You and your mom got here before I did.*

Me to Henry: *Henry, why don't we walk up to the front where there's more people around?*

They resumed walking. I did too but was a few feet from them.

Henry to me: *Will you please stop recording?*

Me: *Not if he's around me.*

Henry to me: *Get away!*

Me: *No, sorry.*

Seth went back to the conversation with Henry about requesting extra time with him.

Well, she has to tell you what day when you request it.

Henry to me frustratingly: *Stop filming.*

Me: *No.*

Seth to Henry: *Do you want me to forward you the way it says so you understand it better? Yes or no?* [Seth is referring to the order and where it says that the kids can ask for extra time.]

Henry: *Yes.*

Seth, about me recording: *Don't worry about that, Henry.*

Henry: *I know, but she's getting herself embarrassed.*

Seth: *What's that?*

Henry: *She's getting herself embarrassed.*

It was interesting how Henry used the wording that Seth used during the cleat incident. When Seth was verbally harassing me at the practice fields, he told me I was "an embarrassment" (along with other disparaging names). Now, in this situation, Henry used the same wording but incorrectly. Because Henry hadn't heard what Seth had said to me at the fields that day, Seth must have used those words to describe me and Henry was now repeating them. This is called "parroting" and refers to when kids incorporate their parent's words or phrases in their own descriptions or complaints. It is most apparent when the words or phrases are above the child's vocabulary level or represent ideas or attitudes that are more adult-like.

As an aside, Seth also discussed what happened that day with the cleats with Gracie. Unbeknownst to me, she had recorded their conversation and later shared it with me. Note that I never, ever asked her to record their conversations. She simply recorded on her own. Perhaps she was better than Henry at seeing through her dad's behavior. Here are the relevant portions of that recording:

> Seth to Gracie, with her going "ok" and "uh-huh" in between strings of his sentences: *He [Henry] wants to be rested for his tournament tomorrow. And all your mom wants to do is take him over there because she's trying to get me mad. You know what I mean? She's not looking out for the best interest of your brother. And somebody besides me has got to figure out how what's best for your brother and you . . . I need your help, Gracie, talking to her about this stuff. Because this ridiculous stuff needs to stop. She's mad at me because I called her unreliable because she was 10, 20, 30 minutes late handing off Henry's shoes. I was*

mad because I could have just gone to her house and gotten them and gotten back in time. But instead, I was expecting that she would be there on time. And I was mad because she was 20 minutes late. Then when she gets there she starts throwing a fit in front of everybody. For 20 minutes I'm sitting there being quiet trying to coach a team and she's over there yelling at every single kid on Henry's football team, embarrassing your brother, humiliating him. Can you imagine if she went to your softball game and did something like that? In front of your friends and you? Right? So, what did I do? I took all of his team and moved them over to the other field so they can't hear her. I walked over there and I was so angry. I said she was a joke, she was an effin' joke, for doing this to her son. She was selfish for trying to embarrass us, embarrassing him. And you know what she did, Gracie? She hit me right in the head . . . hit my hat in my forehead. Did she slap me across the face? No. Did she punch me? No. But she swung her hand around me trying to hit me. I moved my head back; she hit me on the side of my head and got most of my hat. But the fact is, she took a swing at me because she was so angry and mad and frustrated. Okay? The thing is, is that I'm tired of it, Gracie. I'm really tired of it . . . I'm tired of the stress that she's putting on your brother . . . I'm at the point now where I don't care anymore, Gracie. All I want is Henry to be happy and I want you to be happy. I don't want no drama or anything . . . I'm tired of the drama. I'm tired of her doing what she does . . . I'm at the point now Gracie that the next time she does something like that to me I'm gonna call the police and they're gonna arrest her. I don't want to do that. I don't want that to happen . . . Please, Gracie, talk to her, man. I really need you to step up and talk to her about this stuff.

End of recording.

Now back to the recorded transcript after Henry's baseball tournament. We were all still walking toward the parking lot.

Again, Henry referring to me recording: *She's getting herself embarrassed.*

Seth: *Well, it's just the way it goes.*

Henry looked over at me irritatingly, then shook his head back for forth shamefully at me like Seth often did.

Henry: *She's so stupid.*

Seth: *Henry, don't say that; that's disrespectful. Okay? Alright? You can have your opinion, but not to be respectful. Stuff like that will get her angry. And we don't want her angry.*

Henry: *I know.*

Seth: *It's okay. And when everything calms down and she stops getting mad, then we'll start going back to how it used to be. She's doing this right now to get at me, you know that.*

Henry: *Why do I have to go with her?*

Seth: *Because, Henry, she has a right. But all you have to do is just request.*

Henry to me: *I request to be with Dad.*

> Me: *No, it's my period of possession. And Henry, we really need to stop doing this every time; it's getting old.*

> Henry: *So?*

> Me: *I mean, it's like you're setting it up for he and I to argue, Henry. You're going with me. Just let him go, and you'll see him tomorrow.*

We walked out of the ballpark and were on a gravel parking lot/road lined with cars. My car was on the right side of the road.

> Me, pointing to the right side of the road: *I'm down this way, Henry.*

Henry ignored me and continued walking with Seth whose van was in the same direction.

> Me, exasperated: *Henry! Please stop. I'm down this way and you need to come with me. I'm so sick of having this same conversation.*

Henry was completely unresponsive. Seth stopped walking. Then Henry stopped walking.

> Me: *Really, Henry? You're gonna do this again?*

> Seth to me while looking down at his phone: *Just keep walking ahead of me, Kathi.*

I sighed and kept walking toward my car; Henry finally joined me. He just stared at me with a look of contempt. Seth then crossed the road and began walking on the left side; I continued walking on the right. Henry then crossed to the left side and began walking with Seth once again. They picked up their pace, and I sped up. They arrived at Seth's van. He dropped the chair and other stuff he was carrying and began to open the back hatch. Jessica was there waiting to put her chair and bag in the van; she remained silent.

> Me: *Keep walking, Henry; we're this way. Come on. Henry, you don't want to do this. Come on.*

Henry paused for a moment but then started walking toward me.

> Seth: *One second, Henry. Take your bag with you, buddy. What I'll do is I'll text you. Talk to her about it. Discuss when those days will be, okay?*
>
> Henry: *I don't care.*
>
> Seth: *You should care, Henry, because you need to repair that relationship, okay? The relationship between you and her has been damaged from what happened.* [Seth is referring to the incident with the cleats.]

Jessica put her things in their van and started walking to the passenger side. She did not look or talk to me, Seth, or Henry.

> Me, with a very stern voice: *Let's get going, Henry. Henry, it's time to go. It's time to go; come on.*
>
> Henry turned to me: *Shut up!*
>
> Me: *Excuse me?*
>
> Seth: *Hey! Henry!*
>
> Henry, again to me: *Shut up!*
>
> Me: *No. You don't tell me to shut up.*
>
> Seth bent down to Henry: *Hey, come here; look at me. Don't say that. Don't say that to her. Listen to me. Listen to me. I'll email you the stuff. You go with her.*

Henry to Seth: *I want to go with you.*

Seth: *There's not a good reason for it right now. You can spend all day with her. Now at night when she starts ripping me and starts making fun of me and starts making all those bad negative comments, you tell her, "Mom, please stop," and then you call me and then I'll come get you.*

Henry: *What if she takes away my phone?*

Seth: *Well, she can't. You have the right to call me anytime you want to.*

Henry glanced over at me: *But she does that.*

Me: *Let's go, Henry.*

Seth to Henry: *Just don't be disrespectful.*

Henry: *I didn't even do anything last time that was disrespectful and she took it.*

Seth: *I wasn't there to see that.*

Henry turned to me and asked: *What did I do that was disrespectful?*

Me, trying to hurry Henry: *We need to go. It's time to go.*

Seth: *Henry, I'll text you that page and then you can talk to her about . . .*

Henry stopped considering coming with me and started walking toward Seth's van to get in.

Seth: *No, no listen to me. Let's do it the right way be-*

cause what we don't want is her to show up tomorrow and throw a fit like she did at football practice, okay, alright?

Me, firmly: *Let's get going, Henry.*

Seth to Henry: *Her filming us doesn't bother me because I still act the same way whether or not judges are looking at me or not. Okay? It doesn't change the way I act or what I say, okay? Alright, so you remember that no matter who's asking. You're doing the right thing. You don't have to change the way you act or who you contact. Okay? Alright, so, you need be respectful. There's not a good reason for you to come home with me right now. Except that but if the environment at home is . . . is . . . is . . . where she's saying bad things to me about me or she's saying bad things about you then give me a call and we'll figure it out. Okay? Okay? Before then I will give you that page and you can talk to her about the right day she can, at minimum; tell her it's at minimum.*

Henry: *But what about me staying with you all the time?*

Seth: *The kid can decide when they meet with the judge and they will figure it out then.*

Me to Henry: *Let's go!*

Seth to Henry: *The kid and the judge will work together. We'll get that worked out.*

Henry: *When?*

Seth: *When can we? I'll file the paperwork and we'll get that done, okay? We'll work on that.*

Henry and I started walking to my car. I was exhausted, hurt, and angry.

Me to Henry: *You are being so disrespectful to me right now and it's not fair. I have to record your father. And you don't yell at me. Don't act like I'm this horrible mother that I'm trying to make you late and I won't work with your dad. This is not because of me. This isn't because of me, Henry; it's not because of me. And I look forward to the time when you're older and you finally understand it. And you profusely apologize to me for how you treated me.*

Henry: *I'm sick of all this!*

Me, as I put his baseball bag into the trunk: *I'm sick of it, too!*

Henry and I got into my car.

Me: *I mean, give me a break. It's like I can't do anything right. Now are you gonna text your dad and say, "Please help me. I wish I could go with you because Mom is so horrible"?*

I started the car.

Me: *I would like to have a conversation with you. Talk to me. I would like to learn your perspective, Henry. Why am I so horrible right now? Please explain it to me.*

Henry: *You're yelling at me.*

Me: *Okay, let me stop yelling.*

Henry: *And you're recording my dad for no reason.*

Me: *You did not see the way that he was looking at me in there. It was extremely intimidating, which is, do you see how I try to stay away? I don't try to be right there with him. You didn't see how he was looking at me, and when I recorded him, his face was totally different. And that's why I have to."*

End of recording.

PARENTAL ALIENATION

I tried to be patient with Henry's rejection, but it was difficult. I knew it was all coming from Seth. I had read a plethora of books by this time and knew that using the children in this way was typical of a narcissistic abuser. It had also been given a label by psychologists—"parental alienation"—which validated the painful emotions I was feeling and reassured me that I wasn't alone. The more I read, the more I was floored by the intricacies of parental alienation and the methods used by alienating parents to damage the relationship between the child and the targeted parent. They were literally the exact tactics Seth was using—the exact ones! Here's what I learned.

"Parental alienation" refers to a substantial negative change in a child's behavior toward one parent without justification and with whom the child previously enjoyed a good relationship, often to the point where they refuse to visit that parent. There is strong consensus among researchers regarding the behaviors that constitute parental alienation and how they affect the family system. This research concludes that parental alienation is a form of family violence that encompasses coercive control toward the child and targeted parent and, as such, is considered a form of child abuse and intimate partner violence.

Parents who engage in parental alienating behavior use a number of strategies to distance the child from the targeted parent. Again, it was shocking how many Seth had repeatedly engaged in to thwart my relationship with the kids, especially Henry; it was like he was following a playbook. Common behaviors include allowing the child to choose whether they want to spend time with the targeted parent even when that time is court ordered, use of legal and administrative aggression to interfere with the child's relationship with the targeted parent, undermining the targeted parent's authority with the child, and making false allegations of abuse against the targeted parent. Alienating parents additionally engage in schemes to make the targeted parent look like a bad parent as a way to garner evidence against them. For example, it is common for alienating parents to try and micromanage the child while in the targeted parent's care, and when the targeted parent does not respond quickly or fully enough to requests for information, the alienating parent uses such actions as proof that the targeted parent is negligent and uncooperative. Alienating parents also routinely interfere with the child and targeted parent's time together, such as by incessantly texting or calling the child, often inquiring to the child whether they feel safe with the targeted parent. They also send e-mails that revise or fake past events with the purpose of creating a version of reality that meets their objective. For instance, the alienating parent may e-mail the targeted parent and claim that the targeted parent had been neglectful or abusive in some way toward the child with the intention of collecting documentation of poor parenting against the targeted parent to be used in court. Alienating parents also seek to damage the targeted parent's credibility by bad-mouthing the targeted parent to the child, friends, teachers, coaches, and other involved adults in an effort to turn them against the targeted parent. In addition, alienating parents often don't inform the targeted parent about school events, communications with teachers, and details of extracurricular activities, often resulting in the child believing the targeted parent does not care about their achievements.

Although alienated children may resist, disparage, and openly express hostility toward the targeted parent, particularly during transition times between parents, they still tend to enjoy spending time with the targeted parent when away from the power and control of the alienating parent. In line with this, Henry would be withdrawn and disrespectful for the first few days he was this me on my weeks. Eventually Seth's hold would wear off, and Henry would be affectionate and loving toward me. We would sit together for meals, TV, or homework and talk and laugh and play.

Henry would also confide in me about things he refused to talk to his dad about. Usually, it was about his overcommitment in sports and how he didn't enjoy playing this or that or just wanted a break. Gracie would tell me the same thing. I continued to encourage the kids to talk to Seth about it, but they were too concerned about hurting his feelings. Sometimes Henry would talk to me about how Seth would treat him. He would tell me how his dad put him down, made him feel bad about himself, and how he could never make his dad happy. One time, Henry drew a picture of a "hole" he said his dad made in him. He described how each time his dad made a negative comment (e.g., that he was lazy and not trying hard enough to be the best) he would go further and further down the hole. Next to it, he drew a heart and darkened a portion of the heart, which he said represented each deleterious comment his dad made toward him. It was clear to me that he was extremely concerned about pleasing and not disappointing his dad and that he too was suffering from Seth's narcissistic behavior. It broke my heart then, and it breaks my heart now.

I wished that May, the social worker, would have recommended me to get full custody of the children in the social study. I was astonished she hadn't given everything she learned about Seth and his abusive behavior. But it was only a recommendation. Now, it was up to the judge. I hoped that she would come to a better verdict and award me full custody. Certainly, she would see through all the bullshit, right? I could only pray.

It was time for divorce court.

CHAPTER 9: THE JUDGMENT

The day finally arrived; my marriage was officially going to end. Roughly two years after I found the first evidence of my husband's cheating, I found myself in a cold courtroom with him to finalize our divorce. The courtroom looked like any other; it was small with two long tables both facing the judge's bench. As is typical, the judge's bench was raised much higher than the tables, making clear who held the power in the room and who didn't. Seth and his attorney, Chelsea, were sitting at the table to the right of the judge's bench, and my attorney, Lyle, and I were at the table left of the judge's bench, both couples ferociously whispering to each other. Chelsea was dressed in her usual garb: a short, tight pink dress with a zipper from her cleavage to the hem and black platform stilettos. Seth and Lyle both wore suits. I was in a long, boring, conventional black dress, complete with a bow tied at the waist and black flats, just as all the books on divorce had suggested. Apparently, it was important for women to be perceived by the judge as wholesome, innocent, and maternal, especially if they were fighting for custody of their kids. Such double-standard sexist crap—but I did it anyway.

After a few minutes, Honorable Judge Sandy Wilson entered the courtroom from her chambers, which were behind her bench on the left. We all stood and then sat. The judge was a tall, thin, lengthy woman in her mid-sixties with short, wavy dyed-blond hair. I felt like maybe she could have been a beauty queen in her younger years. She wore the customary long black robe, a clear signifier that she was an upholder of law and justice and, as such, was to be treated with dignity and honor. I watched her curiously as she shuffled some papers around and then made herself comfortable at her bench. It was strange to me that this woman, someone I didn't know and had never met, would be making critical decisions about my life that I had to abide by, even if I disagreed with them. I instantly became panicked.

I knew the divorce would be granted, so I wasn't worried about that. It was all the other issues I was concerned about: fault for the divorce, custody of the kids, division of assets and debts, and attorney fees. I learned through my readings that it was all a spin at the roulette wheel depending on the judge overruling the case. Lyle, my attorney, corroborated all that I had read.

"You never know who you're going to get," Lyle had warned. "It could be a judge who is more progressive, or it could be someone who is more conservative. Some judges are more empathetic toward women and some toward men. Some see cheating and abuse as deplorable, while others perceive it as par for the marriage course. Some see working mothers as being a strong role model for their kids, while others see that same woman as selfish and uncommitted. We need to hope you get the former of all these cases."

Indeed, research shows that, while women are awarded custody most of the time, they can no longer assume they are going to prevail in court. Moreover, fathers who contest custody have a good chance of winning joint custody, if not sole custody, should they seek it. And just as my first attorney Harry had cautioned me before I fired him for his own sexist behavior, a woman may be scrutinized and punished for the exact same behavior her husband engages in, including working, dating, going back to school, or moving out of state. Although laws may explicitly mandate equality, the judges who apply those laws often hold mothers to a higher standard. Judges frequently base their decisions on their own biases and subjective interpretations of behavior and events and rarely have to provide a rationale for those decisions. In short, women have lost their advantage in the courtroom, with fathers increasingly winning custody through blatant judicial gender discrimination against divorcing mothers. This is especially the case for narcissistically abusive men who fight tooth and nail against the mother of their children during their divorce, their vindictiveness toward the mother of their children a key motivating factor for the pursuit of custody. Being awarded custody is just another way for such men to control and terrorize the mother of their children. Many mothers divorcing narcissist men simply don't get the justice they deserve from the family law system.

Not only were these misogynistic realities at the forefront of my mind, but I also felt overcome with dejection and grief about the end of my marriage. Here Seth and I were, after fifteen years and two children together, divorcing. I recalled how handsome and charismatic he was when I met him at Jenna's Halloween party and how I thought I would never have a shot at dating him. I remembered falling in love with him and saying an enthusiastic yes to his marriage proposal. I thought about all of our adventurous moves—to Michigan, Kentucky, and Texas—the kids and pets happily in tow. I reminisced about all the things I loved about him—sitting on the backyard swing, making future plans, camping, holidays, and our inside jokes. He was the love of my life. I was so incredibly in love with him throughout our marriage, so much so that I pushed all his bullshit behavior under the carpet. Perhaps I still was. Even after everything he had done and how horribly he had treated me, I still missed him. I took a deep sigh and closed my eyes. Why did it have to turn out this way? I kept thinking of Kelly Clarkson's song "Maybe," that maybe, just maybe, we might meet again and things would work out.

I looked over at Seth who was looking straight ahead. I wanted him to look over at me. I wanted some indication that he too was wondering how and why it came to this. But he didn't; his head never turned in my direction. It felt like a stab to my heart. He was a stranger to me now. The man I had loved so much was now someone I didn't know at all. It felt so odd to miss him, hate him, and not know him all at the same time.

Not long after Judge Wilson arrived to the courtroom, she asked the attorneys to meet her in her chambers to discuss and negotiate our case. That was so bizarre to me. Not only was the judge going to make decisions about our lives, but two attorneys were going to argue each of our cases, *without us even in the room*. It felt like the whole thing was shrouded in secrecy, with a complete eradication of my, or Seth's, voice. They were in chambers for what seemed like hours, Seth and I silently sitting at our respective tables looking at our phones. I could feel my heart beating fast and hard for no reason other than simply nerves. When they finally appeared, the judge and attorneys returned to their seats. Judge Wilson then read her decisions. She started with her verdict on granting the divorce itself.

As a "no-fault" divorce state, divorces in Texas are usually granted on the basis of "insupportability," placing no blame on either party for the termination of the marriage. It is possible, however, to get a "fault" ruling for a divorce if one of the parties seemed responsible for the demise of the martial relationship. Because I had so much evidence documenting Seth's emotional abuse, harassment, intimidation, stalking, and infidelity both during the marriage and separation, Judge Wilson found him guilty and at fault on the grounds of adultery and cruel treatment. When the judge read this decision, I was elated and relieved. Her verdict completely validated my experiences as a victim of narcissistic abuse at the hands of my husband. And now, Seth finally, *finally*, was going to be punished for his horrendous actions. I couldn't wait to hear what she was going to read next. I sat there quietly, now repeating the Smiths' song "Please, Please, Please" in my head, hoping that I would finally get what I want this time.

Next came the ruling regarding the custody of the kids. This was the biggest, most anxiety-provoking, and critical of the judge's decisions. Was the judge going to award Seth sole custody of Gracie and Henry, just as Seth had repeatedly and condescendingly warned me? Or was the judge going to go along with the social worker's recommendation of joint custody? Or, oh please dear universe, would she award me sole custody? I sat there quietly in my chair, my head down, eyes closed, and hands tightly clamped on my lap. I slowly rocked back and forth as to comfort myself for the possible blow. Then she announced it:

"I grant joint custody of the children."

I let out a huge sigh of relief, one I'm sure everyone in the room could hear. After years of speculating and worrying about Gracie's and Henry's fates, now we finally knew. Seth and I would continue co-parenting with a week-on-week-off schedule. It wasn't the full custody outcome I'd hoped for, but I had to accept it. And it was completely in line with the notion that, even when wife abuse is acknowledged by the courts (the judge finding Seth at fault for the dissolution of the marriage based partly on cruel treatment), there is a strong belief in the equal presence of fathers in children's lives even when they have been abusive toward the mother. The family courts simply ignore the existence and effects of violence and abuse toward women in custody determinations, a clear demonstration of gender bias and the ubiquitous patriarchal norms in family law.

The next of Judge Wilson's decisions were shocking and downright unfair, especially given her ruling of fault by Seth for the failure of the marriage. The first was my ask that Seth pay 100 percent of my attorney fees. Judge Wilson denied this request and instead ruled that we each pay for our own attorney fees. Her exact words were as follows:

> *There was a substantial difference in the amount of attorney fees incurred by each party: $6,200 [for Seth] and $22,357 [for me]. Without knowing a great deal more about that difference, I disregarded attorney fees in the division of property and order each party to pay his or her own.*

My mouth dropped to the floor when I heard these numbers. There was absolutely no way that Seth had incurred just six grand in attorney fees. It confirmed what I had suspected: Chelsea knocked down her price because she was seeing Seth intimately or, at the very least, really liked him. Either way, that Seth was charged so little was unbelievable. That the judge didn't pick up on something fishy was astonishing and negligent. My attorney sent the judge a letter the next week challenging her ruling. It read as follows:

> *Regarding attorney fees, Ms. Lord did not copy me on whatever she provided to the Court [regarding the amount of Seth's legal fees]. I have previously notified the Court and Ms. Lord about this failure to provide but I was still never provided a copy. However, in reviewing the discovery responses of Ms. Lord, I have an invoice in the amount of $4,220 and an invoice in the amount of $6,200 for a total of $10,420. I have attached these invoices hereto. While there may still be a great disparity, [Seth's] fees were not $6,200. I would also note that in reviewing the invoices, there was clearly work performed that was not billed for such as preparing discovery responses. I would note*

that in your chambers, Ms. Lord indicated that her fees were in line with mine when I told the Court the approximate amount. As the Court indicated that it would need to know a great deal more about that difference, I would welcome the opportunity to provide the Court with any details it might need to know. One example is the sheer amount of costs my client incurred in challenging a restraining order that was without merit. The fact of the matter is that we immediately went to mediation and the result of the mediation was an immediate return to the status quo before the wrongful filing of the restraining order. [My client] would obviously not have incurred any fees if not for the fault and adultery of [Seth].

In addition to this, Seth also did not have to contribute a dime toward the $50,000 in student loans I took out to support the family while we were in Michigan—another emancipation.

Perhaps her most egregious judgment was the division of the family property and debt. She actually awarded Seth *more* than he was asking. My attorney described it best in the same letter to Judge Wilson questioning the logic of her rulings:

I do not understand the Court's ruling that [my client] was only awarded fifty-five percent (55%) of the marital estate for two reasons. One is that [Seth] stipulated to fault . . . The second reason is that such an award is less than [Seth] submitted to the Court . . . [Seth] submitted a proposed Total Community Property division of sixty-one percent (61%) for [my client] and thirty-nine percent (39%) for [Seth]. [Seth] also proposed a virtual 50/50 of the marital debt and yet the

Court placed a burden of $71,697 on [my client] and only $48,377 on [Seth]. I would appreciate the Court explaining why it decided to punish the non-faulting party by making an award that was less than what the at-fault party proposed.

Judge Wilson's response to my attorney's inquiry about these issues? Silence. Nothing. Nada. In the end, this was how my divorce was settled. Although Seth was found at fault because of his rampant infidelity and narcissistic abuse, he retained 50 percent custody of the kids and did not have to pay me one dime—not for the credit card debt we incurred (perhaps in part because of his cheating), my attorney fees, or for part of the student loans I took out to support the family. Rather, the judge ruled that I owed Seth money—over twenty grand in fact. Where's the justice in that? There isn't any. But judges can make decisions on a whim and be careless in their interpretation of the law without any repercussions. They are assumed to make judgments on good faith with little judicial oversight even if those conclusions are biased, unfair, ignorant, or wrong.

The real cherry on top that day was Judge Wilson's final words to Seth and me as we were gathering our things to leave the courtroom.

"One last thing," she said with an air of patronizing authority. "Be nice to each other."

I just rolled my eyes. It was just another instance of the family court's minimization and perpetuation of men's abuse of women. I now have zero trust in the legal system. It failed to protect me, and it fails to protect millions of other women. Simply put, it propagates patriarchal biases in society, contributing to the very real social problem of husband's separation and divorce abuse toward their wives. It also wasn't lost on me how messed up the family law system must be for women who must also deal with classism, heterosexism, and racism in addition to the sexist bullshit inherent in the courts. As an upper-middle-class, educated, financially independent, heterosexual white woman, I have privileges and resources other women may lack. And I still got fucked over.

Moreover, I once again felt completely victimized and humiliated by Seth. Seth used the courts as a mechanism to continue to exercise coercive control over me and my life, and it felt like, ultimately, he succeeded. He came out of that courtroom essentially unscathed and without any consequences for his years of cheating, lying, and abuse. Although my attorney did what he could, he got me very little. And Seth's attorney, Chelsea, walked out of that courtroom like she'd won a bar fight. That pissed me off. I later learned that Chelsea could have been disbarred for her behavior with Seth. And when my best friend Sheri's ex, Kenny, needed a divorce attorney, he hired Chelsea just to spite us because we despised her so much. One day, when I accompanied Sheri to support her during one of her divorce hearings, I ran into Chelsea as I was leaving the building. I couldn't help but say something.

"Hey, Chelsea," I said complacently.

"Oh, hi, Kathi, how are you?" she responded, surprised to see me.

"You know, not great," I said. "Do you know why? Because of what my abusive ex-husband put me through. The ex-husband *you* represented. And now you're representing Kenny, another abuser. You should be ashamed of yourself representing these abusive men. You know, there's a special place in hell for women who don't help other women." And with that, my favorite quote by Madeline Albright, I walked out the front door of the building.

I never saw Chelsea again after that encounter but heard about her passing away from an alleged alcohol and drug overdose a few years later.

CHAPTER 10: THE LAST-DITCH EFFORT

I was in full celebration mode once the divorce was final. I was a free woman! But the exhilaration didn't last long, and my mental health plummeted. I began crying nearly all the time and had intense feelings of hopelessness, sadness, and loss. I couldn't eat, shower, or even get out of bed. Not even a good glass of red appealed to me. I found this reaction to the finalization of the divorce extremely puzzling and upsetting. Shouldn't I have been relieved and happy? After all, I was freed from Seth's threats, intimidation, and disparagement. But I just couldn't seem to shake the intensity of the grief that my marriage, and my relationship with Seth, was really over. It was like I thought that, once the divorce was settled, I was going to wake up from some horrifying nightmare and return to my happy and fulfilling family life. But it all really happened; the frightening dream was real. My husband Seth actually did do all of those terrible, hurtful, and cruel things. And then he just walked away completely unharmed, leaving me damaged, broken, and alone.

I wondered what my problem was that I couldn't just get over it, that I couldn't get over him. I found myself repeatedly looking through our wedding and family photo albums, aching to have my husband and family back. I had shared a life with that man, and I missed it. We had a history and had made meticulous plans for the future. He was the father of my beloved children and was there, holding my hand and supporting me, when they were born. Waves of nostalgia kicked in, and I began replaying all the positive memories of us together over and over in my head: our picturesque wedding and honeymoon, when the kids were giggly and toddling around the house, all the amazing family trips and holidays, snuggling on the couch together, and the relaxing Saturdays playing and grilling in the backyard. Then I would look at Seth's girlfriend Jessica's Facebook page and see her happily making memories with the man I had called mine and, sometimes, with Gracie and Henry too. She now had the life I so desperately wanted back.

I began to question myself and my decision to leave him. I had vowed to spend the rest of my life with Seth—in good times and in bad—until death do us part, and I had taken that promise seriously. But then, I bolted when the marriage was in trouble. What kind of wife, what kind of person, did that make me? What happened to commitment and loyalty? Where was my understanding, empathy, and forgiveness? He made some mistakes, sure, but don't we all? No one is perfect. And was he really that bad during the marriage? Yeah, he could be a real jerk sometimes, but isn't everyone? I mean, don't all husbands sometimes put down and yell at their wives? How can you not belittle and become angry and annoyed with someone you've been with for years and years, day in and day out? And all his negative comments about my mothering—maybe they were just meant to encourage me to do better, to become the best mother I could possibly be. Plus, don't all men cheat and lie? What made me think I was so special that he wouldn't want to sleep with other women? Maybe he just wanted sexual variety; it didn't mean he didn't love me, right? All his stalking, intimidation, and abuse during the separation—maybe it was just his way of showing he was hurting and that he missed me. And if he was so horrible, why did I miss him so badly? Why was I still suffering?

I decided that my marital expectations were too high and that the kind of marriage I had always wanted—one based on respect, equality, and honesty—was unrealistic. I thought back to when my mom had died twenty-five years earlier and I had to take over caring for my dad. I recalled doing his laundry and thinking to myself that I never wanted the kind of marriage where my main role was to be a good little wife. But maybe that was where I got it all wrong; maybe I didn't make Seth feel enough like a man. Making matters worse, my identity and personality as a strong, independent, confident, feminist woman were likely in contrast to the kind of woman that Seth, and any man, likely sought. I probably made him feel emasculated and like he wasn't needed. And, oh shit, not only was I more educated than him, but I was also the breadwinner of the family. Dammit, I fucked it all up. What stupidity to think my marriage would buck engrained societal ideas about gender, work, family. I really thought we could escape the confines of traditional marriage and the conventional roles of husband and wife, but clearly, we couldn't. Or Seth couldn't. I don't know. Regardless, it didn't work. The experiment failed. I had asked too much from him. I had asked him to embody a mythical man—a feminist, egalitarian, faithful man—one he could never live up to. Maybe I, and not him, caused the death of our marriage.

Soon, I was in a full-blown depression, accompanied by a playlist of songs that I had carefully selected to represent the shitshow I was feeling. I listened to those songs over and over and wept. One song in particular, "Say Something" by A Great Big World, compelled me to do something I never thought I would. I had thought about reaching out to Seth numerous times over the course of the separation to try and have an honest and authentic conversation with him about us and our demise, one where we put all our walls down and all our cards on the table and could be who we were when we met, fell in love, and swore to spend our lives together. I never did, though, because I felt it was useless. But this one evening, I just couldn't resist. I had to reach out to him. I had to talk to my husband. I had to see if he was still there. I had to see if I had really damaged our relationship beyond repair. At the very least, I had to relieve my intense feelings of despair, heartache, and angst even if it meant making a fool of myself. I just didn't care at that point. So, I wrote him an email. When I finished what I wanted to say, I looked up to the sky (well, ceiling) and said a little prayer. I looked back at my laptop screen and paused for a moment, my mouse hovering over the Send button. Was I doing the right thing? Was I going to regret this? *Fuck it.* I hit Send.

> *Seth,*
>
> *I can't believe I'm doing this. We have been through hell and back . . . and then some. These have been the most difficult and traumatic years of my life. I am going to admit it: I am still in love with you. I have always been in love with you and will always be in love with you. You are the love of my life. OK there, I said it. I have no idea what this admittance means or how it affects you, me, and/or the kids. I have not thought it through. I need you to do some soul searching. Do you feel the same way? Do you have any desire to figure this out? Reconcile? Therapy? Do you have any feelings left for me? I miss you. And I hate you at the same time. I just need to voice how I am feeling. I cannot seem to get over us. Please give this some thought. I have no idea where to go from here or how to proceed. I guess I just need to know where you stand. Are we really over? Do you have any feelings left? Do you think about repairing us? Would you like to try? Would you like to be a family again? As you can imagine, this is incredibly difficult for me to send. I beg that you please keep*

this message between us. I am the woman you married and the mother of your children. Please do not share this message. I promise to never share this conversation with anyone as well. Let's respect each other enough to do that – for Gracie and Henry. I'm totally putting my heart out there on this one. I'm very nervous and anxious about sending this to you. I look forward to your response. Please take your time and think about what I'm saying. And please keep it between us. I promise I will. I understand it may take some time for you to respond.

-Kathi

It was late in the evening when I sent the email, so I knew I likely wouldn't hear from him until the next morning. I got ready for bed and snuggled in with Peanut and Cooper, anxious about what was to come. I slept surprisingly well that night, though, perhaps because I had finally gotten so many intense feelings off my chest. When my alarm rang bright and early, I instantly reached for my laptop. No new emails. I sighed deeply. *That's okay*, I reassured myself. *He probably hasn't even seen it yet.* But by dinner time, I still hadn't heard from him. Why wasn't he responding? Oh, shit, did I not send the email? I went to my Sent folder and confirmed that I had. I started freaking out, pacing the room. I began coming up with reasons why he hadn't yet replied. Maybe there was a glitch in the system and my email didn't go through. Or maybe his computer was on the fritz. Maybe he had been in a horrible car accident and was bleeding out somewhere. Maybe he had received the email and he and Jessica were laughing about it over dinner. I decided the most likely reason was that he thought I was messing with him and it was all just a big joke. I plopped down on the couch and crafted another message. Just to clarify.

Seth,

I'm feeling very distressed and really, really stupid because you haven't even acknowledged my message. My message is genuine. I can see that you might be weary of its legitimacy. I would be, too. I'm being real and I'm surrendering everything we have been doing for years now. I just wonder if we are really done. I need to know if you have any need or desire to "just see." I'm not saying I want to get back together. I'm not saying I want you to break up with Jessica. I'm not saying I forgive you. I am asking if you would like to find peace, calm, and if it is even a possibility that we could conceivably be together at some point. I'm done with hating each other. I'm done with putting each other down. I'm done with finger pointing and blaming. I want to (at least) be cordial and eventually even be friends. I want this to end Seth. I am 100% willing and interested in exploring therapy to help repair a semblance of a relationship. I am willing to do that. Let's finally do the healthy thing - let's get beyond this. If we end up in a marriage, just friends, or healthy co-parents, I am ready to do this with you. I really need you to acknowledge these messages. All you have to say is "Got it" or "Confirm" or "OK" - just something. And again - I plead we keep this between you and I. We cannot figure this out (even a friendship or healthy co-parenting relationship) with others' input. I think this is something only you and I (and possibly a therapist) can figure out. I have not told anyone of my olive branch to you nor do I intend to (they might commit me . . . not kidding). You can trust me on this. I am being genuine. Do you want to end this too?

Please acknowledge me. One last thing: Even if you are not interested in anything I have said, please acknowledge by saying something like "Got your messages. I'm not interested." I would appreciate that.
-Kathi

In less than thirty seconds, a new email was in my inbox. It was him.

I received your message. Trying to compose a reply.

I read Seth's words as my body slowly melted into the couch. I just sat there, my eyes darting around the room. I didn't feel pleased, or relieved, or sad, or even curious. I felt appalled, but not by him—by me.

THE SHAME

I didn't recognize myself or who I had become. This woman, this new me, had reached out to her abuser and told him she loved him and missed him. She apologized to him and practically took blame for the marriage failing. She asked him to reconcile. The old me—before I found that first text from Jackie from Married and Flirting, before I learned about all the cheating websites, before I knew about the affairs with Carly and Angela and likely numerous other women, before the verbal attacks, harassment, stalking, intimidation, smear campaigns, and isolation, before trying to damage my relationship with the kids, before alienating Henry—would have never, ever even considered being with such a malicious, sadistic man. In fact, she would have told him to go fuck himself. The process of separation and divorce from a narcissistic abuser had changed me into someone weak, insecure, and cowardly, someone wholly shameful, someone as sick as he was.

Seth had finally done it; he had attained his ultimate objective. I had internalized everything he had drilled into me time after time, year and year. I now effusively and fully believed it. I really was stupid, pathetic, crazy, a joke, an embarrassment, and crazy. I was gross and ugly. I was unlovable and worthless. Just like Johnny Cash in "Hurt," a song that fully resonated with me at the time, I was an empire of dirt. Seth had beaten every morsel of self-love out of me, his figurative fists strong and hard, hitting me repeatedly nonstop until I lay there lifeless and unable to return the slightest reciprocal swat. He had slaughtered my soul, and he had bludgeoned my light. He had executed me, and all by a calculated and steady stream of narcissistic abuse. I now looked down upon myself, like a jurist adjudicating the morality of a perpetrator of a heinous crime, and felt nothing but contempt. I snickered a little under my breath. *Touché*, Seth. *Touché*.

More than anything, though, I was exhausted. So tremendously tired from being so completely broken, I just wanted to go to sleep and never wake up. I needed rest, real rest—permanent rest. I again turned to music for comfort and understanding, listening on replay to two songs that perfectly represented what I was feeling, "Alone Again, Naturally" by Gilbert O-Sullivan and "Asleep" by the Smiths. The former held distinct meaning for me in that it was the song my Aunt Barbie had committed suicide to generations earlier. I was just a baby when she died and I don't remember ever meeting her, but I would hear about her now and then and how that song was playing on repeat on her record player when they found her.

I found myself envious of Barbie's brave decision. She had done it; she had stopped her psychological suffering. Oh, how wonderful that sounded, to be free from it all—no more hurt, no more grief, no more loneliness. The thought of ending it all comforted me like a warm soft blanket. It didn't sound scary or cryptic but peaceful and beautiful. And I missed my mom. It had been so long since she'd died, when I was only a teenager, and she was the only thing that was going to make me feel better. If I left this earthly place, I could see and hug her again. I could cry on her lap. I would feel loved. I wanted to be in that world, another world. The Smiths' suicide lullaby was exactly what I sought.

Out of curiosity, I started researching ways to unalive myself. I decided that firearms, hanging, jumping off a building, or slitting my wrists were too bloody and violent. If I was to ever really do it, I would do something serene and painless where I would just slowly slip away. I thought pills might be my best bet, but that I would really have to plan because I had nothing in the house that would do the trick. Perhaps I would poison myself; carbon monoxide poisoning seemed simple enough and required no special pills or weapons. I decided that carbon monoxide poisoning would be my method of choice if it ever came down to it. It was interesting how I thought about it so matter-of-factly, like I was planning for a trip or considering a new recipe. I put my new-found information in my back pocket, so to speak, and went along my daily life hating myself. I had no intention of acting on what I had learned.

But then, one evening a few days later, that changed. The kids were at Seth's (whom I had again blocked so had no idea if he had responded to my last-ditch-effort email), and I was listening to music that consoled me. But this time, instead of feeling calmer, I stood up and started frantically pacing the room, Peanut and Cooper following me with their curious, concerned eyes. An intense surge of grief, heartache, and hopelessness overcame me and infiltrated my every cell, muscle, and bone. I dropped hard to the floor, and I began uncontrollably sobbing. Thoughts began bombarding my brain one after the other so quickly that one would begin before the other ended. *I'm so sick of this! I'm so tired of feeling this way! I'm never going to get better! I'm never going to heal and be happy again! I hate this! I hate my life! I want out! I want this agony to end!* I was so completely overwhelmed by the repeated and sudden nature of these destructive cognitions that every bit of energy I had in my body dissipated into the air. I couldn't even pick my head up off the floor it was so heavy. Then suddenly—*Stop!*

I placed my sweaty palms on the floor and began to push myself up, my head hanging low like a ragdoll's. I got to my feet, placed my hands on my knees, and slowly and deliberately stood up. I stood there for just a few moments, my face strong and stoic but wet with tears. In that moment, I made the conscious decision. It was time. This was it. I was done. I even said it out loud, but with a whisper. "I'm done." Then I went into motion.

THE GARAGE

I walked directly to my bathroom, went to pee, brushed my hair and put it up in a ponytail, and put some Vaseline on my lips. I then went to my dresser, found my favorite pair of fluffy blue socks, and put them on keeping my balance by jumping on one foot and then the other. I grabbed the blanket and a pillow off my bed and headed toward the garage.

"C'mon, boys," I said to Peanut and Cooper as I walked through the living room and then the kitchen grabbing my car keys on the counter along with way. "We're going to go take a nice nap." I was calm and resolute. I already felt better.

I got into my gray Camry on the driver's side, the dogs right behind me. I shut the car door once we were in and started the ignition. I then turned off the lights and radio and looked at the boys who were looking at me curiously in the passenger seat. "This is it, boys. I love you so much." I put the blanket over my body and the pillow behind my head. Immediately both dogs jumped on my lap wanting to be as close to me as they possibly could. It was a tight fit, especially with the steering wheel poking into us. I decided to move us to the backseat, so I got back out of the car and entered the door behind the driver's seat, the dogs jumping from the front to the back seat before I could even close the door. I grabbed the blanket and pillow and made a little comfy bed for us, the car engine humming in the background. I lay my head softly on the pillow. It felt cool and comfortable against my face. I sighed gently as a tear ran from the corner of my eye, down the bridge of my nose, to my lips.

"I love you, Gracie. I love you, Henry. I'm so sorry," I whispered.

Then I closed my eyes. It was all going to be over soon. I couldn't wait.

After a few minutes, Peanut and Cooper became restless, whining and scratching the window to get out of the car. They were obviously anxious and confused about what was happening. I hated seeing them so uncomfortable and decided it wasn't fair to them to end their lives just because I wanted them with me when I passed. *Just another example of what a horrible person I am*, I thought. So, I sat up, got out of the car, and led them back into the house. As I headed back out the door, I stopped. What if no one found me for a while? What would happen to my sweet dogs? I wanted to make sure someone knew they were home alone, so I grabbed my phone from the kitchen counter and I texted a few words to my best friend Sheri:

> *I'm done. The boys are home alone. Please take care of them.*

It was late, nearly 2:00 a.m., so she wouldn't get the message for a few hours. I knew when she did, though, that she would immediately come get them and take them in. They were in excellent and loving hands with her, and that comforted me. I set the phone down, kissed and hugged Peanut, and then Cooper, tears now gushing down my face.

"I love you so much, boys, so much."

Then I returned to the running car, rested my head back on the pillow, and fell fast asleep.

CHAPTER 11: THE HOSPITAL

I could hear a man's voice determinedly yelling in the distance.

"Get her out! Get her out!"

At the same time, I could feel my back against another man's chest, his arms wrapped tightly around me and his hands clamped just above my breasts. He was lifting me out of the back seat of my car, my head bobbing forward like a newborn baby. The blanket that was my cocoon fell from my body to the cement floor. I was groggy but not unconscious. I could open my eyes but only wide enough to see the spinning red and white lights of the ambulance, which illuminated the car and garage against the night's darkness. Within seconds, I was on a gurney inside an ambulance.

"Kathi, can you hear me?"

It was a different voice than that of the man who had yelled to get me out of the car and more inquisitive than demanding. He was holding a flashlight directly into my eyes while holding my left eye wide open with his fingers. I nodded a yes, that I could hear him, my head pulling back a little.

"Good. My name is Dennis. I'm an EMT, and you're on your way to the hospital. Can you tell me what you were doing in the back seat of the car, Kathi?"

Of course, I knew—I wanted to end it all—but I couldn't speak. I just nodded yes again.

"Why were you in the back seat, Kathi? Can you tell me why?"

I started getting a bit annoyed with his questions. I was tired and I just wanted to sleep. I was glad he was there, though. I felt safe and secure. Even though I knew it was his job to take care of me, it still felt good that someone gave a shit. Then I passed out.

When I woke up, I was lying in a hospital bed in the ER. I slowly lifted my head and sluggishly looked around. The curtain was drawn around my bed so I couldn't see much. More than anything it was noisy, with people talking and machines beeping. I looked down at my right arm; I was connected to an IV. I wondered how long I had been there and how the ambulance even found me in the first place. I started to cry. I was tremendously relieved that my attempt was unsuccessful but still felt heavy with intense hopelessness and shame. And I was hungry. I closed my eyes and hoped that a nurse would come check on me soon. I was too exhausted to find any help button that might be by my bedside.

The swift opening of the curtain made me abruptly open my eyes to see a man standing there. Because he wasn't wearing scrubs, I assumed him to be a social worker, and I was right. He sat down in a chair to the left of me.

"Hi, Kathi. I'm Jeff. How are you feeling?" he asked compassionately.

"I'm ok." I spoke very quietly, which was unlike me.

"Do you know why you're here, in the ER?"

I nodded affirmatively.

"Good. The doctors are running some tests, and we will find out the results soon. In the meantime, I'm here to find out what brought you here. Can you tell me what's been going on with you?"

I responded surprisingly quickly and resolutely and much louder than my previous words.

"I've gone through a devastating divorce, and my ex-husband is an abusive asshole. I'm tired of it."

Then I looked down, almost embarrassed. It seemed so simple and stupid when I said it aloud. I tried to kill myself because of a jerk ex? How dumb could I be? I felt the need to elaborate and provide a more representative account of the hell I had been living in. I calmed my voice a bit.

"This has been the worst and most difficult time of my life, full of grief, despair, abuse, and harassment. It has all had a tremendous toll on my mental health, and I'm in a near-constant state of anxiety and depression. I just wanted it to end. I wanted the pain to stop. It's like I can't seem to get over it. I don't seem to be healing at all."

"I'm so sorry, Kathi. But you know there is help out there. There is help available to you. Do you feel suicidal right now?"

I nodded no.

"Good. Will you let us help you? Will you let us help you get better?"

I nodded yes and began to weep.

"I'm so happy to hear that. What is going to happen now is we will move you to a psychiatric facility because you have to be under surveillance for seventy-two hours. That is standard after a suicide attempt. We are looking for a bed now. I'll let you know once we've found one. Until then, can I get you anything?"

"Yes, I'm really hungry. Can you get me something to eat and drink please?"

"Sure," he said with a gentle nod.

A few minutes later, he brought me some water in a paper cup and a dry turkey, cheese, and lettuce sandwich on white bread. I scarfed it down and then fell asleep. It was near midnight when I was again awakened by Jeff loudly pulling open the curtain once again.

"Ok, we have found a bed for you at Cedar Crest Hospital. Your ride will be here shortly. You might want to use the bathroom; it's over a two-hour drive away."

"Okay, thanks."

When I walked out of the bathroom, a wheelchair was waiting for me. A nurse, who was holding onto the handles of the chair, kindly motioned for me to sit, which I did. Jeff approached me and handed me his business card.

"Please call me if you have any questions. Oh, and is there anyone you would like us to call, to let know you're ok?"

I hadn't even thought about that. I really didn't want to talk to anyone, but people might be worried about my whereabouts and I was really concerned about Peanut and Cooper.

"Um, yeah, I'd like you to call my best friend Sheri, but I don't have her phone number memorized," I replied concerningly.

"That's ok. We have Sheri's number. She's the one who called the ambulance. She just happened to get up out of bed to use the bathroom and saw your message. She loves you very much, you know. We will give her a call and let her know that you are on your way to Cedar Crest."

"Oh, okay. Thank you."

I sighed deeply as a profound, warm sensation of love encircled me. I was so grateful to have Sheri in my life.

Then Jeff reassured me, "You're going to get through this, Kathi. I promise."

The nurse pushed me through the halls of the ER to the entrance where there was a black sedan with two large men waiting, one in the driver's seat and one in the front passenger seat. The nurse opened the back seat door, handed me a blanket, and gestured for me to get in. The driver then got out, walked around the car to the nurse, and signed some form I hadn't noticed the nurse was holding on a clipboard. He then shut the back seat door and got back into the driver's seat. I immediately realized that those two men were not only there to escort me from point A to point B, but to keep me under control and contained. I was their cargo, a woman with a mental health problem, who might freak out or try to bolt at any moment.

It was a strange feeling. That wasn't me at all, but they didn't know that. Their mission was to watch over the woman who had tried to kill herself and deliver her safely to her destination. We didn't say one word to each other the entire drive. I just lay down in the back seat and let myself be rocked gently by the road, the two men's faint chatter serving as a soothing distraction.

CEDAR CREST HOSPITAL AND
RESIDENTIAL TREATMENT CENTER

It was roughly 3:00 a.m. when we arrived at the hospital, so everything was dark and quiet. The two men who had escorted me by sedan from the ER to the psychiatric facility walked me from the car to the tiny intake office where another man was waiting. The driver again signed a form, and my two chaperons were off.

"This way, Kathi," said a heavyset man in his late twenties, clearly the night shift. I followed him to a small office with several desks. He motioned for me to sit at the first desk, so I sat down on one side and he sat on the other. He began asking me routine questions, like my birthday and if I had any diagnosed mental illnesses. I answered his questions, and he wrote them down. He wasn't particularly comforting or empathic, just doing his job. When he was done with his questioning, he walked me along a little lighted path to another building close by. He didn't say a word along the way, nor did I. When we reached our destination, he entered a code to get into the building.

Just beyond the entrance was a small stark waiting room with a dingy couch and several wooden chairs.

"Hey, Pete. I'll buzz you in," said a woman sitting at a desk behind a thick glass partition.

You could hear the large metal door to the right of us unlock as she did. I was surprised by the security at first but then quickly realized it made sense given we were in a psychiatric ward. *Oh, shit,* I thought, *I'm gonna be locked in!* I wasn't allowed to leave, or come and go as I pleased, while I was a patient there. I had to be accounted for and watched. I didn't feel great about it, but that was irrelevant; I had no choice.

We walked through the door, and it forcefully shut and locked behind us; I even jumped a little.

"This is the nurse's station," described Pete as he pointed to the left.

The area was about as large as the waiting room and held three desks. It was partitioned by the same thick glass that separated the nurse's station from the waiting room. Before long, I began using the recognized term for the nurse's station: "the fishbowl."

"The common room is directly in front of us; you'll find a TV, books, and writing supplies in there. And down these halls to the left and right are the room corridors. I'll take you to yours now. You're in room 17."

He brought me to a room with two twin beds with white sheets and a blanket, a set of white drawers, and a white plastic chair. The room had a window (that didn't open) and its own bathroom. It was exactly what you would expect for a room in a psychiatric hospital. It held the bare minimum and absolutely nothing that could be used as a weapon against oneself or someone else—no pictures, no hangers, no lamps, nothing.

"This is where you'll stay. You're lucky you get your own room. There's a change of clothes for you and some toiletries on the bed. Wake up is at six thirty and breakfast is at seven thirty. You'll see the doctor shortly after that. Any questions?"

I nodded no, and he left, closing the door behind him. I brushed my teeth and hair and washed my face. The water was cold, but it felt good. Then I changed my clothes and got into bed. I was asleep before my head hit the pillow.

I was awakened by a knock on my door the next morning.

"Good morning, dear. It's time to get up," a woman's voice sang as she opened the door.

I unsealed my eyes and groggily glanced over at her. I had only slept a few hours, so it was agonizing to even think about getting up.

"I'm one of the day nurses. My name's Maria. When you're ready, you can go to the common room. Don't forget to make your bed."

I so badly wanted to go back to sleep, but I followed my orders and slothfully got myself presentable. I grabbed a coffee with cream from the small shared coffee area along the way to the common room. I was so nervous I could actually feel my heart beating, having absolutely no idea what, or whom, to expect.

There were only a few people in the common room when I arrived. One, a woman, was asleep on a long yellow couch to the right of me, and the other two, both men, were sitting in chairs at the large oval table that took up most of the space. The men were blowing on coffee and talking about something seemingly related to the military. They looked up at me in unison, likely curious about the newest addition.

"Hi," I said softly with an uneasy smile as I went to sit on another, empty, couch.

As more and more residents arrived to the room, maybe fifteen in total, it became louder and livelier as if they were all longtime friends. I decided I would sit silently and just observe. I casually watched them, slowly sipping my coffee, wondering why they had been hospitalized.

It didn't take long to discover everyone's diagnosis. About half the group was there for alcohol rehabilitation, with most of them also suffering from post-traumatic stress disorder (PTSD). I later learned that Cedar Crest was the closest psychiatric facility to nearby Killeen, home to U.S. Army Military Base Fort Hood. Fort Hood is one of the largest military bases in the world and is the largest active-duty armored post in the U.S. Armed Forces. There are nearly forty thousand soldiers who work on Fort Hood. Who knew? Perhaps not surprising, then, most of the residents were associated with the military and base. The remaining patients had various other disorders, including two who had schizophrenia (both heard voices that would communicate regularly with them, even whilst in the group), one who was a cutter, and the woman sleeping on the couch who was a full-fledged meth addict. Then there was me, a middle-aged woman with a suicide attempt resulting from a devastating divorce and a narcissistically abusive ex-husband. My situation seemed so modest compared to the others, but the longer I was there, the more it became clear that I had more in common with the group than I would have ever thought.

I stayed quiet and to myself until after breakfast when it was my turn to visit with the medical doctor, Dr. Hemmer. Our first visit was solely about my test results from the ER and my medication use. He first pronounced that he was relieved to report that my vitals were all normal and there was no indication of brain damage from the carbon monoxide exposure during my attempt. That last bit of information freaked me out; it never even occurred to me that I could have suffered brain damage from my impulsive decision. He then asked what medications I was currently taking and, for consistency, prescribed my routine hypothyroid and reflux meds. He also upped my antidepressant and prescribed a new medication to help me sleep.

There was a strict and precise schedule at the hospital for when we would wake up, eat meals, take medications, have therapy, exercise, and go to bed. We did not have regular access to computers or phones and were told that we were now completely and officially "off the grid." If you wanted contact with the outside world, you had to get approval for who you were communicating with and why, and you only had a one-hour window in the evening to do so. I quickly got clearance to contact my sister Jill (to inform the family I was safe), Sheri (to bring me some personal items and thank her for being my best friend), and my work colleague Wendy (to inform the university of what Wendy described only as my "medical emergency"). Fortunately, it was near the end of the fall semester, and I only had one day left of my classes until the online final exams. That last class was simply canceled, which likely thrilled the students. There was the issue of grading those final exams, however, and I did eventually get special authorization from the hospital to use a computer for that purpose. If my students only knew their feminist psychology professor was grading their exams under lock and key at a psychiatric facility because of her husband's psychological abuse. Sheri took the two-hour trek out to bring me some clothes and toiletries the next day. It was so nice to see her when she arrived, and she assured me she was taking good care of Peanut and Cooper and that she would do whatever she could to support me, including bringing my kids for a visit should I be staying at the hospital for any real length of time.

I also got approval to email, ugh, Seth. I unblocked him and then crafted an email informing him that I was in a psychiatric healing center to work on my mental health (I didn't divulge the attempt), that he would need to care for the kids for at least a few more days (it was nearing the end of his week of possession) and possibly longer, and to please tell the kids that I was okay and I loved them very much. His reply was:

> *Kathi,*
>
> *I am 100% in support of you getting help so that you can be the most productive, supportive, caring, loving mother to our kids. During this whole ordeal I have done my best to protect the kids from our ugliness and keep them sheltered from all of our disputes. I will do my best to continue to do that. It is best for everyone that we get along in a civil non-adversarial manner.*

I am glad that you are finally getting the help and the
support you need. I have been very worried for your
well-being for a long time. I will do nothing but be
positive about this situation. I will continue to send
the message that you love them and care for them with
all of you heart, and your time away will do nothing
but make you a better mother.
-Seth

I did not respond to Seth's message. By this time, I had been in the hospital for a few days and I had completed numerous rounds of intensive individual and group therapy (being in the hospital was akin to having months and months of therapy each day) and was beginning to understand that his years of narcissistic abuse had led to major psychological trauma. My only concern was taking full advantage of my time at the hospital to immerse myself in more treatment, learn tools and strategies to really begin to heal, and, hopefully, begin to find and love myself again. As I neared the seventy-two-hour mark of being a resident at the hospital—the time when I could officially be released—the medical doctor and therapists made clear that I should stay; they recommended at least another week. On their urging, I decided to remain at the hospital and did so for nearly three full weeks. Truth be told, it was an easy decision to stay. I actually liked being there. I relished the freedom of no obligations or responsibilities. I savored focusing solely on me, my mental health, and my healing. I absorbed feeling understood, supported, and cared for. I began laughing, smiling, and having—it feels strange to say—fun with the other patients. When you're with people 24/7 and have all admitted you need professional help with whatever issues you are dealing with, you become very close very quickly.

I bonded most deeply with Erin, the meth addict, and George, a soldier who was struggling with alcohol abuse and PTSD. It was interesting; you would never guess that they were dealing with mental health issues upon first meeting them. Erin was a beautiful freckly redhead who was making a name for herself as a successful business manager; she was hospitalized at the insistence of her husband who was in the military. She and I were always telling sarcastic, off-hand jokes to each other, which helped lessen the seriousness of where we were. George, whom I grew to have a bit of a crush on, was incredibly handsome with his deep dark skin, massive smile, and warm demeanor; he always went out of his way to make me feel comfortable and seen. I also grew especially close to one of the nurses, Dericia. As a devoutly Christian black woman with an underprivileged background, some might assume we would have little in common, but we connected instantly. We would talk for hours about philosophy, spirituality (for me) and religion (for her), and healing from our experiences of abuse at the hands of men. What I appreciated most about being at the hospital, though, was being far, far away from Seth. It was extremely liberating and made me feel like I actually had control over my own life. In short, I felt hopeful.

I was diagnosed with PTSD after about a week at the hospital. Although I was somewhat surprised by the diagnosis, I probably shouldn't have been. I certainly knew I had experienced horrific narcissistic abuse by Seth, but I hadn't made the connection between narcissistic abuse as a form of trauma and PTSD. All I knew was that I felt helpless, empty, worthless, inferior, and alone. Seth's abuse had fucked me up so badly that I couldn't see what was right in front of me. I was shocked, too, that my previous therapists hadn't made the seemingly obvious connection, or myself, for that matter, with a background in psychology. Nonetheless, the formal diagnosis of PTSD brought me great comfort and strength. I finally felt acknowledged, understood, and validated for what I had gone through. I wasn't crazy, pathetic, deficient, dumb, or worthless; I had been made to feel that way.

I immediately asked the hospital psychologists for any and all information they had about PTSD and spent every free minute reading about it. I also received special privileges to use the computer to do additional research on how PTSD relates to narcissistic abuse and divorce. In my exploration of these topics, I learned about a specific form of trauma—"betrayal trauma"—that was completely relevant to what I had experienced. In the end, it was clear that I had not only been traumatized for years by Seth's detestable behavior, but that it had occurred in a social context I had been teaching my students about for over a decade: a patriarchal society that minimized, legitimized, and perpetuated men's abuse and violence toward women. Together they—Seth and sexist societal norms—made the perfect storm, one that left me completely defeated and dominated, just like so many other women. Let me don my professor cap to describe what I found after days of researching these topics.

TRAUMA AND TRAUMATIC EVENTS

Psychologists define "trauma" as resulting from an overwhelmingly shocking, frightening, dangerous, or scary experience or event or one that involves serious injury, sexual violence, or an evident threat to life. People who have experienced such events often immediately feel emotional and physical shock, withdrawal, numbness, confusion, and speechless terror. Traumatic events can even produce permanent physiological changes in our body and brain chemistry. Trauma changes who we are as a person and leaves an imprint that affects our relationship with ourselves, others, and the social world. Being betrayed, going through a divorce, or experiencing narcissistic abuse can all lead to trauma under extreme circumstances.

"Betrayal trauma" refers to a situation in which trust is critically violated by a person or an institution we rely on for care, safety, resources, and survival, such as child sexual abuse, intimate partner violence, or the discovery of a spouse's sex addiction. Because women are substantially more likely to be victims of trauma at the hands of someone close to them, especially men, betrayal trauma is particularly relevant to women, their relationships with men, and their subordination in society. Victims of betrayal trauma, again especially women, report more negative outcomes—including depression, anxiety, disassociation, memory lapses, self-blame, shame, suicidality, trust issues, and physical health complaints—compared to those with other forms of trauma, demonstrating that trauma perpetrated by a close male is especially damaging for women. Thus, for women but not for men, trauma that results from abuse within close relationships is much more serious than trauma inflicted by strangers. Moreover, because of the interconnected relationship between the victim and the perpetrator, it can be extremely difficult for the victim to break free from the abuse. A betrayed wife, for example, may share a home, children, and finances with the offender, making severing ties an exceptionally challenging and lengthy process, particularly when she feels unsupported by the oppressive social norms and messages maintaining that "all men lie and cheat" or that "all men lash out at their wives." This material on betrayal trauma completely resonated with me and began to help me understand why I was so traumatized by Seth's deceit and infidelity. I trusted and relied on Seth to love me, care for me, and keep me safe. He did none of those things with his rampant adultery. That I was experiencing all of the negative outcomes associated with betrayal trauma further solidified that I was suffering from trauma because of his duplicity.

"Divorce trauma" can occur when a marital divorce causes significant distress, shock, grief, or hurt. Divorces that are sudden, unusual, high-conflict, or that involve infidelity, cruelty, or abuse may be particularly traumatic. Divorce trauma, I learned, is especially applicable to women divorcing abusive men. The tactics abusive husbands use during a divorce to maintain power and control over their wives—such as custody and visitation battles, intentionally prolonging the case, manipulating finances, intimidation and harassment, and disparaging the wife's character as a person and mother—can be highly traumatizing for women exiting abusive marriages. It is also common for abusive male spouses to belittle, demean, verbally attack, and even physically strike their wives during the divorce process. Women's traumatic symptoms in response (e.g., anxiety, depression, anger, self-blame, shame) may in turn be perceived by judges, attorneys, and custody evaluators as evidence that women are mentally unstable, resulting in her losing custody of the children, the family home, and other assets. These consequences are exacerbated by inadequacies within the court system, such as the tendency for courts to minimize abuse and lack of education and training in abuse dynamics, which only facilitate the power and control male abusers perpetuate over their female partners. Thus, not only can women experience trauma from the divorce itself, but from biased divorce litigation processes as well. Wow! This was right in line with my divorce from Seth, from his abusive behavior toward me during the divorce process to my inequitable treatment by the courts and legal system. Moreover, my divorce had all the features that make divorces traumatic—it was unexpected, strange, and toxic, and it involved cheating, malice, and mistreatment. There was no doubt that I was experiencing trauma because of my divorce.

Finally, in "narcissistic abuse trauma," the constant stream of degradation, manipulation, gaslighting, rejection, etc. can represent a series of stressful events that result in trauma because the target's nervous system never has the chance to stabilize, leaving her in a constant state of tension. Adding to this, victims often feel confused as to why they have such a difficult time leaving or moving on from the relationship even though they recognize it as abusive. This can exacerbate the damage to a target's self-identity, making her feel weak, shameful, worthless, unlovable, and deserving of the abuse. Other outcomes of narcissistic abuse trauma are similar to those of betrayal and divorce trauma (e.g., anxiety, self-blame, shame). This research also made perfect sense to me. I had been in a narcissistically abusive relationship with Seth for years, especially during the divorce. It was now no surprise to me why I felt such shame and self-loathing and why I was having difficulty moving on from him. I was experiencing trauma from his narcissistic abuse.

As alluded to above, psychologists have begun to regard trauma as a highly social phenomenon that can be facilitated or hindered by societal and cultural factors, thereby influencing an individual's experience of trauma and the chances of developing trauma-related disorders like PTSD. This is important because it suggests that a victim's experience of trauma is affected by injustices in the larger social environment. For example, men's dominance, power, and control in the larger society can exacerbate women's experiences of abuse trauma from men because that abuse can be easily delegitimized and ignored by the larger culture. In my situation, for instance, how I was treated by the family court system during my divorce deleteriously affected my mental health, intensifying the damage Seth had already caused. That Seth saw no repercussions for any aspect of his traumatic abuse exemplifies how he, as a man in society, benefitted from patriarchy and therefore was destined to come out unscathed. As such, not only was Seth culpable for causing my trauma, but larger social systems, and gender oppression in particular, was as well.

One other important thing to note—because women as a group may experience trauma from abusive men similarly as a result of their subordinated status in society, their traumatic abuse experiences can be considered a form of collective trauma. In other words, men's abuse of women in society traumatizes all women, regardless of the extent to which they have personally experienced abuse. Psychologists uphold that, when trauma is acknowledged by a group as collective, it lessens the likelihood of perceiving the trauma as a solely individual experience. This, in turn, can serve as a form of protection against the negative consequences of trauma. Thus, it is critical that collective traumatization by men toward women be identified, labeled, and shared by women.

The above research is compellingly clear that women can experience trauma and traumatic symptoms in response to betrayal, divorce, and narcissism from their male partners and that the trauma can be intensified by larger social systems and institutions. The research also suggests that women who have experienced trauma from betrayal, divorce, and/or narcissistic abuse may develop post-traumatic stress disorder (PTSD). I certainly did.

POST-TRAUMATIC STRESS DISORDER (PTSD)

According to psychologists, trauma can lead to post-traumatic stress disorder (PTSD) if trauma symptoms persist beyond thirty days and are severe enough to interfere with aspects of daily life like family, school, or work. The symptoms must also not be attributable to medication, substance use, or other illness. Early classifications of PTSD maintained that one-time events such as a violent personal attack, natural or human-caused disaster, accident, or military combat could lead to PTSD. The definition has since been reevaluated to also consider prolonged, chronic exposure to stressful events that cause extreme emotional distress, including, for example, a drawn-out toxic divorce or longstanding abusive relationship. This persistent, repeated form of trauma can result in what is called "complex post-traumatic stress disorder (C-PTSD)." Neither PTSD nor C-PTSD are considered a form of mental illness but as a response to exposure to trauma.

Usual symptoms of both forms include flashbacks, nightmares, insomnia, distraction, dissociation, depersonalization, memory lapses, startle reactions, aggression, and substance abuse. Feeling emotionally numb, tense, angry, irritable, and guilty and experiencing depression, shame, guilt, fear, embarrassment, humiliation, and abandonment are also very common. People with PTSD and C-PTSD also tend to practice "avoidance"—avoiding people and situations that remind them of the trauma—which are called "triggers." "Hypervigilance" (being on "high alert") and "hyperarousal" (feeling constantly agitated) are also likely. Individuals with these disorders may also lose interest in things they previously enjoyed, have intense reactions and emotions that seem disproportionate to the current situation, and begin to feel negatively about oneself, others, and the world. These disorders can lead to suicide ideation, suicide attempts, and actual suicide. Disturbances in emotion regulation, self-concept, interpersonal relationships, and physical health occur more frequently in individuals diagnosed with C-PTSD compared to individuals diagnosed with PTSD.

This newfound knowledge of PTSD and C-PTSD hit the nail on the head for me. I was a textbook case, especially for C-PTSD. I had experienced multiple forms of trauma because of my husband that—along with the societal values surrounding male dominance, power, and control—catapulted me into developing the disorder. What I learned also gave me the strength and courage to not only label and accept that I was a victim and survivor of spousal abuse trauma, but to socially acknowledge and share my story with other women to help heighten awareness of how men's abuse toward women leads to collective trauma for women. If it could happen to me—an independent, highly educated, feminist psychology professor—it could happen to anyone. This was pivotal for me in making meaning out of Seth's abuse so that I could begin to really move on and reenter the world as a whole person again.

ROLLING MY EYES

At some point during this period, I received another email from

Seth. He stated that he wasn't sure that I had received his response to my last-ditch-effort email (you know, the senseless email where I essentially asked him to reconcile and that hurled me into such shame that it landed me in the backseat of a running car in a closed garage), so he wanted to resend it. Apparently, he had sent his response shortly after I had sent my email, but I hadn't known because I had blocked him and, oh yeah, was in the ER. I so deeply regretted sending the email, especially because now I was learning how I got to that terrible point in the first place and why I would consider reuniting with someone so harmful. It sickened me to think how much he likely enjoyed receiving that email and what he may have written in response. I even considered not reading it, but I just couldn't help myself. Here's his email response to my ill-conceived olive branch:

> *Kathi,*
>
> *How am I supposed to take this email? Forget everything you have done? You have emailed Jessica several times trying to bully and intimidate her. You have shared every detail about us with her in attempt to break us up, you have attempted to humiliate me to her, and even insulted her for being with me. You have also threatened her physical harm. You have told multiple people that you feel threatened and are scared of me. You tell people I stalk and harass you. So, I am supposed to forget all of that from the heart-filled email you sent? Yes, I feel sorry for you and hope you get your mind right. I still can't believe you lie about being a victim of abuse, when in reality, you were the one [who was abusive]. I have been the victim of you. I do not wish to humiliate you. You are the mother of my children and deserve that respect. And, we also need to have a conversation in the very near future about*

Jessica and I's relationship. Just wanted to explain my point of view and maybe you can print it up and show it to your therapist. Again, I am relieved for you and the kids that you are getting help with your issues and problems. Get better.
-Seth

I just rolled my eyes when I read his response. The degradation, gaslighting, minimizing, and blaming were his modus operandi and to be expected. But it didn't have nearly the same effect on me this time. This time felt different. This time I stood up for myself.

Seth,
It seems you have interpreted my email as admittance of wrongdoing. You should not perceive it this way. Everything I did and said was true - you have been and continue to be emotionally abusive, and have stalked and harassed me. I told you numerous times that I was extremely distressed by your presence and asked you to leave me alone. You refused. It also seems you have interpreted my current situation as some kind of mental illness or disorder that just appeared; that I am "getting the help and support I need" to overcome what a horrible, sick person you perceive me to be. This is not the reason. YOU are the cause of why I am here. YOU caused the trauma. YOU are personally responsible for my PTSD. YOU are to blame. But once again, you skirt responsibility for all of this. If you really "cared about my well-being" you would not continue to emotionally abuse me and would sincerely apologize for the hurt and pain you have caused me. I have learned a lot the short time I have been here. You are toxic

in my life and nearly destroyed me. And I do not see any reason for us to have a conversation about you and Jessica. I'm glad that you have found someone that you are a good match with. I will never interfere in your relationship. I was only doing what I thought was right - to forewarn another woman of likely hurt and pain. However, she has decided to stand by you given these warnings. Again, you seem to be a very good match. It's time for me to move on and be happy again.
-Kathi

Hitting Send on that message represented the beginning of the end of Seth's once-impenetrable hold on me. Because of the intensive therapy I had at the hospital, the comprehensive research I did on PTSD and C-PTSD as a result of betrayal, divorce, and narcissistic abuse trauma, and the support and care from the hospital patients and staff, the indignity and darkness that had enveloped and surrounded me began to lift. I began feeling tough and resilient, like the person I was before this nightmare. I was slowly coming back and was ready to heal.

But I missed Gracie and Henry tremendously. Thankfully, I was able to get permission from the hospital for them to come for a visit. I called Sheri to confirm a few times that were good for her, then reached out to Seth to coordinate Sheri picking up the kids from his home. Perhaps not surprisingly, he refused to let Sheri bring the kids and instead insisted that he be the one to bring them. His stance, of course, was totally in line with his seeming insatiable desire for coercive control. I knew I had to accommodate him if I wanted to see my babies. So, I obliged even though it made me want to vomit.

THE KIDS' VISIT

I felt like a kid on Christmas Eve, patiently and excitedly waiting for Santa to deliver his troves of toys, the night before Gracie and Henry's visit. I just wanted to hug and kiss them and tell them how much I loved them. It would be my first time seeing them since my failed suicide attempt, and I thanked the universe constantly that I didn't succeed. I treasured them more than anything and was angry and disappointed at myself for making a choice that could have harmed them forever. I knew firsthand how devastating it is to lose a mother early in life and almost put them in the same situation. It was done, though, and now I was focused on healing and recovering from the trauma I had experienced from their father. As the most important people in my life, I vowed to be the best mom I could be by once again becoming the strong, loving, happy, feminist woman I once was. They deserved that.

"Mommy! Mommy!" the kids squealed as they entered the waiting area of my temporary abode.

My arms were stretched out wide to greet them, and I swallowed them up as they fell into my body. Love and warmth enclosed me; they were my joy. I kissed each of their heads and squeezed them tight. I could see Seth on the other side of the glass doors watching us. He then entered the building.

"You got them, ok?" he asked me, almost like we were good friends.

"Yeah," I replied with a nod.

"Enjoy your mom, kids." Then he left.

"Guess what, Mommy! Guess what!" Gracie asked elatedly as the doors closed behind Seth. She was barely able to control her enthusiasm.

"What, honey? Tell me!" I was eager to hear about whatever she wanted to tell me.

"Daddy and Jessica are getting married! And Henry and I are going to be in the wedding! He asked Jessica to marry him last night!" She was grinning ear to ear.

"Really? That's so exciting!" I feigned.

"Yeah, Mommy," said Henry. "It's all we talked about on the drive to come see you. After we're done visiting you, we are going to a special dinner to celebrate!"

"Oh, wow, that's unbelievable!" I responded with a little laugh. And it was. It was God-dammed fucking unbelievable. "Wait, did Jessica come with you?" I looked over at Gracie inquiringly.

"Yeah, the four of us, me, Henry, Daddy, and Jessica drove up together. They are going shopping while we visit you and then we are going out to a fancy restaurant!"

"Well, that's great. You both sound really happy about this!"

What an odd and disturbing choice for Seth to make, to propose to a woman the day before he takes his children to visit their "sick" mother in a mental hospital. Fucking incredible. I was damned, though, if I was going to let their shocking announcement affect my mood or my precious time with them.

The visit went by like the speed of light. Before I knew it, Seth and Jessica were pulling up in the parking lot, there to pick up my kids to go for a celebratory engagement dinner while I went back into a psychiatric hospital to heal from my trauma. I just shook my head. It all now made impeccable sense why Seth refused to let Sheri bring Gracie and Henry to visit me. He wanted to bring them, he wanted Jessica to be with him, and he wanted the kids to excitedly arrive with the thrilling pronouncement that he was getting married. He wanted the opportunity to take another deep, jolting, bloody stab. Oh, how the timing was perfect, he must have thought. How could I be more down than being in a psychiatric ward? In what other situation could I be so vulnerable and helpless? It was ideal. He must have been overjoyed with the anticipation of the kids running in to tell me his glorious news. *Same ole Seth. Same ole mind games. Same ole narcissistic bullshit. Sorry, Seth, not gonna work this time. I'm coming back, I'm healing, and your chain has been severed.*

Dericia, the nurse I had become so close to while in the hospital, was waiting for me on the other side of the bolted door when my visit with the kids was over. She could tell something big had happened by the look on my face. I told her about Seth's engagement and confirmed that I was just fine. She looked at me in a way that said, "What an asshole," and shook her head with condemnatory disbelief. And I really was okay. Of course, her gigantic hug didn't hurt. We then smiled compassionately at each other and strode arm in arm to the common room, our chests protuberantly proud and strong.

THE UNEXPECTED LETTER

Seth's engagement was on my mind the rest of the day and the next morning, which I embraced. I wanted to really let myself process it, as well as any and all emotions that surfaced. I didn't feel dejected, jealous, or resentful, though. Rather, I felt a sense of profound ease and contentment. It was the first time in years that I actually believed I was going to survive the hell I had endured and—what's more—was going to thrive. I sighed deeply, gently closing my eyes. It was a new feeling, and I wanted to cherish it. I was deeply grateful too for my time at the hospital. I wished I had sought that kind of treatment and support a lot sooner, certainly before I had made the rash decision to end it all. I looked forward to when Dericia would arrive for work; she was my main source of encouragement and I wanted to thank her. When she did arrive, she immediately went looking for me, ecstatic to share some news.

"I have something wonderful to share!" The happiness she emitted was overwhelming.

"What? What is it? What's going on?" I was so curious.

"I have a letter for you!" She elatedly waved a piece of paper high in the air.

"A letter? From who?"

"Someone very important!"

"Who?" I couldn't even imagine who it could be from.

"Well, I was fast asleep last night when all of the sudden I was woken up by a beautiful, soothing presence. It told me to get a pen and paper. It wanted to use me to write you a letter. It came from God. God used me to write you a letter."

My jaw fell to the floor as she handed me the letter. I'm not a religious person, so it was a little difficult for me to believe that God had spoken through Dericia's ballpoint pen. Then I read the letter.

Pg. 52 – The Fate of the Wicked
Numbers 16:21 God said separate yourself from (your opponent) so HE (God) can consume him "In A Moment!"

Kathi, that visit [Seth bringing the kids] was designed by evil to throw you off. Mentally you are being beat down so he can feel superior to you. Because he knows as it stands, you are beyond him and deep in his heart he hates you for who you are because someone that loves you couldn't do a thing like that. You are too wonderful, and delightful, you are a warm beam of light on a cloudy day. And instead of him basking in your light, he has envied and loathed what he was not able to achieve and his thoughts became dark and cold, and the only power he had was your desire to love him so instead of embracing your affection he rejected it which broke you down. That was his only tool. He had to beat you down for being successful and to satisfy his nothingness that he brought upon himself.

Whatever your relationship might be with God, He loves you so much that He cannot bear to see you being mistreated so what has taken place is by design. But just so you can understand, imagine if you will that someone just walked up to your child and SLAPPED HER SO HARD she fell to the ground and slid across the floor (see how you feel right now?). That's how angry God gets (but more) when someone hurts His daughter, meaning you. Because just as you would jump in defense of your child, so shall God defend you. In spite of what you've overlooked or ignored, tolerated or accepted, there is a line in God's heart that will not be crossed concerning you. Just as you would not allow someone to injure your child as you stand on the sidelines and watch.

There's a reason you came to this place [the hospital]. It was to give you rest from a weary journey. To un-yoke you from the dead corpse of a situation and for you to begin to embrace the freedom you deserve. God put you in a place of examples. He then gave you two versions of one person. Erin [the meth addict] is the splitting image of my life. I was her once upon a time. The only difference was my drug was love and I was abused because I did anything to get it. However, I lived a vulgar existence because I looked for it from people who were incapable and did not love themselves, and my immaturity did not allow me to make a healthy assessment. I became bitter and cruel . . . but God. He stepped in before I became a crusty barnacle due to the abuse of my fleeting drug and overdosed me with a love beyond my ability to explain. Now I deal the dope I once craved. And I'm hoping you become addicted. ☺

Hand written by me . . . Instructed by God.

I don't know if that letter came from spirit, the universe, God, or just Dericia, but it sent chills down my spine and gave me an overpowering sense of peace and love. I knew after reading it that something had changed in the matrix and that a new component had been added to the algorithm of my life. It was clear and undeniable confirmation. I had made it. I prevailed. Seth's hold on me was over.

A NEW COMMITMENT

It was time to fall back in love with myself. That meant inundating myself with self-love, self-compassion, and self-respect. It also meant self-forgiveness; I needed to forgive myself for staying with Seth all those years, for allowing him to have coercive control over me and my life, and for nearly leaving Gracie and Henry without a mom. I decided that, in order to do so, I needed to find my fight, turn what happened to me into something good, and have an amazing life. This was now my purpose, and I was ready for it.

A few days later, I was released from the hospital. Sheri was there in the parking lot waiting with a big hug and an even bigger smile.

"You've got this!" she said supportively.

"Yes. Yes, I do," I agreed, also beaming.

As we drove away, I started emphatically singing what was to be my new chorale: Alicia Keys' "Girl on Fire."

I had come full circle. The committed feminist professor who had taught thousands of students about patriarchy from a university lectern, and who was ultimately committed to a psychiatric ward because of it, had finally made the best and most important commitment of all: a commitment to herself and to bringing other women her story.

THE COMMITTED PROFESSOR PLAYLIST

"One Less Bell to Answer," 5th Dimension

"Everything I Own," Bread

"Against the Grain," Garth Brooks

"Side of the Road," Lucinda Williams

"Widow of a Living Man," Ben Harper

"Rolling in the Deep," Adele

"Friend of Mine," Liz Phair

"Please Bleed," Ben Harper

"Jar of Hearts," Christina Perri

"You Lost Me," Christina Aguilera

"Back to the Old House," The Smiths

"Rock Me," Liz Phair

"Cannonball," Damien Rice

"Smile," Lily Allen

"Get Lucky," Daft Punk

"Maybe," Kelly Clarkson

"Please, Please, Please," The Smiths

"Say Something," A Great Big World

"Hurt," Johnny Cash

"Alone Again, Naturally," Gilbert O-Sullivan

"Asleep," The Smiths

"Girl on Fire," Alicia Keys

REFERENCES

DeKeseredy, W. S., Dragiewicz, M., & Schwartz, M. D. (2017). *Abusive endings: Separation and divorce violence against women* (Vol. 4). University of California Press.

Domestic Abuse Intervention Programs. (2024, April). *Understanding the power and control wheel.* https://www.theduluthmodel.org/wheels/

Fischel-Wolovick, L. (2018). *Traumatic divorce and separation: The impact of domestic violence and substance abuse in custody and divorce.* Oxford University Press.

Freyd, J. J. (1996). *Betrayal trauma: The logic of forgetting childhood abuse.* Harvard University Press.

Gagnon, K. L., Lee, M. S., & DePrince, A. P. (2019). Victim–perpetrator dynamics through the lens of betrayal trauma theory. In *The Abused and the Abuser* (pp. 131–140). Routledge.

Harman, J. J., & Biringen, Z. (2016). *Parents acting badly: How institutions and societies promote the alienation of children from their loving families.* CreateSpace Independent Publishing.

Harman, J. J., Kruk, E., & Hines, D. A. (2018). Parental alienating behaviors: An unacknowledged form of family violence. *Psychological Bulletin, 144*(12), 1275–1299.

Herman, J. L. (1992). Complex PTSD: A syndrome in survivors of prolonged and repeated trauma. *Journal of Traumatic Stress, 5*(3), 377–391.

Maercker, A., & Hecker, T. (2016). Broadening perspectives on trauma and recovery: A socio-interpersonal view of PTSD. *European Journal of Psychotraumatology, 7*(1), 29303.

Maercker, A., & Horn, A. B. (2013). A socio-interpersonal perspective on PTSD: The case for environments and interpersonal processes. *Clinical Psychology & Psychotherapy, 20*(6), 465–481.

Morningstar, D. (2017). *Out of the fog: Moving from confusion to clarity after narcissistic abuse.* Morning Star Media.

Morningstar, D. (2017). *Start here: A crash course in understanding, navigating, and healing from narcissistic abuse.* Morning Star Media.

Murphy, Clare (2024, April). *A new power and control wheel.* https://speakoutloud.net/intimate-partner-abuse/new-power-and-control-wheel/

National Institutes of Mental Health. (2024, April). *Coping with traumatic events.* https://www.nimh.nih.gov/health/topics/coping-with-traumatic-events

National Institutes of Mental Health. (2024, April). *Post-traumatic stress disorder.* https://www.nimh.nih.gov/health/topics/post-traumatic-stress-disorder-ptsd

Office of Violence Against Women, U.S. Department of Justice. (2024). *Domestic violence.* https://www.justice.gov/ovw/domestic-violence.

Resick, P. A., Bovin, M. J., Calloway, A. L., Dick, A. M., King, M. W., Mitchell, K. S., . . . & Wolf, E. J. (2012). A critical evaluation of the complex PTSD literature: Implications for DSM-5. *Journal of Traumatic Stress, 25*(3), 241–251.

Sharples, A. E., Harman, J. J., & Lorandos, D. (2023). Findings of abuse in families affected by parental alienation. *Journal of Family Violence*, 1–11.

Smith, G. R., & Abrahms, S. (2007). *What every woman should know about divorce and custody: Judges, lawyers, and therapists share winning strategies on how to keep the kids, the cash, and your sanity.*

Penguin Publishing Group.

Twenge, J. M., & Campbell, W. K. (2009). *The narcissism epidemic: Living in the age of entitlement.* Simon and Schuster.

Van der Kolk, B. (2014). *The body keeps the score: Brain, mind, and body in the healing of trauma.* Penguin Books.

Warshak, R. A. (2010). *Divorce poison: How to protect your family from bad-mouthing and brainwashing.* Harper Collins Books.

Watson, L. B., & Ancis, J. R. (2013). Power and control in the legal system: From marriage/relationship to divorce and custody. *Violence Against Women, 19*(2), 166–186.

Winner, K. (1996). *Divorced from justice: The abuse of women and children by divorce lawyers and judges.* ReganBooks.

Zaffuto, G. (2016). *From charm to harm: And everything else in between with a narcissist.* CreateSpace Independent Publishing.

BIOGRAPHY

Dr. Kathi Miner grew up the youngest of five children in a loving and close family in Southern California. She received a BA in psychology and social behavior from the University of California, Irvine, an MA in experimental psychology from Southern Methodist University, and a PhD in psychology and women's studies from the University of Michigan, Ann Arbor. She joined academia as an assistant professor of social and organizational psychology at Western Kentucky University and then became an associate professor of industrial-organizational psychology and women's and gender studies at Texas A&M University. Her academic research focused on diversity, inclusion, and respect in the workplace. In particular, she examined how disrespectful and exclusionary interpersonal experiences in work environments affect the personal and professional trajectory, health, and well-being of employees, especially women. She has published over fifty articles in prestigious peer-reviewed journals and received nearly $5 million in grants to conduct her academic research on these topics. The devastating effects of her abusive marriage and divorce drove Kathi to write her memoir to share her experiences with other women. She left academia to focus on this project and to have a more direct influence on women's experiences in the workplace. Kathi now works as a diversity and inclusion specialist for a large energy company in the Middle East where she lives with her two small dogs, Peanut and Prince. She also has two grown children, both of whom live in Texas. Kathi enjoys nature, travel, cooking, writing, fitness, live music, and wine tasting.

Made in United States
North Haven, CT
18 January 2025

64606519R00163